PRINCIPLES OF
PROGRAMMING LANGUAGES

Prentice Hall International
Series in Computer Science

C. A. R. Hoare, Series Editor

BACKHOUSE, R.C., *Program Construction and Verification*
BACKHOUSE, R.C., *Syntax of Programming Languages: theory and practice*
DE BAKKER, J.W., *Mathematical Theory of Program Correctness*
BJÖRNER, D., and JONES, C.B., *Formal Specification and Software Development*
BORNAT, R., *Programming from First Principles*
BUSTARD, D., ELDER, J., and WELSH, J., *Concurrent Program Structures*
CLARK, K.L., and MCCABE, F.G., *micro-Prolog: Programming in logic*
DROMEY, R.G., *How to Solve it by Computer*
DUNCAN, F., *Microprocessor Programming and Software Development*
ELDER, J., *Construction of Data Processing Software*
GOLDSCHLAGER, L., and LISTER, A., *Computer Science: a modern introduction (2nd edn)*
HAYES, I. (ed.), *Specification Case Studies*
HEHNER, E.C.R., *The Logic of Programming*
HENDERSON, P., *Functional Programming: application and implementation*
HOARE, C.A.R., *Communicating Sequential Processes*
HOARE, C.A.R., and SHEPHERDSON, J.C. (eds), *Mathematical Logic and Programming Languages*
INMOS LTD, *Occam Programming Manual*
INMOS LTD, *Occam 2 Reference Manual*
JACKSON, M.A., *System Development*
JOHNSTON, H., *Learning to Program*
JONES, C.B., *Systematic Software Development using VDM*
JONES, G., *Programming in occam*
JOSEPH, M., PRASAD, V.R., and NATARAJAN, N., *A Multiprocessor Operating System*
LEW, A., *Computer Science: a mathematical introduction*
MACCALLUM, I., *Pascal for the Apple*
MACCALLUM, I., *UCSD Pascal for the IBM PC*
PEYTON JONES, S.L., *The Implementation of Functional Programming Languages*
POMBERGER, G., *Software Engineering and Modula-2*
REYNOLDS, J.C., *The Craft of Programming*
SLOMAN, M., and KRAMER, J., *Distributed Systems and Computer Networks*
TENNENT, R.D., *Principles of Programming Languages*
WATT, D.A., WICHMANN, B.A., and FINDLAY, W., *ADA: language and methodology*
WELSH, J., and ELDER, J., *Introduction to Modula-2*
WELSH, J., and ELDER, J., *Introduction to Pascal (2nd edn)*
WELSH, J., ELDER, J., and BUSTARD, D., *Sequential Program Structures*
WELSH, J., and HAY, A., *A Model Implementation of Standard Pascal*
WELSH, J., and MCKEAG, M., *Structured System Programming*
WIKSTRÖM, Å., *Functional Programming using Standard ML*

PRINCIPLES OF PROGRAMMING LANGUAGES

R. D. TENNENT

Department of Computing and Information Science
Queen's University, Kingston, Canada

PRENTICE HALL

NEW YORK   LONDON   TORONTO   SYDNEY   TOKYO

First published 1981 by
Prentice Hall International (UK) Ltd,
66 Wood Lane End, Hemel Hempstead,
Hertfordshire, HP2 4RG
A division of
Simon & Schuster International Group

Printed and bound in Great Britain by
SRP Ltd, Exeter

Library of Congress Cataloging-in-Publication Data

TENNENT, R D   1944—
  Principles of programming languages.

  Bibliography: p.
  Includes index.
  1. Programming language (Electronic computers)
I. Title.
QA76.7.T47   001.64'24   80-24271
ISBN 0-13-709873-1

British Library Cataloguing in Publication Data

TENNENT, R D
  Principles of programming languages.

  1. Programming languages (Electronic computers)
  2. Electronic digital computers – Programming
  I. Title
  001.64'24   QA76.7
  ISBN 0-13-709873-1

---

11 12   93 92

ISBN 0-13-709873-1

to Liz

CONTENTS

8 PARAMETERS 117

9 DEFINITIONS AND BLOCKS 127

10 JUMPS 147

11 CONCURRENT PROCESSES   165

12 TYPES   179

PREFACE

This book is a systematic exposition of the fundamental concepts and general principles underlying programming languages in current use. It may be used as a text for courses in computing science and software engineering programs, and as a reference by advanced programmers, programming theorists, and programming language implementers, describers and designers. Linguists and logicians may also be interested to see how the methods of mathematical logic may be applied to formal languages that are much more complex than the traditional logical calculi.

The material and the presentation have been strongly influenced by the approach to programming language theory founded by Dana Scott and the late Christopher Strachey at Oxford University, particularly the first chapter of *A Theory of Programming Language Semantics* by Robert Milne and Strachey (Chapman and Hall, London, and Wiley, New York). But I have emphasized intuitive concepts, rather than formalism and mathematical theory. I hope that this will help to make their work accessible to a wider audience.

Readers are expected to have enough programming experience to appreciate the basic ideas of programming methodology (importance of program correctness, readability and modularity, as well as efficiency; separation of levels of abstraction; stepwise refinement), and to have a reading knowledge of PASCAL, which is used as a standard example throughout. There are also "case studies" of interesting aspects of several other languages used in practice, but no attempt is made to give complete descriptions of languages, or to discuss experimental languages. The emphasis is on significant differences and similarities between linguistic concepts. The only mathematical prerequisite is a basic knowledge of sets and functions.

Undergraduates with adequate programming experience and mathematical maturity can cover all the material in the order presented in two terms. For students with weaker backgrounds, the "starred" sections (on the principles underlying Scott's theory of computation) may be omitted. It is also possible to use the final chapter as the outline of an introductory graduate course in formal description of programming languages, referring to material in earlier chapters as needed.

There are exercises, project suggestions and an annotated bibliography at the end of almost every chapter. An additional bibliography of suggested readings on each of the programming languages mentioned in the text is given in an appendix.

I am very grateful to everyone who gave me suggestions and comments on various drafts, particularly Michael Gordon, Robert Milne, Tony Hoare, David Barnard, Mike Jenkins, Molly Higginson, David Leeson, Bill O'Farrell, John Gauch and Bruce Stratton. The remaining errors, obscurities and prejudices are my responsibility. I would also like to thank Michael Levison for his help in preparing the manuscript with his IVI text-editing system and the Natural Sciences and Engineering Research Council of Canada for financial assistance.

R. D. T.

PRINCIPLES
OF
PROGRAMMING LANGUAGES

The meaning of a sentence must remain unchanged when a part of the sentence is replaced by an expression having the same meaning.

G. FREGE (1892)

1 INTRODUCTION

1.1 PROGRAMMING LANGUAGES

A programming language is a system of notation for describing computations. A useful programming language must therefore be suited both for *describing* (i.e., for human writers and readers of programs), and for *computation* (i.e., for efficient implementation on computers). But human beings and computers are so different that it is difficult to find notational devices that are well suited to the capabilities of both. Languages that favor humans are termed *high-level*, and those oriented to machines *low-level*.

Let us consider some extreme examples of programming languages. In principle, the most "powerful" language for any computer is its machine language, which provides direct access to all of the resources of that computer. However, programs in such a language cannot conveniently be implemented on *other* computers. Furthermore, it is very difficult to write or read machine-language programs. Human beings cannot cope with the complete lack of structure in both programs (sequences of machine instructions) and data representations (sequences of machine words).

It might be thought that "natural" languages (such as English and French) would be at the other extreme. But, in most fields of science and technology, the formalized symbolic notations of mathematics and logic have proved to be indispensable for precise formulation of concepts and principles and for effective reasoning. However, in their full generality the notational devices of mathematics are not even implementable on computers, for deep reasons that will be discussed later.

There is a language called LAMBDA (invented by D. Scott) that has many of the properties of conventional mathematical notations and is as expressive as possible: *all* and *only* the operations that apparently are possible to compute are definable in LAMBDA. These properties make it useful as a specification language and in theoretical studies of computability.

But LAMBDA is so far removed from conventional computers that, though implementable in principle, it would not be practical as a *programming* language.

In short, an ideal programming language would combine the advantages of machine languages and mathematical notations, but achieving this aim has proved to be a very difficult problem. Many existing languages have only managed to combine countless "features" into a jumble that is neither easy to implement nor a pleasure to use.

There are so many programming languages and most are so complex and irregular that it would be nearly impossible and certainly pointless to learn *every* feature of *every* existing programming language (or even of the dozen or so more important ones). Fortunately, there is a great deal of *conceptual* overlap between programming languages, even those that on the surface appear to be quite dissimilar. Almost every practical programming language has mechanisms for dynamically updating storage, introducing symbolic names, transferring control, structuring data, defining procedures, and so on. In every language, these mechanisms are governed by the same general principles.

It is on these fundamental concepts and general principles that this book concentrates. Understanding them will make it easier to use, describe, compare, implement, and design programming languages.

It will be convenient to use a single programming language as a standard example in this book. PASCAL has been chosen because it is widely known and has been one of the most successful at reconciling conflicting design criteria (though it is certainly not the final step in the evolution of programming languages!) The reader is assumed to have a reading knowledge of PASCAL as well as experience in programming with some high-level language. Jensen and Wirth (1974) or a comparable description should be available for reference. Minor variants or extensions of PASCAL will be described and discussed when convenient or necessary to illustrate a point. Several case studies of other well-known languages will provide a broader perspective. Appendix A is a bibliography of suggested readings for each of the programming languages discussed. It should be noted that many of the program fragments used as examples are intended only to illustrate language concepts and do not necessarily exemplify good programming style.

1.2 SYNTAX, SEMANTICS AND PRAGMATICS

It is traditional when dealing with languages of all sorts to try to separate concerns with form, the subject of *syntax**, from concerns with meaning, the

---

*Important technical terms are introduced in bold italic face.

field of *semantics*. Consider the simple "language" of *binary numerals*. Some examples of binary numerals are

0
1
101
0101
10011010

A communication in this language evidently consists of a finite sequence of characters '0' and '1'. This is just syntax however, and says nothing about what such a communication is intended to *mean*.

The usual interpretation for such numerals is that each numeral denotes a *natural number* (i.e., zero or one of its successors). For example, '101' and '0101' both denote the number five, the fifth successor of zero. Numbers are "abstract" mathematical concepts, whereas the digit strings that appear on paper are numerals, that is to say, symbolic representations or descriptions of numbers. Many other languages have this same set of numbers as their meanings: decimal numerals, Roman numerals, and so on.

In general, then, *syntax* is concerned with only the format, well-formedness, and compositional structure of communications in a language, and *semantics* with their meaning.

The **pragmatics** of languages have to do with their origins, uses, and effects. So, the pragmatic aspects of programming languages include language implementation techniques, programming methodology, and the history of programming-language development. In this book, important pragmatic considerations will be pointed out wherever appropriate, but systematic expositions of programming methodology, language implementation, and history are outside its scope.

The criterion for correctness of a language processor is that it implement the syntax and semantics of the language. However, because of pragmatic factors, processors often do not meet their specifications for all possible programs and data. For example, suppose that the language of binary numerals were to be "implemented" by representing numbers in a storage register of fixed size. It is evidently impossible for every numeral in the language to be correctly implemented as specified.

If a processor is unable to meet its specifications for some input, it should signal this with an appropriate warning message. Otherwise, it is termed **insecure**. Output from an insecure processor must be treated with suspicion unless it can be verified that the program has not breached any of the insecurities.

An important goal of programming language design is to make it easier for implementers to eliminate insecurities without incurring severe penalties in execution time or storage space. Unfortunately, with most current computer designs, some kinds of programming error cannot be detected economically, so that the goal of eliminating insecurities should also be taken up by computer designers.

1.3 SYNTAX-DIRECTED SEMANTICS

Programmers are encouraged to program in a "structured" way, that is to say, to use the *syntactic* structures of their programming language to help them systematically develop and more clearly express the *semantic* structure of their algorithms. Similarly, languages are best *described* by basing specifications of their semantics on an appropriate syntactic description. Programming languages are so complex that a structured approach is almost essential for conceptual understanding.

As a simple example of syntax-directed semantic description, consider again the language of binary numerals. The syntax of this language may be precisely specified as follows:

(a) Characters '0' and '1' are binary numerals.
(b) If N is a binary numeral, then N with a '0' or a '1' appended to the right of it is also a binary numeral.
(c) These are the only binary numerals.

Rule (a) describes the two *elementary* (i.e., nondecomposable) syntactic forms. Rule (b) describes the two *composite* forms; in this rule, the binary numeral N referred to is an example of what is termed an ***immediate constituent*** (of a composite syntactic form). Rule (c) specifies that the set of binary numerals is to be the *smallest* set meeting requirements (a) and (b).

Note that this syntactic description specifies not only the criteria for well-formedness of a binary numeral, but also its ***phrase structure,*** that is to say, how it is analyzed into immediate constituents, and these into their

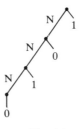

Fig. 1.1

immediate constituents, and so on, until elementary forms are reached. For example, the phrase structure of binary numeral '0101' may be depicted by the tree shown in Fig. 1.1. The process of determining the phrase structure of text is known as *parsing.*

A specification of the meaning of (i.e., the number denoted by) every binary numeral may now be based on the above syntactic description as follows:

(a) Binary numerals '0' and '1' denote numbers zero and one, respectively.

(b) If N is a binary numeral that denotes number n, then (i) N with '0' appended to the right of it denotes number $2 \times n$, and (ii) N with '1' appended to the right of it denotes number $2 \times n + 1$.

For example, consider numeral '0101'. Working from the leftmost character,

'0'   denotes zero, using rule (a);
hence, '01'   denotes $2 \times 0 + 1 = 1$, using rule (b), part (ii);
hence, '010' denotes $2 \times 1 = 2$, using rule (b), part (i);
hence, '0101' denotes $2 \times 2 + 1 = 5$, using rule (b), part (ii).

Each non-terminal node of the phrase structure tree for '0101' may be "labelled" with the semantic object denoted by the corresponding phrase (Fig. 1.2). Thus semantics chases denotation up the syntax tree (with apologies to W. V. Quine).

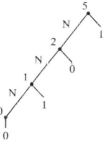

Fig. 1.2

The above description of the syntax and semantics of binary numerals is an example of what is known as the *denotational* approach to language description. The general idea is simply to specify the meanings of (i.e., the semantic objects denoted by) elementary forms directly, and the meanings of composites in terms of the meanings of their immediate constituents. This "structured" approach has a long history in logic and linguistics. Subsequent chapters will explain how *programming* languages may be described denotationally.

EXERCISES

1.1 Suggest two "unusual" semantic interpretations for binary numerals.

1.2 Suppose that rule (b) of the definition of the syntax of binary numerals were changed to
(b)   If N is a binary numeral, then N *prefixed* by a '0' or a '1' is also a binary numeral.
Define the usual semantics of binary numerals using this syntactic description.

1.3 Describe the syntax and usual semantics of binary numerals with fractions, such as '101.0101'.

*1.4 Prove that, according to the syntax and semantics given, *every* finite binary numeral has a *unique* meaning, using mathematical induction on the length of the numerals.

*Solutions to starred exercises require a higher level of mathematical maturity.

PROJECT

Write an essay on the history of one of the major programming languages.

BIBLIOGRAPHIC NOTES

There is a large literature on programming language design. Three papers by Hoare [1.6, 1.7, 1.9] are especially recommended. The language LAMBDA was described by Scott [1.15].

The trichotomy between syntax, semantics, and pragmatics was proposed by Morris [1.12, 1.13] and Carnap [1.2]. The history of programming languages is discussed in papers by Knuth and Pardo [1.10] and Hoare [1.8], in a book by Sammet [1.14], and in a conference proceedings [1.18]. There are large literatures on programming methodology and language implementation; see, for example, collections edited by Gries [1.5], and Bauer and Eickel [1.1], respectively.

The denotational approach to language description may be traced back to Frege [1.4], Carnap [1.3], and Tarski [1.17]. Its use for formal description of programming languages was developed by Scott and Strachey [1.16]. Montague [1.11] gave a denotational description of a fragment of a natural language.

1.1 Bauer, F. L. and J. Eickel (eds.). *Compiler Construction, An Advanced Course*, Springer, Berlin (2nd edition, 1976).

1.2 Carnap, R. *Introduction to Semantics*, Harvard University Press, Cambridge (1942).

1.3 Carnap, R. *Meaning and Necessity, A Study in Semantics and Modal Logic*, University of Chicago Press, Chicago (1947, enlarged edition 1956).

1.4 Frege, G. "Über Sinn und Bedeutung"; *Zeitschrift für Philosophie und Philosophisches Kritik* **100**, 25–50 (1892); English translations in *Readings in Philosophical Analysis* (eds., H. Feigl and W. Sellars), pp. 85–102, Appleton-Century-Crofts, New York (1949), and *Translations from the Philosophical Writings of Gottlob Frege* (eds., P. T. Geach and M. Black), pp. 56–78, Blackwell, Oxford (2nd edition, 1960).

1.5 Gries D. (ed.). *Programming Methodology*, Springer, New York (1978).

1.6 Hoare, C. A. R. "Prospects for a better programming language", in *High Level Languages*, Infotech State of the Art Report 7, pp. 328–43, Infotech Ltd., Maidenhead, England (1972).

1.7 Hoare, C. A. R. *Hints on Programming Language Design*, technical report CS–403, Computer Science Dept., Stanford University, Stanford, California (1973).

1.8 Hoare, C. A. R. "High level languages, the way behind", in *High Level Languages, The Way Ahead*, British Computer Society conference proceedings (ed., D. Simpson), pp. 17–25, NCC Publications, Manchester (1973).

1.9 Hoare, C. A. R. "The high cost of programming languages", in *Software Systems Engineering*, pp. 413–29 (papers presented at the European Computing Conference, London, 1976), Online Conferences Ltd., Uxbridge, England (1976).

1.10 Knuth, D. E. and L. T. Pardo. "The early development of programming languages", in *Encyclopedia of Computer Science and Technology*, vol. 7, pp. 419–93, Marcel Dekker, New York and Basel (1977); also technical report CS–562, Computer Science Dept., Stanford University, Stanford, California (1976).

1.11 Montague, R. "English as a formal language", in *Formal Philosophy, Selected Papers of Richard Montague* (ed., R. Thomason), pp. 188–221, Yale University Press, New Haven, Conn. (1974).

1.12 Morris, C. W. *Foundations of the Theory of Signs*; International Encyclopedia of Unified Science, vol. 1, no. 2, University of Chicago Press, Chicago (1938).

1.13 Morris, C. W. *Signs, Language and Behavior*, Prentice-Hall, New York (1946).

1.14 Sammet, J. E. *Programming Languages, History and Fundamentals*, Prentice-Hall, Englewood Cliffs, N.J. (1969).

1.15 Scott, D. S. "Data types as lattices", *SIAM J. on Computing*, **5** (3), 522–86 (1976).

1.16   Scott, D. S. and C. Strachey. "Towards a mathematical semantics for computer languages", in *Proc. of the Symposium on Computers and Automata* (ed.,
J. Fox), pp. 19–46, Polytechnic Institute of Brooklyn Press, New York
(1971); also: technical monograph PRG–6, Programming Research Group,
University of Oxford (1971).

1.17   Tarski, A. *Logic, Semantics, and Meta-mathematics*; Oxford University
Press, Oxford (1956).

1.18   Wexelblat, R. L. (ed.). *Proc. of the History of Programming Languages Conference*, Los Angeles, Aug. 1978, ACM Monograph, Academic
Press, New York (1980).

2 SYNTAX

The main aim of this chapter is to analyze the syntactic structure of programming languages. However, the study of syntax cannot be divorced entirely from semantics. Exercise 1.2 demonstrated that a language may have more than one syntactic description, and that one of these may be considerably more convenient for *semantic* specification.

For more complex languages, it is also necessary to *classify* syntactic phrases according to the kinds of meaning they denote, much as "parts of speech" like nouns, adjectives, and verbs are distinguished in the study of natural languages. For example, in the context

> **if** $g=3$ **then** $\cdots$

fragment '$g=3$' has a (Boolean) value and is an *expression*, whereas in the context

> **const** $g=3$;

the same fragment gives identifier 'g' a local meaning and is a *definition*. Other important syntactic classes are *commands* (such as '$g:=3$') and *sequencers* (such as '**goto** 3'). In this chapter, we shall see how such syntactic distinctions are motivated by semantical considerations. Detailed discussion of semantics will appear in subsequent chapters.

2.1 EXPRESSIONS

2.1.1 Literals

For now, our view of expressions is simply that they are those program phrases that are *evaluated*. The simplest form of expression is the *literal*: an elementary expression whose value is defined by the language and cannot be changed by the programmer. Literals are also known as "constants" or "denotations". Here are some examples in PASCAL:

    6349
    2.37E$-$28
    'A'
    'STRING'
    nil
    [ ]

As always, it is important not to confuse syntactical and semantical entities. Note that syntactically *distinct* literals may have the *same* values (e.g., '4' and '04'). More significantly, a programming language need not provide literals for *all* of the values expressible in it. For example, in PASCAL the two Boolean values are not expressible by literals. (Symbols '*true*' and '*false*' are pre-defined to have these values, but are not literals because a programmer may *re*-define them if he chooses.) Many programming languages omit literals for some of the values expressible in them in order to reduce the amount of specialized notation.

2.1.2 Operators

One way that composite expressions may be formed is by the use of *operators*, such as '+'. For example, if E_1 and E_2 are expressions, then the construct $E_1 + E_2$ is also an expression with E_1, E_2, and the operator as its immediate constituents. Its value is determined by the operation denoted by operator '+' from the values of operands E_1 and E_2. (For now, we ignore the possibility of illegal uses of operations, such as

    2+'A'

and

    3 **div** 0

which are "trapped" before or during evaluation.) A construct of the form $E_1 + E_2$ may itself be a sub-expression of a larger expression, and such nesting may in principle be done to arbitrary depth.

Note that the value of $E_1 + E_2$ depends on the *values* of immediate constituents E_1 and E_2, but not on any *other* properties of them, such as whether they are syntactically elementary or composite. Furthermore, the value of $E_1 + E_2$ is independent of the *pragmatic* difficulty of evaluating E_1 and E_2. Expressions '4', '1+3', and '1+1+1+1' are distinct, both syntactically and pragmatically, but are *semantically* equivalent because their values are the same.

2.1.3 Bracketing

In PASCAL, expression '2+3*4' is analyzed as having the phrase structure of Fig. 2.1 rather than that of Fig. 2.2. To obtain the semantic effect of the second of these, a programmer may write '(2+3)*4'. In PASCAL, the value of (E) is that of its immediate constituent, E, but the parentheses may affect the way text is parsed into phrase structures.

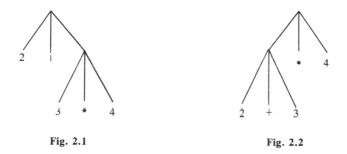

Fig. 2.1   Fig. 2.2

Note that syntactic patterns such as $E_1 * E_2$ and immediate constituent symbols such as E_1 and E_2 stand for *parsed* expressions (i.e., phrase structures), and not merely text. For example, the value of $E_1 * E_2$ may be described as the product of the values of E_1 and E_2. But this would not be accurate if E_1, E_2, and $E_1 * E_2$ stood for text fragments '2+3', '4', and '2+3*4', respectively.

2.1.4 Identifiers

An *identifier*, like a literal, is a symbolic name, but its value may be defined or re-defined by the programmer, even if it is a pre-defined ("standard") identifier. Because of identifiers, the values of expressions are dependent on their computational context. We shall term this contextual information the *state* of the computation.

For now, we are not going to be precise about exactly what a state is or how the value of an identifier occurrence is extracted from it. The significant point is that the possible occurrence of identifiers in expressions now requires us to distinguish between

(a)   the *value* of an expression **relative to** a particular state and
(b)   the *meaning* that an expression denotes.

For example, expression '$x+1$' does not *by itself* have a value, but it does denote a meaning. Roughly, the meaning denoted by an expression yields a value as "output" when given a state as "input". Note however that none of the forms of expression we have discussed so far *change* the state, so that when evaluating a composite such as $E_1 + E_2$ relative to some state, all of its sub-expressions are evaluated relative to that *same* state.

Expressions are semantically equivalent when they denote the same meanings, that is to say, when they would have equal values relative to *every* possible state. For example, addition is a commutative operation, so that '$x+1$' is equivalent to '$1+x$'.

2.2 COMMANDS

A command is essentially a request for an "irreversible" *change* in the current computational state, and so we speak of **executing** a command relative to some state in order to obtain a new state. For example, the effect of executing **assignment** command '$x := x+1$' relative to some state is to produce a new state that differs only in that the value of 'x' is greater by one. Commands are often called "statements", but this term is also applied to phrases that have distinct kinds of meaning, such as declarations and sequencers, so that we shall avoid its use.

Commands are used in programming languages to give a programmer control over storage media that permit over-writing, without requiring him to explicitly mention the states in his programs. If the only practical large-scale storage devices were "read only", there would be little reason to have commands in programming languages.

It is possible for a programming language to have no forms of command. These have been termed *applicative* languages. The sub-language of LISP known as "pure" LISP or as LISP 1.0 is one example, and the language LAMBDA mentioned in Section 1.1 is another. (Of course, *processors* for such languages may still take advantage of conventional storage devices.) Some programming theorists think that it is easier to reason about properties of programs expressed in languages that do not involve the semantic complexities of *imperative* constructs (i.e., assignments and other forms of command).

As with expressions, there are both *elementary* and *composite* forms of command. An example of an elementary form of command is the **null** command, which has no effect on the state. In PASCAL it is expressed by the absence of an explicit command, that is to say, by the null text string.

The assignment is an example of a composite command. The two immediate constituents of an assignment are expressions which we shall term its **source** and **target**. In most languages (including PASCAL) the targets of assignments cannot be arbitrary expressions. For example,

$$x+1 := \cdots$$

is not allowed. The class of expressions that may be used as assignment targets will be termed *l-expressions* ("*l*" for "left" or "location"). *L*-expressions are often called "variables", but we shall avoid this term to prevent confusion with its use by mathematicians to designate non-constant identifiers (i.e., parameters), and its use by programmers to designate storage as well as *l*-expressions.

Some of the more important composite forms of command are known as **control structures** and may be classified as follows:

(1) *Sequential composition.* In this form of command, the effect of the construct is that obtained by executing each of the sub-commands once in a pre-determined sequence. In PASCAL, this is expressed by use of the semi-colon: if C_1 and C_2 are commands, then the effect of composite command C_1; C_2 is that of C_1 followed by that of C_2. Symbol C (possibly with subscripts or primes) will consistently be used to designate arbitrary (parsed) commands, in the same way that E has been used to stand for arbitrary (parsed) expressions.

(2) *Selection.* A **selective** (or "conditional") command is a construct whose effect is obtained by executing *one* of its sub-commands (or is null), as determined by the value of a sub-expression. Examples of selective control structures are the **if** and **case** forms of command in PASCAL.

(3) *Repetition.* A *repetitive* (or "iterative") command is a construct whose effect is obtained by repeatedly executing a sub-command, with the number of repetitions usually determined by evaluating one or more sub-expressions. Examples of repetitive control structures are the **for, while,** and **repeat** forms of command in PASCAL. For the present we ignore the possibility of *non-termination* of execution due to "infinite" looping in repetitive forms.

(4) *Bracketing.* Symbols 'begin' and 'end' in PASCAL play the same role for commands as do parentheses '(' and ')' for expressions. The effect of **begin** C **end** is simply that of C itself, but the brackets may be used to control parsing. For example, in PASCAL a command of the form

$$\textbf{if } E_1 \textbf{ then if } E_2 \textbf{ then } C_1 \textbf{ else } C_2$$

would be parsed so that the **else** part matches the *second* **if**. If a programmer wanted the **else** part to match the *first* **if**, he would use brackets (and, for readability, indentation) as follows:

```
if E₁ then
begin
    if E₂ then C₁
end
else C₂
```

We have seen that several forms of command have expressions as immediate constituents. Programming languages generally also allow commands to be components of expressions in some contexts. For example, suppose that the following form of *expression* were added to PASCAL:

```
begin
    C
result E
```

(A similar construct, with syntax **begin** C ; E **end** is found in the language ALGOL W.) Its value is to be that of sub-expression E evaluated *after* execution of command C. But evaluation of this composite expression may also be expected to change the state, because of the effects of executing C. These state changes are known as the *side effects* of the expression evaluation.

For example, the value of

```
begin
    a := sqr(a);
    b := sqr(b)
result a+b
```

is the sum of the squares of the original values of a and b. But this evaluation *also* has the side effect of squaring a and b.

Side effects are often confusing to program readers because they are *unexpected*: the familiar expressions of conventional arithmetic and algebra do not have side effects. Furthermore, whenever a composite expression has more than one sub-expression (such as $E_1 + E_2$), it is necessary to take into account the *order* of their evaluation because side effects of one sub-expression may affect the value yielded by another. If expression evaluation cannot change the state, the order of sub-expression evaluations is semantically insignificant (except for possible jumps and error traps). For these reasons, the use of side effects is generally regarded as poor programming practice, except in special circumstances such as during program debugging.

2.3 DEFINITIONS

2.3.1 Definitions and Commands

A simple example of a definition in PASCAL is

   const $i = -j$;

This seems similar to *assignment*

   $i := -j$

but the latter is a command and has an *irreversible* effect on the computational state. In contrast, the effect of a definition normally is "undone" later. Consider the composite form

   D
   begin
      C
   end

in PASCAL, where D stands for a definition. This form of command is termed a **block**. In block

   const $i = -j$;
   begin
      $\cdots i \cdots$
   end

the effect of interpreting the definition is to define identifier 'i' to denote the value of '$-j$' for the execution of the sub-command. When control leaves the block, some previously defined meaning of 'i' will be restored.

   The localized association of an *identifier* to a *value* established by a definition is termed a **binding**, and the region of program text in which a binding is effective is known as its **scope**.

   In contrast, the effects of commands (such as '$i := -j$') need not be localized to any pre-determined part of the program. For example, in

   $i := -j$;
   begin
      $\cdots i \cdots$
   end

the effect of updating *i* will persist until execution of another assignment to it, rather than be localized to the second command. To help maintain the important conceptual distinction between definitions and assignments, the term "binding" should *not* be used for the associations set up by executing assignments.

2.3.2 Environments and Stores

The semantics of blocks and definitions are most conveniently described if the computational state is partitioned into two components: the ***environment***, which is used as a record of identifier bindings, and the ***store***, which is used as a record of the effects of assignments. Expressions, definitions, and commands are all interpreted relative to a complete state, that is to say, *both* an environment *and* a store. But the "outputs" for these three syntactic classes differ:

(a) an expression yields a value (and, if necessary to allow for side effects, a new store);

(b) a command yields a new store; and

(c) a definition yields a new environment.

For example, the meaning of composite command C_1 ; C_2 may be specified by describing the effect of executing it relative to an environment and a store. First, sub-command C_1 is executed relative to the original environment and store; this will yield a new store. Then, sub-command C_2 is executed relative to the *original* environment and the *new* store. This yields another store, which is the overall result of executing the whole composite.

Note that by separating the environment and the store it is not necessary to *explicitly* "undo" any changes to the environment made during the execution of C_1. They are implicitly undone merely by stating that C_2 is executed relative to the *original* environment. It is the responsibility of language processors to manipulate their representations of environments to have the effects specified, but the details of how this is done need not be included in the semantic description.

As a second example, consider execution of a block command

> D
> **begin**
>   C
> **end**

relative to an environment and a store. First, definition D is executed relative to the original environment and store. This yields a new environment, and sub-command C is executed relative to this environment and the store. The store yielded by executing C becomes the overall result for the block. As before, the command as a whole has no persistent effect on the environment; however, definition D does have a *local* effect on the environment used for execution of sub-command C.

Finally, consider evaluating an expression of the form

> **begin**
>   C
> **result** E

relative to an environment and store. Command C is executed and yields a new store. Then sub-expression E is evaluated relative to the original environment and this new store. The resulting value and store are the overall results for the whole evaluation.

2.3.3 Declarations

Some forms of definition affect the store as well as the environment. For example, interpretation of *declaration*

> **var** x : *integer*;

in PASCAL has the effect of allocating an area of storage suitable for storing integers. This "new" (i.e., currently unused) storage becomes the local meaning of identifier 'x', so that assignments to 'x' in the scope of the declaration will update the contents of this storage area. Thus, the declaration has an effect on the store, because the storage allocated must somehow be marked as being currently "in use". Consequently, interpretation of a declaration has the effect of yielding a new store as well as a new environment. The other forms of definition in PASCAL affect *only* the environment.

Storage allocated by a **var** declaration in a PASCAL block may be *reclaimed* by a processor when execution of the block has terminated, because this storage will no longer be accessible. Such storage reclamation has no semantic effect, but it is an important pragmatic aspect of the language, because it permits a simple and efficient stack-oriented approach to storage management.

2.3.4 Type Expressions and Static Expressions

In declaration

> **var** x : *integer*;

the role of identifier '*integer*' is to specify the *type* of the bound identifier, '*x*'. Type information has three purposes. Firstly, it is used to simplify implementation; for example, it is easier and more efficient for an implementation to allocate storage for integers only, rather than for arbitrary values.

The second function of type information is to allow checks of the compatibility of operations and arguments before execution; for example, in the scope of the declaration above, expression '**not** *x*' would be in error because the type of operand '*x*' is not compatible with the type expected by Boolean operator '**not**'.

Finally, type specifications are often useful during program development and can improve program readability.

In declaration

> **var** *x* : *integer*;

'*integer*' is a type *identifier*. PASCAL also allows *composite* type expressions, as in

> **var** *a* : **array**[*Boolean*]**of** *integer*;

in which type construction **array**[T_1]**of** T_2 is used, where T_1 and T_2 are sub-expressions. It is also possible in PASCAL for the programmer to bind an identifier to a type by means of a **type** definition, as in

> **type** *t* = **array**[*Boolean*]**of** *integer*;
> **var** *a* : *t*;

A syntactic class in PASCAL that is closely associated with type expressions is what we will term the *static expressions*. These are simply expressions that are sufficiently restricted that they may be straightforwardly evaluated "statically", i.e., before program execution. Static expressions are required in certain contexts in PASCAL, such as in subrange type expressions, as **case** labels, and as the right-hand sides of **const** definitions.

2.4 PROCEDURE INVOCATIONS AND DEFINITIONS

2.4.1 Invocations

The syntactic form

> I($\cdots$, E_i, $\cdots$)

in PASCAL, where I is an identifier, is what will be termed a procedure *invocation* (or "call"). It might be an *expression*, in which case the identifier must be a **function** name, or a *command*, in which case the identifier is a **procedure** name. Sub-expressions E_i are the *actual parameters* of the invocation, and their values will be termed the *arguments* of the procedure.

How should we describe the meaning of an invocation? The most obvious approach is to express the effect of an invocation in terms of an execution of the program fragment that *defined* the **procedure** or **function** name elsewhere in the program. The identifier would therefore be regarded as the name of a *syntactic* entity.

This approach is conceptually unsatisfactory, however, because *distinct* procedure descriptions may have the *same* meanings, just as different numerals may denote the same number. For example, consider how many semantically equivalent array-sorting procedures may be written. Procedures are not merely devices for abbreviating program texts. Programmers are encouraged to use procedures to separate levels of abstraction in the development of large programs. Our explanation of the semantics of procedures should similarly distinguish between the abstract meaning of a procedure (*what* it does) and the concrete text that describes it (*how* to do it).

Let us recall at this point an important mathematical notion; a *function* (or "mapping" or "operation") is a correspondence between the elements of two given sets such that for *each* element of one set there corresponds (exactly) *one* element of the other set. If a function *f* maps *a* to *b*, then *b* is termed the *result* of *applying* *f* to argument *a*. If **A** is the set of arguments of a function *f*, and **B** is the set of its possible results, then this may be written $f: \mathbf{A} \rightarrow \mathbf{B}$. Functions are regarded as equal just if they have the same set of arguments, the same set of possible results, and the same result for every argument.

In conventional mathematical terminology, the sets of arguments and possible results of a function are known as its "domain" and "codomain", respectively. In this book, the term *domain* will designate any set that is the set of arguments or the set of possible results of a function used in describing a programming language.

Here are some examples of functions over the domain of integers:

(a) For any integer k, there is a *constant* function that maps every argument into k.
(b) The *squaring* function maps any argument n to n^2.
(c) The *identity* function maps any argument n to n.
(d) The *negation* function maps any argument n to $-n$.

Now, consider invocation expression

$$sqr(i+j)$$

in PASCAL. Suppose that it is being evaluated in an environment in which identifier '*sqr*' has its pre-defined (standard) meaning. If we assume that the squaring function mentioned above *is* this meaning, then the value of the invocation expression may be described as the result of applying the value of the procedure identifier to the value of the actual parameter. Note that we do *not* need to be concerned with *how* the squaring function is described or implemented. Therefore, we have described the meaning of the invocation *denotationally*, that is, in terms of the meanings of its immediate constituents, just as we did for other composite forms of expression and command.

Of course, this example is unusually simple. In general, the so-called "functions" describable in PASCAL require a more elaborate semantic model to account for side effects of invocations and dependencies on the states at definition and invocation. These issues will all be discussed later.

For the present we consider only the problem of terminology: it seems inappropriate to use the term "function" for entities that in general seem not to behave like mathematical functions. We will therefore adopt the following conventions: the term "function" will *only* refer to the usual mathematical notion (except when reference is made to a syntactic entity as a "**function definition**".) The term *procedure* will designate the meaning of identifier I in *all* forms of invocation $I(\cdots,E,\cdots)$. If it is necessary to distinguish between kinds of procedure, they will be termed *expression* procedures, *command* procedures, and so on.

2.4.2 Procedure Definitions and Abstracts

In the previous section, we considered the semantics of invocations and saw that it was possible in a very simple case to describe the meaning of the composite form in terms of the meanings of its immediate constituents. By using a pre-defined procedure it was possible there to avoid issues relating to how procedures may be set up by the programmer. In this section we discuss procedure *definitions*, sometimes called "sub-programs".

Again, complexities of the general case (such as recursion, parameter conventions, and non-local identifiers) may be temporarily avoided by considering the following rather simple example:

```
function sqr(n : integer) : integer;
  begin
    sqr := n*n
  end;
```

We would expect this to define the *same* procedure as the standard meaning for identifier '*sqr*', that is to say, the squaring procedure.

Note that there are really *two* kinds of "definition" involved here. Firstly, there is the "definition" of a certain semantic entity, in this case the squaring procedure. Secondly, this procedure is given a name by means of a definition of identifier '*sqr*'; this is essentially similar to the forms of definition in PASCAL that have been discussed already. In some programming languages, these two aspects are expressed by distinct syntactic features and it will be helpful conceptually to treat them separately.

Consider then the following re-arrangement of the **function** definition:

$$sqr = \mathbf{function}(n \ : \ integer) \ : \ integer;$$
$$n*n;$$

This is not syntactically legal in PASCAL, but similar constructions appear in several other languages. If the phrase on the right-hand side of the '=' symbol is regarded as an *expression* whose value is the squaring procedure, then this construct as a whole may be regarded as an ordinary definition of the form I = E, with the usual effect of locally binding identifier I to the value of expression E. But how can

$$\mathbf{function}(n \ : \ integer) \ : \ integer;$$
$$n*n$$

be regarded as an *expression*? Note in particular that sub-expression '$n*n$' cannot be evaluated when the procedure is *defined* because the value of the *formal parameter*, n, is not yet known!

The explanation is that to define the procedure we are only interested in the meaning denoted by '$n*n$', and not its value at the time of definition. Recall that it was suggested that the meaning of an expression could be regarded as yielding a value *when* evaluated relative to a state. Therefore, the value of expression

$$\mathbf{function}(n \ : \ integer) \ : \ integer;$$
$$n*n$$

may be defined in terms of the meaning of '$n*n$', as follows: it is the procedure whose result for any (integer) argument is the value of '$n*n$' relative to a state in which the value of 'n' is that argument. Of course, this procedure *is* the squaring procedure. Note that three distinct values are involved in this explanation:

(a) the squaring procedure, which is the value of the whole expression,
(b) the argument, n, for any application of this procedure, and
(c) the result, $n*n$, for this particular argument.

Again we see that it is possible to specify the meaning of a composite form solely in terms of the meanings of its immediate constituents.

The specification of a procedure by a syntactic description of its result for a typical argument is an example of a linguistic device known in some branches of mathematics as *abstraction*. This term is appropriate because the semantically irrelevant properties of the description are indeed "abstracted away". For example, the PASCAL definition in Fig. 2.3 is syntactically and pragmatically quite different from the definition of '*sqr*' given earlier; but the procedures they define happen to be *semantically* indistinguishable.

```
function sqr(m : integer) : integer;
  var i,s : integer;
  begin
    s := 0;
    for i := 1 to abs(m) do
      s := s+abs(m);
    sqr := s
  end;
```

Fig. 2.3

Expressions like

```
function(n : integer) : integer;
  n*n
```

will be termed **abstracts**. In PASCAL, this form of expression is *implicit* in **function** and **procedure** definitions, but similar constructs appear in other languages and notations. For example, the analogous constructs are

```
proc(int n) int: n*n
```

in ALGOL 68,

```
(LAMBDA (N) (TIMES N N))
```

in LISP, and

$$n \mapsto n.n$$

in algebra.

It may be helpful to compare the concept of procedural abstraction to a more familiar form of abstraction. In mathematics,

$$\{n \in \mathbf{N} \mid n^2 \leq 2 \times n\}$$

is generally understood to denote the subset of elements of $\mathbf{N}$ whose squares are not greater than their doubles. It is an example of a *set* abstract. Its value is a set, determined by the meaning of formula '$n^2 \leq 2 \times n$', just as a procedural abstract has a procedure as its value, determined by the meaning of its body. For example, compare the set abstract above with procedural abstract

$$\textbf{function}(n : natnum) : Boolean;$$
$$sqr(n) \leq 2*n$$

which defines the characteristic function for the set.

The analog of procedure invocation for sets is set membership testing. For example, if

$$S = \{n \in \mathbf{N} \mid n^2 \leq 2 \times n\},$$

then

$$i \in S$$

would have value *true* just if i is an element of the set (i.e., if $i^2 \leq 2 \times i$), and *false* otherwise.

2.5 SEQUENCERS AND LABELS

2.5.1 Sequencers

Conventional computers have the property that *any* location in their fast store may be treated as the next instruction to be executed. Language processors make use of this to implement control structures and procedures. Sequencers are provided in programming languages to allow programmers to use this flexibility more directly. The only sequencers in PASCAL have the form

goto N

where N stands for a numeral.

The presence of sequencers in a programming language creates two significant semantic difficulties that control structures and procedures alone do not. The first is the problem of explaining the meaning of a construct like 'goto 13' in terms of the meaning of its immediate constituent, numeral '13'. Evidently the *numerical* significance of the numeral is irrelevant in this context. The numeral is just being used to designate the point in the program that is to be the destination of the "jump". But what is the *semantic* counterpart of a "program point"?

The second difficulty is that, with the semantic model we have been using, an expression evaluation or command execution is expected to yield a value, or an updated store, or both. For example, we defined the effect of

$$C_1 ; C_2$$

to be the effect of C_2 relative to the store *after* execution of C_1. But now suppose C_1 is a command that contains a **goto**, as in

begin···; **goto** 13;···**end**; C_2

Then this description would be incorrect because the sequencer may cause a "jump" out of the whole construct and C_2 will not be executed at all. Similarly, "evaluation" of sub-expression E_1 in $E_1 + E_2$ will not yield a value if E_1 contains an invocation of the procedure defined by

function *escape* : *integer*;
   begin goto 13 **end**;

which results in a jump to a context far removed from the original addition expression. The introduction of sequencers into a language has repercussions on the interpretation of almost all syntactic classes.

We are not going to attempt to solve these semantic problems at this point. But it should be noted that some programming theorists think that sequencers impair the readability and verifiability of programs, and recommend that their use be avoided. Others insist that languages without sequencers would be too inflexible. We shall return to these issues in Chapter 10.

2.5.2 Labels

In PASCAL a command may be labelled by prefixing it by a numeral and a colon, as in

13: $x := x + 1$

This establishes a local meaning for the numeral and is therefore similar to a *definition*.

In PASCAL, the procedure definition that encloses a labelled command is also required to contain a "declaration" of the label, as in

label 13;

But this form of "declaration" does not have any real semantic significance. It is required in PASCAL merely to simplify syntactic analysis of programs in which labels are used before the program points at which they are defined, as in

begin
    ⋮
    goto 13;
    ⋮
    13: $x:=x+1$;
    ⋮
end

2.6 FORMAL SYNTAX

It would be possible to specify the syntax of programming languages informally, as was done with the language of binary numerals in Chapter 1. But it is much more convenient to use a specialized formal notation. Notation that is used in describing the syntax or semantics of a language is termed a *meta-language*. In this section, we shall discuss meta-languages for describing syntax.

2.6.1 Abstract Syntax

The syntactic structure of a language may be conveniently summarized by simply listing all of the possible forms for each of the syntactic classes. This is termed the *abstract syntax* of the language. The abstract syntax of PASCAL is specified in Appendix B. The first section lists the syntactic classes along with the symbols that stand for arbitrary elements of the classes. In the second section, the alternatives for each of the non-elementary classes are listed to the right of a '::=' symbol, separated by occurrences of symbol '|'.

2.6.2 Concrete Syntax

An abstract syntax tells us what syntactic structures are available in a language, but does not specify which strings of characters are well-formed program texts, nor their phrase structures. For example, the abstract syntax of PASCAL tells us that

> **if** E **then** C

and

> **if** E **then** C **else** C

are possible phrase structures for commands, but does not specify whether

> **if** a **then if** b **then** p **else** q

is a well-formed command text or, if it is, whether it is to be analyzed so that the **else** part matches the first or the second of the **then** parts. Such issues are settled by a ***concrete syntax*** (or "grammar").

Backus–Naur Formalism (BNF) is a well-known meta-language for specifying concrete syntax. An example is given in Fig. 2.4. The first rule specifies that (the textual representation of) an expression is either a term or an expression followed by an addition operator (*addop*) followed by a term. The interpretation of the other rules is similar.

$\langle expression \rangle$	$::=$	$\langle term \rangle \mid \langle expression \rangle \ \langle addop \rangle \ \langle term \rangle$
$\langle term \rangle$	$::=$	$\langle factor \rangle \mid \langle term \rangle \ \langle multop \rangle \ \langle factor \rangle$
$\langle factor \rangle$	$::=$	$\langle identifier \rangle \mid \langle literal \rangle \mid (\langle expression \rangle)$
$\langle identifier \rangle$	$::=$	$a \mid b \mid c \mid \cdots \mid z$
$\langle literal \rangle$	$::=$	$0 \mid 1 \mid 2 \mid \cdots \mid 9$
$\langle addop \rangle$	$::=$	$+ \mid - \mid$ **or**
$\langle multop \rangle$	$::=$	$* \mid / \mid$ **div** $\mid$ **mod** $\mid$ **and**

Fig. 2.4

These rules specify the *phrase structures* for texts analyzable as expressions, terms, factors, and so on, and not merely *what* texts are recognizable. For example,

> $a+b*c$

is recognized as an expression whose phrase structure is

> $\langle expression \rangle \ \langle addop \rangle \ \langle term \rangle$

where the term is '$b*c$'. Similarly,

$$a*b+c$$

is analyzed as having the phrase structure

$$\langle expression \rangle \; \langle addop \rangle \; \langle term \rangle$$

where the term is 'c'. Therefore, '$a+b*c$' is equivalent to '$a+(b*c)$', and '$a*b+c$' is equivalent to '$(a*b)+c$'. In short, the syntax specifies that multiplication operators take *precedence* over (or "bind more tightly than") addition operators.

Similarly,

$$a-b-c$$

is analyzed as an expression of the form

$$\langle expression \rangle \; \langle addop \rangle \; \langle term \rangle$$

where the sub-expression has the same form. Therefore, '$a-b-c$' is equivalent to '$(a-b)-c$'. That is, the syntax specifies that the addition operators (and also the multiplication operators) *associate* to the left.

A syntactic description is termed *ambiguous* if, for any text, it specifies more than one phrase structure. For example, consider replacing the first rule in the syntax above by

$$\langle expression \rangle ::= \langle term \rangle \mid \langle expression \rangle \; \langle addop \rangle \; \langle expression \rangle$$

This would recognize the same set of texts, but for a text like

$$a-b-c$$

there would be two possible phrase structures. Because '$(a-b)-c$' is not equivalent to '$a-(b-c)$', these two phrase structures would have distinct meanings. It is certainly undesirable to have an ambiguous syntax, but there is no *general* method possible for testing whether a syntax is ambiguous. However, it is often possible to prove that a *particular* syntax is unambiguous.

BNF is not the only notation in use for specifying formally the concrete syntax of programming languages. Appendix C is a description of the concrete syntax of PASCAL that uses *syntax diagrams*. Their interpretation should be evident. Every path through a diagram in the direction of the arrows represents a possible analysis for that kind of text.

2.6.3 Context-sensitive Syntax

A significant limitation of notations like BNF and syntax diagrams is that they specify only the *context-free* aspects of the syntax of a language: each rule describes the phrase structures possible solely in terms of their sub-structures. But contextual information is necessary to specify that texts like

> **const** $i=32$;
> **begin**
> $\vdots$
> $i:=i+1$;
> $\vdots$
> **end**

and

> **var** i : *integer*;
> **begin**
> $\vdots$
>   **not** i
> $\vdots$
> **end**

are ill-formed.

There is no widely accepted notation for specifying such context-sensitive constraints, and they are often expressed informally. Unfortunately, an informal description is often incomplete or imprecise, particularly if it is not based on a formal description. Most of the incompatibilities between and inconsistencies within PASCAL processors are attributable to incomplete and imprecise specification of its syntax. An approach to describing context-sensitive syntax formally will be discussed in Chapter 13.

EXERCISES

2.1 In PASCAL the meanings of operators such as '+' are pre-defined and unchangeable; that is, they are analogous to *literals*. Would it be possible to have operators that are analogous to *identifiers*?

2.2 Give an example of a PASCAL fragment that is semantically equivalent to the null command, yet is syntactically different from it.

2.3 Compare the effects of the following PASCAL blocks:

(a) **const** $a = 1$;
    procedure p;
      const $a = 2$;
      begin
        write(a)
      end {p};
    begin
      p;
      write(a)
    end

(b) **var** a : integer;
    procedure p;
    begin
      $a := 2$;
      write(a)
    end {p};
    begin
      $a := 1$;
      p;
      write(a)
    end

2.4 According to Appendix B, none of the forms of expression in PASCAL have command components. How is it possible for an expression to have side effects?

2.5 According to Appendix B, parameter specifiers, Q, have the same syntax as formal parameters, P. Why is it appropriate to distinguish these classes?

2.6 Describe a reasonable semantics for expressions of the form

    D
    begin
      C
    result E

where D is a definition (possibly a declaration), C is a command, and E is an expression.

2.7 The *composition* of two functions $f : A \rightarrow B$ and $g : B \rightarrow C$ is the function $g \circ f : A \rightarrow C$ defined by the rule that a is mapped into $g(f(a))$. Show that for any $h : C \rightarrow D$,

$$h \circ (g \circ f) = (h \circ g) \circ f$$

2.8 Does evaluation of an abstract (as described in Section 2.4.2) have side effects?

2.9 A label in PASCAL is analogous to an identifier in that its meaning as a label is definable by the programmer. Is it conceivable for a language to have a *pre-defined* label identifier? What about a *literal* label? Suggest possible applications of these concepts if they are feasible.

2.10 The concrete syntax of COBOL has been described using the following notational conventions:

(a) The vertical bar of BNF is replaced by alternatives arranged vertically and enclosed in braces:

$$\left\{ \begin{array}{l} \text{alternative}_1 \\ \text{alternative}_2 \\ \vdots \\ \text{alternative}_n \end{array} \right\}$$

(b) Optional constructs or optional alternatives are indicated by enclosing them in square brackets:

$$\begin{bmatrix} \text{option}_1 \\ \text{option}_2 \\ \vdots \\ \text{option}_n \end{bmatrix}$$

(c) Repetition of a construct is indicated by appending an ellipsis " ··· ".
(d) Key words that are not underlined have no effect and may be omitted. (They are known as "noise words".)

For example, the syntax of the ADD statement in COBOL may be expressed as follows:

$$\underline{\text{ADD}} \quad \begin{Bmatrix} \langle \textit{identifier} \rangle \\ \langle \textit{number} \rangle \end{Bmatrix} \quad \begin{bmatrix} , \langle \textit{identifier} \rangle \\ , \langle \textit{number} \rangle \end{bmatrix} \quad \cdots$$

$$\underline{\text{TO}} \langle \textit{identifier} \rangle [\underline{\text{ROUNDED}}] \quad \begin{bmatrix} , \langle \textit{identifier} \rangle [\underline{\text{ROUNDED}}] \end{bmatrix} \quad \cdots$$

$$[; \text{ON } \underline{\text{SIZE}} \; \underline{\text{ERROR}} \quad \langle \textit{statement} \rangle]$$

Express this with a syntax diagram.

2.11 Part of the concrete syntax given in the 1960 Report on ALGOL 60 is effectively as follows:

⟨statement list⟩
    ::=⟨statement⟩
    | ⟨statement list⟩ ; ⟨statement⟩

⟨statement⟩
    ::=⟨assignment⟩
    | **if** ⟨expression⟩ **then** ⟨statement⟩
    | **if** ⟨expression⟩ **then** ⟨statement⟩ **else** ⟨statement⟩
    | **begin** ⟨statement list⟩ **end**

In the 1963 Revised Report on ALGOL 60, this was changed to

⟨statement list⟩
    ::=⟨statement⟩
    | ⟨statement list⟩ ; ⟨statement⟩

⟨statement⟩
    ::=⟨unconditional statement⟩
    | **if** ⟨expression⟩ **then** ⟨unconditional statement⟩
    | **if** ⟨expression⟩ **then** ⟨unconditional statement⟩
                  else ⟨statement⟩

⟨unconditional statement⟩
   ::=⟨assignment⟩
   | **begin** ⟨statement list⟩ **end**

(a)   Give an example that shows why the original syntax was unsuitable and why the revised syntax is an improvement.

(b)   What would be the advantage of the following syntax:

⟨statement list⟩
   ::=⟨statement⟩
   | ⟨statement list⟩ ; ⟨statement⟩

⟨statement⟩
   ::=⟨balanced statement⟩
   | ⟨unbalanced statement⟩

⟨balanced statement⟩
   ::=⟨assignment⟩
   | **begin** ⟨statement list⟩ **end**
   | **if** ⟨expression⟩ **then** ⟨balanced statement⟩
                    else ⟨balanced statement⟩

⟨unbalanced statement⟩
   ::=**if** ⟨expression⟩ **then** ⟨statement⟩
   | **if** ⟨expression⟩ **then** ⟨balanced statement⟩
                    else ⟨unbalanced statement⟩

2.12   In the language APL, all operators have the same precedence and associate to the right. Give a concrete syntax with these properties for expressions whose abstract syntax is

   B   literals
   I   identifiers
   O   operators
   E   expressions

   E ::= B | I | OE | EOE | (E)

PROJECT

Work out an abstract syntax for some other programming language. To facilitate comparison with PASCAL, try to use the same syntactic classes and symbols as in Appendix B.

BIBLIOGRAPHIC NOTES

Programming languages without commands and their use have been described by McCarthy [2.12], Landin [2.11], Burge [2.5], Ashcroft and Wadge [2.1], Backus [2.3], Henderson [2.7], Warren [2.18], Morris et al. [2.15], and others. The *environment* concept was first used for programming-language description by Landin [2.9]. The separation of the "state" into environment and store components was described by Scott and Strachey [2.17]. The term "sequencer" was introduced by Milne and Strachey [2.14]. Arguments pro and con sequencers may be found in Landin [2.10], Dijkstra [2.6], and Knuth [2.8]. The concept of abstract syntax was introduced by Landin [2.9] and McCarthy [2.13]. The notation used in Appendix B is essentially that of Scott and Strachey [2.17]. BNF was introduced by Backus [2.3] and popularized in the reports on ALGOL 60 [2.16]. Much more information on (concrete) syntax and parsing may be found in a book by Backhouse [2.2].

2.1   Ashcroft, E. A., and W. W. Wadge: "LUCID, a non-procedural language with iteration", *Comm. ACM*, **20** (7), 519–26 (1977).

2.2   Backhouse, R. C. *Syntax of Programming Languages, Theory and Practice*, Prentice-Hall International, London (1979).

2.3   Backus, J. "The syntax and semantics of the proposed international algebraic language of the Zurich ACM-GAMM Conference", *Proc. Int. Conf. Information Processing*, pp. 125-32, UNESCO, Paris (1959).

2.4   Backus, J. "Can programming be liberated from the von Neumann style? A functional style and its algebra of programs", *Comm. ACM*, **21** (8), 613–41 (1978).

2.5   Burge, W. H. *Recursive Programming Techniques*, Addison-Wesley, Reading, Mass. (1975).

2.6   Dijkstra, E. W. "**Go to** statement considered harmful", *Comm. ACM*, **11** (3), 147–8 (1968).

2.7   Henderson, P. *Functional Programming, Application and Implementation*, Prentice-Hall International, London (1980).

2.8   Knuth, D. E. "Structured programming with **goto** statements", *Comp. Surveys*, **6** (4), 261–301 (1974).

2.9   Landin, P. J. "The mechanical evaluation of expressions", *Comp. J.*, **6** (4), 308–20 (1963).

2.10 Landin, P. J. *Getting Rid of Labels*, Univac Systems Programming Research report, New York (1965).

2.11 Landin, P. J. "The next 700 programming languages", *Comm. ACM*, **9** (3), 157–64 (1966).

2.12 McCarthy, J. "Recursive functions of symbolic expressions and their computation by machine, pt. 1", *Comm. ACM*, **3** (4), 184–95 (1960).

2.13 McCarthy, J. "Towards a mathematical science of computation", in *Information Processing 1962*, Proc. IFIP Congress, 1962, pp. 21–28, North-Holland, Amsterdam (1963).

2.14 Milne, R. E. and C. Strachey. *A Theory of Programming Language Semantics*, Chapman and Hall, London, and Wiley, New York (1976).

2.15 Morris, J. H., E. Schmidt, and P. Wadler. "Experience with an applicative string processing language", *Conf. Record of the 7th ACM Symposium on Principles of Programming Languages*, pp. 32–46 (1980).

2.16 Naur, P. (ed.). "Revised report on the algorithmic language ALGOL 60", *Comm. ACM*, **6** (1), 1–20 (1963); also in *Comp. J.*, **5,** 349–67 (1963), and *Numerische Mathematik*, **4,** 420–52 (1963).

2.17 Scott, D. S. and C. Strachey. "Towards a mathematical semantics for computer languages", in *Proc. of the Symposium on Computers and Automata* (ed., J. Fox), pp. 19–46, Polytechnic Institute of Brooklyn Press, New York (1971); also: technical monograph PRG-6, Programming Research Group, University of Oxford (1971).

2.18 Warren, D. H. D. "Logic programming and compiler writing", *Software Practice and Experience*, **10** (2), 97–125 (1980).

3 DATA

As mentioned in Section 2.4.1, argument and result sets of functions used in describing the semantics of a programming language are termed *domains* (or "data types"). For example, the semantics of binary numerals given in Section 1.3 specifies a mapping having (parsed) binary numerals as its domain of arguments and natural numbers as its domain of possible results.

Every domain has associated with it certain "essential" operations. We shall describe these as the operations with which the domain is *equipped*. For example, the domain of binary numerals is equipped with two "constant" operations whose results are the elementary numerals, '0' and '1', and two operations that construct composite numerals of the forms N0 and N1 from arguments N. Similarly, the domain of natural numbers is equipped with a "constant" operation that produces the number zero, and an operation that constructs the successor of any number. Additional operations on numbers (such as addition and multiplication) may be defined using these basic operations.

The domains that are needed to describe programming languages can be much more complex than the sets of numerals and numbers. Indeed, the diversity and complexity of elementary and structured data in programming languages seem overwhelming at first. PASCAL alone has numbers, characters, Boolean values, enumerations, pointers, arrays, records, sets, files, procedures, and labels. Other languages have S-expressions and lists (LISP), multi-dimensional arrays (APL), strings and patterns (SNOBOL4), and so on. Furthermore, sets of semantic constructs such as environments and stores, and syntactic classes such as expressions, commands, and definitions must all be regarded as domains as well.

Yet we shall see that a remarkably small number of general domain operations will allow us to *construct* domains that model all of these features of programming languages. These domain constructions are described in Section 3.1. Section 3.2 presents several examples of the use of these domain constructions in modelling the "data types" of three well-known programming languages. Certain pragmatic and theoretical limitations on domain construction will be considered in Section 3.3.

3.1 DOMAIN CONSTRUCTIONS

3.1.1 Products of Domains

Consider type expression

> **record**
> > *i* : *integer*;
> > *c* : *char*
>
> **end**

in PASCAL. It describes a domain that consists of all ordered pairs whose first components are integers and whose second components are characters. In general, for *any* sets **A** and **B,** the set of all ordered pairs, (a,b), with $a \in A$ and $b \in B$, is termed the (Cartesian) ***product*** of **A** and **B**, written $A \times B$. Note that if **A** is a set with na elements and **B** is a set with nb elements, set $A \times B$ contains $na \times nb$ elements.

Domain $A \times B$ is equipped with two operations that select the **A** and **B** components, respectively, of arguments in $A \times B$. These are termed the ***projection*** functions for the product. In PASCAL the projection operations for record types are expressed by ***field selection*** *l*-expressions of the form

$$L.I$$

By using ordered *n*-tuples, the product construction may be generalized to allow any number *n* of "factors", as in $A_1 \times A_2 \times \cdots \times A_n$. For any domain **D**, we shall write D^n for

$$D \times D \times \cdots \times D \qquad (n \text{ factors})$$

i.e., for the domain of all ordered *n*-tuples of elements of **D**. For $n=0$, we adopt the convention that $D^0 = \{null\}$, that is to say, the singleton set whose only element is *null*.

3.1.2 Sums of Domains

Consider type expression

> **record case** *tag* : *Boolean* **of**
> > *true* : (*i* : *integer*);
> > *false* : (*c* : *char*)
>
> **end**

in PASCAL. Each of the elements in the domain it describes is *either* an integer *or* a character, together with a Boolean component to differentiate the two possibilities. In general, for *any* sets **A** and **B**, their *sum* (or "disjoint union", or "co-product"), written **A**+**B**, is defined to be the set of ordered pairs (*true*, *a*) for all $a \in$ **A**, and (*false*, *b*) for all $b \in$ **B**; that is,

$$\mathbf{A}+\mathbf{B}=\{(true,\ a)\mid a \in \mathbf{A}\} \cup \{(false,\ b)\mid b \in \mathbf{B}\}$$

If sets **A** and **B** contain *na* and *nb* elements, respectively, then set **A**+**B** has *na*+*nb* elements, even if **A** and **B** have elements in common.

Domain **A**+**B** is equipped with two operations that construct elements of **A**+**B** from arguments in **A** and **B**, respectively. These are termed the *injection* functions for the sum. By using *n* "tags", the sum construction may be generalized to allow any number *n* of terms, as in $\mathbf{A}_1+\mathbf{A}_2+\cdots+\mathbf{A}_n$.

3.1.3   Function Domains

Consider type expression

array[*char*]**of** *integer*

in PASCAL. Each of the elements in the domain it describes may be regarded as being a *function* mapping characters into integers, because each array determines a *unique* integer "component" for *every* character "subscript". In general, if **A** and **B** are *any* sets, then **A**→**B** is defined to be the set of all functions whose set of arguments is **A** and whose set of possible results is **B**. If sets **A** and **B** contain *na* and *nb* elements, respectively, then set **A**→**B** contains nb^{na} elements, because there is a choice among *nb* possible results for each of the *na* arguments.

Domain **A**→**B** is equipped with the operation of *application*, which, for any *f*: **A**→**B** and $a \in$ **A**, determines the result of applying *f* to *a*. In PASCAL, the application operation for array types is expressed by *subscripting* *l*-expressions of the form

L[E]

3.1.4   Recursive Definitions of Domains

The fourth (and last) domain construction principle that we need will allow us to construct *infinite* domains. Consider the PASCAL-like definition

type *string* = **record case** *isnull* : *Boolean* **of**
        true : ( );
        false : (*first* : *char*; *rest* : *string*)
    end;

This is *not* legal in PASCAL (for pragmatic reasons we shall discuss in Section 3.3.1), but the intent should be clear. Each of the elements of the domain it describes is either null, or is not null and consists of a *'first'* component, which is a character, and a *'rest'* component which is a string.

The mathematical counterpart of this **type** definition is the following *equation*:

$$Q = \{null\} + (H \times Q) \tag{3.1}$$

where **H** is the domain of characters. Consider now the set whose elements are

$$(true, null)$$

and

$$(false, (h, (true, null)))   \text{for all } h \in H,$$

and

$$(false, (h_1, (false, (h_2, (true, null)))))   \text{for all } h_1, h_2 \in H,$$

and so on. It may be verified that if this set is termed **Q**, it is a solution to equation (3.1); that is, every element of **Q** is an element of $\{null\} + (H \times Q)$, and every element of $\{null\} + (H \times Q)$ is an element of **Q**. In fact, this set is the *smallest* solution of equation (3.1).

In general, we shall regard a domain equation of the form

$$D = \cdots D \cdots$$

as *defining* **D** to be the smallest solution of the equation. The construction is termed **recursive** because the name of the domain being defined "recurs" on the right-hand side of its definition.

For any domain **D** and $d_1, d_2, \cdots, d_n \in D$, it will be convenient to use the notation

$$\langle d_1, d_2, \cdots, d_n \rangle$$

to stand for

$$(false, (d_1, (false, (d_2, \cdots (false, (d_n, (true, null))) \cdots))))$$

for $n \geq 0$, and regard the solution of

$$S = \{null\} + (D \times S)$$

as being the domain of all such finite *sequences* of elements of **D**. We shall use **D*** to designate this domain.

If $s=\langle d_1,d_2,\cdots,d_n\rangle$ for $n>0$, then

$$first(s)=d_1,$$
$$rest(s)=\langle d_2,d_3,\cdots,d_n\rangle,$$

and

$$last(s)=d_n.$$

The important operation of sequence **concatenation** will be designated '⌢':

$$\langle d_1,d_2,\cdots,d_n\rangle^\frown\langle d_{n+1},d_{n+2},\cdots,d_{n+m}\rangle$$
$$=\langle d_1,d_2,\cdots,d_n,d_{n+1},\cdots,d_{n+m}\rangle.$$

Concatenation of sequences is an **associative** operation; that is, $s_1{}^\frown(s_2{}^\frown s_3) = (s_1{}^\frown s_2){}^\frown s_3$, for all sequences s_1, s_2, and s_3.

As another example of recursive domain definition, consider the equation

$$N = \{zero\}+N \tag{3.2}$$

It may be verified that its smallest solution is the set whose elements are

$$(true,zero)$$
$$(false, (true,zero))$$
$$(false, (false, (true,zero)))$$
$$(false, (false, (false, (true,zero))))$$
$$\vdots$$

so that if we let 0 designate $(true,zero)$ and define $successor(i)$ to be $(false,i)$, then it is clear that equation (3.2) may be regarded as a definition of the domain of natural numbers (i.e., 0 and its successors).

Further examples of recursive domain definition will be given in Section 3.2 and the exercises. The question of whether solutions to such domain equations always exist will be taken up in Section 3.3.2.

*3.1.5 Approximation and Limit Domains

The infinite domain that is the smallest solution to a recursive domain definition is the *limit* of a sequence of domains that "approximate" it. For example, consider again equation (3.2):

---

*Starred sections assume a higher level of mathematical maturity and may be skipped without loss of continuity.

$$\mathbf{N} = \{zero\} + \mathbf{N}$$

Now, define a sequence of domains $\mathbf{N}_i$, for $i \geq 0$, as follows:

$$\mathbf{N}_0 = \{\ \} \text{ (i.e., the empty set)}$$

$$\mathbf{N}_{i+1} = \{zero\} + \mathbf{N}_i$$

Note that each domain in the sequence (except the initial one) is defined by using the equation, but with the recursive occurrence of the domain name replaced by the preceding domain in the sequence, so that there is no longer any circularity. Therefore,

$$\begin{aligned}
\mathbf{N}_1 &= \{zero\} + \mathbf{N}_0 \\
&= \{(true,zero)\} \\
&= \{0\}
\end{aligned}$$

$$\begin{aligned}
\mathbf{N}_2 &= \{zero\} + \mathbf{N}_1 \\
&= \{(true,zero), \ (false, \ (true,zero))\} \\
&= \{0, \ successor(0)\}
\end{aligned}$$

$$\begin{aligned}
\mathbf{N}_3 &= \{zero\} + \mathbf{N}_2 \\
&= \{(true,zero), \ (false,(true,zero)), \ (false,(false,(true,zero)))\} \\
&= \{0, \ successor(0), \ successor(successor(0))\}
\end{aligned}$$

and so on.

The elements of each $\mathbf{N}_i$ are 0 and its successors up to, but not including, the ith. Domains $\mathbf{N}_i$ may be regarded as finite *approximations* to (i.e., subsets of) the desired infinite solution of the equation, so that if we take the *limit* of this sequence to be the union of all of these approximating domains, we obtain the set of all the natural numbers, the desired solution of the equation.

It may be verified that the same technique works with equation (3.1). In subsequent chapters, we shall see several other examples of the use of approximations and limits to construct solutions to recursive definitions, regarded as equations.

*3.1.6 Domain Isomorphism

It is often useful to know that two domains, though not equal as sets, are nonetheless "effectively equivalent" in the sense that they may be interchanged in semantic descriptions. This may be defined rigorously as follows: two sets, $\mathbf{A}$ and $\mathbf{B}$, are *isomorphic*, written $\mathbf{A} \cong \mathbf{B}$, if there exists a one-to-one correspondence between them:

$$\{a_1, a_2, \cdots, a_i, \cdots\}$$

$$\downarrow \quad \downarrow \quad \downarrow$$

$$\{b_1, b_2, \cdots, b_i, \cdots\}$$

More formally, $A \cong B$ just if there are functions $f: A \to B$ and $f^{-1}: B \to A$ such that

$$f(f^{-1}(b)) = b \text{ for all } b \in B$$

and

$$f^{-1}(f(a)) = a \text{ for all } a \in A$$

It may be verified that $\cong$ is an equivalence relation; that is,

(a) $A = B$ implies $A \cong B$,
(b) $A \cong B$ implies $B \cong A$, and
(c) $A \cong B$ and $B \cong C$ imply $A \cong C$.

Here are some examples of set isomorphisms involving the product, sum, and function domain constructions:

$$A \times B \cong B \times A$$
$$(A \times B) \times C \cong A \times (B \times C) \cong A \times B \times C$$
$$A + B \cong B + A$$
$$(A + B) + C \cong A + (B + C) \cong A + B + C$$
$$(A \times B) + (A \times C) \cong A \times (B + C)$$
$$(A \times B) \to C \cong A \to (B \to C)$$
$$(A + B) \to C \cong (A \to C) \times (B \to C)$$

These are valid for all sets A, B, and C. Furthermore, if $0 = \{\}$ and 1 is any singleton set, then

$$A \times 1 \cong A, \qquad A \times 0 \cong 0$$
$$A + 0 \cong A$$
$$A \to 1 \cong 1, \qquad 1 \to B \cong B$$

Domain constructions $\times$, $+$, and $\to$ have the following substitution properties with respect to isomorphism: if $A \cong A'$ and $B \cong B'$, then

$$A \times B \cong A' \times B'$$
$$A + B \cong A' + B'$$
$$A \to B \cong A' \to B'$$

Note that many other operations (such as union and intersection) do *not* have these properties.

3.2 THREE CASE STUDIES OF DOMAIN CONSTRUCTION

3.2.1 S-expressions and Lists in LISP

Values in LISP are termed *S-expressions*, which is a contraction of "symbolic expressions". An S-expression may be either an *atom*, which is written as a symbol, such as

A
APPLE
PART2

or a *pair*, written in the form

$$(S_1 \, . \, S_2)$$

where S_1 and S_2 stand for arbitrary S-expressions. Some examples of pairs are

(A . B)
(A . (B1 . B2))
((U . V) . (X . (Y . Z)))

The domain of S-expressions may therefore be defined as the solution of the equation

$$S = A + (S \times S)$$

where **A** is the domain of atoms.

An important subset of the S-expressions consists of what are known as *lists* and satisfy the following constraints:

(a)   An atom is a list just if it is the atom 'NIL',
(b)   A pair $(S_1 \, . \, S_2)$ is a list just if S_2 is a list.

That is, the domain of lists is defined by

$$L = \{NIL\} + (S \times L)$$

for which the solution is **S*** when atom 'NIL' is regarded as the null list.

Therefore, lists in LISP are sequences whose components are S-expressions. The following S-expressions

> NIL
> (APPLE . NIL)
> (A . (B . (C . NIL)))
> ((APPLE . A2) . NIL)

are all lists.

Lists are more conveniently expressed in "list notation":

$$(S_1 \quad S_2 \quad \cdots \quad S_n)$$

for $n \geq 0$ is an abbreviation of

$$(S_1 . (S_2 . (\cdots (S_n . NIL) \cdots)))$$

For example,

(A B C)	abbreviates	(A . (B . (C . NIL)))
(A)	abbreviates	(A . NIL)
( )	abbreviates	NIL

and

Note the difference between the *pair* '(A . B)', which is not a list, and the *two-component list* '(A   B)' which may also be written '(A . (B . NIL))'. Note also that 'A' and '(A)' are not equivalent, because the latter abbreviates the pair '(A . NIL)'.

S-expressions are the *values* manipulated by LISP programs; but LISP *programs* are also S-expressions. For example, the notation for literals in LISP is

> (QUOTE   S)

where S is an S-expression. Syntactically, this is just a two-component list; the first component is atom 'QUOTE' and the second is S-expression S. Semantically, its *value* (relative to any state) is S-expression S. For example, the value of

> (QUOTE   APPLE)

is atom 'APPLE', and the value of

> (QUOTE (A . B))

is pair '(A . B)'. In LISP an unquoted atom used as an expression is an *identifier* (unless it is 'NIL' or 'T', which, for convenience , are exceptions to this rule, and always denote themselves.)

An expression of the form

$$(E_0 \ E_1 \ E_2 \ \cdots \ E_n)$$

for $n \geq 0$, is an *invocation*. The value of E_0 is the procedure, and the values of E_1 to E_n are its arguments.

LISP provides five primitive operations for constructing, selecting, and testing S-expression values. Procedure 'CONS' constructs a pair from its two arguments. For example, the value of

(CONS   (QUOTE   A) (QUOTE   B))

is '(A . B)'. of course, the actual parameters of an invocation need not be literals. For example, the value of

(CONS   (QUOTE   A)   (CONS   (QUOTE B)   NIL))

is '(A B)'.

Procedures 'CAR' and 'CDR' (rhymes with "rudder") require a pair $(S_1 . S_2)$ as an argument and return components S_1 and S_2, respectively. (The names of these procedures come from the machine instructions used to implement them in the first implementaion of LISP.) For example, the values of

(CAR (QUOTE (A . B)))

and

(CDR (QUOTE (A . B)))

are 'A' and 'B', respectively.

It is important to understand the results of procedures CONS, CAR, and CDR on list arguments. If the value of E_2 is a list, then the value of

(CONS E_1 E_2)

is that list with the value of E_1 prefixed onto it as its new first component. Therefore, the value of

(CONS   (QUOTE   A)   (QUOTE   (B C D)))

is list '(A B C D)'.

The result of applying **CAR** and **CDR** to a list argument is the *first* component of the list and the *rest* of the list, respectively. For example, the values of

(CAR   (QUOTE   (A   B   C   D)))

and

(CDR   (QUOTE   (A   B   C   D)))

are 'A' and '(B C D)', respectively. Note also that the values of

(CONS   (QUOTE   A)   NIL)
(CAR   (QUOTE   (A)))

and

(CDR   (QUOTE   (A)))

are '(A)', 'A', and 'NIL', respectively.

The remaining two primitive procedures in LISP are *predicates*, which for LISP means that their result is one of atoms 'NIL' (representing *false*) and 'T' (representing *true*). If the values of E_1 and E_2 are atoms, then the value of

(EQ E_1 E_2)

is 'T' if both arguments are the *same* atom, and 'NIL' otherwise. The value of

(ATOM   E)

is 'T' if the value of E is an atom, and 'NIL' if it is a pair.

It is surprisingly easy to program very complex manipulations of hierarchically structured symbolic data with just these five primitive operations on the domain of S-expressions and some additional mechanisms for selective evaluation, procedural abstraction, and recursive definition.

3.2.2 Arrays in APL

All the values in APL are termed *arrays*. The simplest kind of arrays are termed *scalars* and are said to have *rank* 0. A scalar is either a number or a character. Here are some examples of scalar-valued literals:

Numbers	*Characters*
8	'A'
2.087	' '

If **R** and **H** are the domains of numbers and character values, respectively, then

R+H

is the domain of all arrays of rank 0.

An array of rank 1 is known as a *vector* and is a homogeneous n-tuple of numbers or characters, for $n=0, 1, 2, \cdots$. Some examples of vector-valued literals in APL are given in Table 3.1. Note that there are no literals for numeric vectors of length 0 or 1, or character vectors of length 1; such values are expressible in other ways.

n	Vector of numbers	Vector of characters
0		$''$
1		
2	3 2.087	'TO'
3	1 2 3	'CAT'

Table 3.1   Vector literals in APL

The domain of all arrays of rank 1 is

$$\sum_n \left[\mathbf{R}^n + \mathbf{H}^n \right]$$

where, in general,

$$\sum_i \mathbf{D}_i = \mathbf{D}_0 + \mathbf{D}_1 + \mathbf{D}_2 + \cdots$$

Note that there are *two* vectors with zero components, one from $\mathbf{R}^0$, and one from $\mathbf{H}^0$.

Arrays of higher rank may be obtained in the same manner. A *matrix* (array of rank 2) is a "table" of components, consisting of $n_1 \geq 0$ rows, each of length $n_2 \geq 0$ with all $n_1 \times n_2$ components being either numbers or characters. The domain of all arrays of rank 2 is then

$$\sum_{n_1, n_2} \left[\mathbf{R}^{n_1 \times n_2} + \mathbf{H}^{n_1 \times n_2} \right]$$

Note that for any n, there are *two* $n \times 0$ matrices, and these are distinguished from the $n' \times 0$ matrices for any n' different from n, and from all the $0 \times m$ matrices, though all have zero components.

In general, an array of rank r is a homogeneous r-dimensional hyperrectangle of numbers or of characters:

$$\sum_{n_1,\cdots,n_r} \left[\mathbf{R}^{n_1 \times n_2 \times \cdots \times n_r} + \mathbf{H}^{n_1 \times n_2 \times \cdots \times n_r} \right]$$

The vector whose components are the r numbers $n_1, n_2, \cdots, n_r$ is known as the *shape* of such an array. Therefore, the shape of the shape of a value is a vector whose single component is the rank of that value.

The domain of *all* APL arrays is then the sum of the domains of arrays of rank r, for $r = 0, 1, 2, \ldots$:

$$\sum_{r} \sum_{n_1,\cdots,n_r} \left[\mathbf{R}^{n_1 \times n_2 \times \cdots \times n_r} + \mathbf{H}^{n_1 \times n_2 \times \cdots \times n_r} \right]$$

Note that the zero-component vectors are distinguished from the zero-component matrices, and similarly for higher rank arrays. Also, scalars are distinguished from single-component vectors, which are in turn distinguished from single-component matrices and arrays of higher rank.

APL provides many operations for construction, selection, and manipulation of arrays. By using operations on entire arrays it is possible to describe many complex computations without using explicit iterations and subscripting.

3.2.3 Strings and Patterns in SNOBOL4

The language SNOBOL4 is used primarily for describing computations on character strings. If $\mathbf{H}$ is the domain of character values, the domain of strings is $\mathbf{Q} = \mathbf{H}^*$. Examples of literal strings in SNOBOL4 are

$$\begin{array}{l} '' \\ 'A' \\ '\,\,' \\ 'CAT' \end{array}$$

If a string is an n-tuple of characters, the characters are numbered from 0 to $n-1$, inclusive, that is to say, zero-origin addressing.

Pattern matching is the operation used in SNOBOL4 to *analyze* strings. It can be a very complex operation, possibly involving procedural abstraction, side effects, and jumps. Only a subset of the pattern-matching facilities will be discussed here. This will permit a relatively simple model for patterns.

The most basic kind of pattern value is simply a string. A pattern string of length n is said to *match a subject string from character position i up to* (but not including) *position* $i+n$ if characters i to $i+n-1$, inclusive, of the subject are equal to the successive characters of the pattern string. The match *fails* if the subject is too short or if for some $j<n$ the jth character of the pattern string is not equal to character $i+j$ of the subject.

For example, the pattern string $'$GRAM$'$ matches the subject $'$PRO-GRAMMER$'$ from position 3 up to position 7, but fails to match from any other position. Note that the *null* pattern string always matches successfully, and that a null subject string is matched only by the null pattern.

The pattern operation of *alternation* produces patterns that can match a subject string in more than one way. If E_1 and E_2 are expressions whose values are the patterns p_1 and p_2, respectively, then expression

$$E_1 \mid E_2$$

has as its value a pattern that matches a subject from some position in all the ways that p_1 or p_2 match from that position. For example, the value of

$$'EA' \mid 'E'$$

is a pattern that matches subject $'$BEAD$'$ from position 1 up to positions 3 and 2.

The second important operation on patterns is *concatenation*, expressed in SNOBOL4 by juxtaposition of pattern-valued expressions separated by at least one blank:

$$E_1 \quad E_2$$

The concatenation of patterns p_1 and p_2 is a pattern that matches a subject from character position i in all the ways that p_1 can match from position i up to position $i+n$ *and* p_2 can match from $i+n$. For example, the value of

$$'EA' \quad 'D'$$

matches the subject $'$BEAD$'$ from positions 1 up to 4, because $'$EA$'$ matches from positions 1 up to 3, and $'$D$'$ matches from positions 3 up to 4.

As a more complex example, consider the pattern expressed by

$$('BE' \mid 'B') \quad ('ET' \mid 'AD')$$

This will match any of the subject strings

> 'BEET'
> 'BEAD'
> 'BET'
> 'BAD'

from character position 0.

Many other patterns and pattern operations are available in SNOBOL4. For example, if the value of identifier 'N' is the number n, the value of 'POS(N)' is a pattern that matches any subject string in the same way as the null pattern, but only at character position n of the subject.

A convenient way to model patterns mathematically is to regard them as *functions* applicable to arguments (q,i), where q is a subject string and i is the position at which a match is to be attempted. The result of applying a pattern to (q,i) is the *sequence* $\langle j_1,j_2,\cdots,j_m\rangle$ of all positions j_k such that the pattern matches from position i up to (but not including) character j_k of the subject. Positions j_k are in the order that they would be discovered by the pattern-matching algorithm in SNOBOL4 processors. The pattern-match operation itself (not discussed here) only makes use of j_1 (i.e., the first component of such result sequences), but all possible match positions are required to describe the pattern operations of concatenation and alternation. If a match fails, the result will be the null sequence $\langle\rangle$ (i.e., with $m=0$). The domain **P** of patterns is therefore

$$\mathbf{P} = (\mathbf{Q}\times\mathbf{N})\rightarrow\mathbf{N}^*$$

For example, if the pattern derived from the null string is applied to (q,i), where q is a string and i is a position in q, the result is the one-component sequence $\langle i\rangle$. The result of applying the pattern derived from a non-null string such as 'GRAM' to (q,i) is either the one-component sequence $\langle i+4\rangle$ if the substring from positions i to $i+3$, inclusive, of q is equal to 'GRAM', or the null sequence if the match fails.

The operations of alternation (|) and concatenation (⁀) of patterns may then be formally defined using concatenation of sequences as follows:

$$(p_1 \mid p_2) \, (q,i)=p_1(q,i)⁀p_2(q,i)$$

and

$$(p_1⁀p_2) \, (q,i)=p_2(q,j_1)⁀p_2(q,j_2)⁀\cdots⁀p_2(q,j_m)$$

where

$$\langle j_1,j_2,\cdots,j_m\rangle = p_1(q,i)$$

In the definition of pattern concatenation, if $p_1(q,i)$ is the null sequence $\langle\ \rangle$, then so is $(p_1{}^\frown p_2)\ (q,i)$.

For example, let p_1 and p_2 be the values of SNOBOL4 expressions

$$\text{'BE'} \mid \text{'B'}$$

and

$$\text{'ET'} \mid \text{'AD'}$$

respectively. Then,
$$p_1(\text{'BEAD'}, 0)=\langle2,1\rangle$$
but
$$p_2(\text{'BEAD'}, 2)=\langle4\rangle \qquad \text{and} \qquad p_2(\text{'BEAD'},1)=\langle\ \rangle$$
so that
$$(p_1{}^\frown p_2)\ (\text{'BEAD'}, 0)=\langle4\rangle^\frown\langle\ \rangle=\langle4\rangle$$
Similarly,
$$p_1(\text{'BET'}, 0)=\langle2,1\rangle$$
but
$$p_2(\text{'BET'}, 2)=\langle\ \rangle \qquad \text{and} \qquad p_2(\text{'BET'},1)=\langle3\rangle$$
so that
$$(p_1{}^\frown p_2)\ (\text{'BET'}, 0)=\langle\ \rangle^\frown\langle3\rangle=\langle3\rangle$$

3.3 LIMITATIONS ON DOMAINS

3.3.1 Pragmatic Limitations

We have already seen (Section 3.1.4) that it is possible to write PASCAL-like recursive **type** definitions analogous to recursive domain definitions. For example,

$$\begin{aligned}
&\textbf{type } \textit{natnum} = \textbf{record case } \textit{iszero} = \textit{Boolean } \textbf{of} \\
&\qquad\qquad \textit{true} : (\ ); \\
&\qquad\qquad \textit{false} : (\textit{pred} : \textit{natnum}) \\
&\qquad \textbf{end};
\end{aligned}$$

is the analog of $N = \{\textbf{zero}\}+N$, and

$$\begin{aligned}
&\textbf{type } \textit{sequence} = \textbf{record case } \textit{isnull} : \textit{Boolean } \textbf{of} \\
&\qquad\qquad \textit{true} : (\ ); \\
&\qquad\qquad \textit{false} : (\textit{first} : d\ ; \textit{rest} : \textit{sequence}) \\
&\qquad \textbf{end};
\end{aligned}$$

is the analog of $S = \{null\} + (D \times S)$. But such definitions are *not* allowed in PASCAL. The difficulty is not conceptual, but pragmatic: the domains described contain an *infinite* number of elements, so that it is not possible to predict before execution how much space will be adequate to represent *any* element of the domain. The same problem arises with all infinite domains.

Several approaches to implementation of infinite domains are possible. One is analogous to the usual treatment of *numerical* domains such as the integers: impose an *a priori* bound on the number of elements that will be represented. If an attempt is made to compute an element outside of this finite subset ("overflow"), the computation should be aborted.

A second approach to implementation is to allocate space as it is required when values are computed. This is more complex for the implementer, but, of course, more convenient for the programmer. The recursively defined domains of LISP, APL, and SNOBOL4 are implemented in this way.

A compromise between these two approaches, using "pointers", is available in many languages, including PASCAL, and will be discussed later.

*3.3.2 Theoretical Limitations

So far, no *theoretical* limitations have been imposed on domains, or on the functions allowable between domains. But if we insist that domain elements and functions be *computable* (i.e., implementable in principle), then this seems unrealistic because a value computable in a finite amount of time can only contain a finite "amount of information". However, this does *not* mean that domains cannot contain values with *infinite* information content. For example, the squaring function is a computable value that specifies an *infinite* number of argument–result correspondences. As another example, it is possible to write a program to compute the decimal representation of the real number $\pi/10$ as a file of decimal digits

$$31415926535\cdots$$

and, indeed, to implement arithmetic operations on real numbers to arbitrary precision. The squaring function and the decimal representation of $\pi/10$ are computable values with *unbounded* "information content". We shall term them *infinitary* values.

The apparent contradiction between the computability of some *infinitary* values and the constraint of *finite* computation may be resolved by realizing that computable infinitary values must be the *limits* of finitely computable *approximations* to them. For example, in a finite computation only a finite number of the argument–result correspondences of the squaring function can be determined. But, more and more information about this function may be obtained by doing more and more computation. Furthermore, all such approximation sequences converge to the *same* limit, the squaring function. Similarly, only finite files of digits can be generated in finite time, but it is possible to obtain arbitrarily good approximations to an infinitary value by computing for a sufficiently long time.

The difference between a limit value and a finitely computable approximation to it is known as *truncation error* in connection with numerical computation. But, it is a *general* principle of computation that domains can contain values with unbounded information content only if these values are the limits of finite approximations to them. This limitation on domains explains our use of a special term "domain" for sets of *computable* values.

Now, let us consider functions over domains. Suppose that the domain of arguments of a function f includes an infinitary element d with unbounded information content. In a finite computation d can only be approximated, so that if f is to model a feasible computation it must be possible to approximate $f(d)$ as closely as desired by using some finite approximation to d. Therefore, if $d_0, d_1, d_2, \cdots$ is any sequence of better and better approximations that converge to d, the function f must satisfy

$$\lim_{i \to \infty} f(d_i) = f(\lim_{i \to \infty} d_i)$$
$$= f(d)$$

It will then be possible to obtain as good an approximation as necessary to $f(d)$ by computing $f(d_i)$ for some *finite* approximation d_i. This is reminiscent of the ϵ–δ definition of continuity in calculus; functions that satisfy this kind of condition are termed **continuous**. In general, for a function to be computable, it must be continuous at all arguments, that is to say, preserve limits of approximations in domains (where the notion of approximation has to do with the "amount of information" represented by the values).

As an example of a *discontinuous* function, let $\mathbf{T} = \{true, false\}$ and $\mathbf{T}^\infty$ be the domain of finite and infinite sequences of truth values such that s_1 approximates s_2 just if s_1 is a prefix (initial segment) of s_2; then consider function

$$all: \mathbf{T}^\infty \to \mathbf{T}$$

such that $all(s_\infty) = true$ for $s_\infty = \langle true, true, true, \cdots \rangle$ (i.e., the infinite sequence whose components are all *true*), and $all(s) = false$ otherwise. But now consider the finite sequences

$$s_i = \langle true,\ true, \cdots, true \rangle$$

with i components for $i=0,1,2,\cdots$, whose limit is s_∞. Then,

$$\lim_{i \to \infty} all(s_i) = \lim_{i \to \infty} false = false$$

yet

$$all(\lim_{i \to \infty} s_i) = all(s_\infty) = true$$

so that function *all* is not continuous. But it is evidently not computable either because it requires an implementation to change a result from *false* to *true* after checking an *infinite* number of components.

There are analogs of the product, sum, function domain, and limit constructions and the notions of domain isomorphism and approximation that meet the conditions discussed in this section (that is, infinitary values are elements of domains just if they are limits of finite approximations to them, and functions are continuous). Furthermore, it can be shown that in this framework "smallest" solutions to recursive domain definitions using operations ×, + and → *always* exist. This is not true if *arbitrary* sets and functions are allowed; for example, if V→V must contain *all* the functions from V to V, then the *only* solution of equation

$$V = D + (V \to V)$$

is a trivial one when **D** is the empty set. But if V→V is taken to be the domain of all *continuous* functions, then "smallest" solutions do exist, for *any* domain **D**. This is a significant result because domain equations such as this are needed to define semantic domains for many programming languages.

In subsequent chapters, we shall see several applications of the general principles discussed in this section.

EXERCISES

3.1 In PASCAL, what are the counterparts for records with variant parts of the injection functions for a domain sum?

3.2 (a) A *binary tree* (with nodes labelled by elements of a domain **D**) is either null or a 3-tuple (b_1, d, b_2), where $d \in D$, and b_1 and b_2 are binary trees. Define domain **B** of binary trees.

(b) A *tree* (with nodes labelled by elements of **D**) is an ordered pair (d,f), where $d \in \mathbf{D}$ and f is a *forest*, that is, a (finite) sequence of trees. Define domains **T** of trees and **F** of forests.

(c) Show that $\mathbf{B} \cong \mathbf{F}$.

3.3 Define the domain of *list structures* in LISP, that is to say, lists each of whose components is either an atom (other than 'NIL') or a list structure. Assume that **A** is the domain of atoms other than 'NIL'.

3.4 Define in PASCAL-like notation a type that describes the LISP domain of S-expressions.

3.5 For a programmer, how would domain

$$\sum_r \sum_{n_1,\cdots,n_r} [\mathbf{H} + \mathbf{R}]^{n_1 \times n_2 \times \cdots \times n_r}$$

differ from the domain of APL arrays? Suggest reasons why this domain was not adopted by the implementers of APL.

3.6 Refer to documentation on SNOBOL4 and define the built-in patterns or pattern-valued operations REM, FAIL, LEN(N), POS(N), TAB(N), and ARB.

3.7 What patterns are the *identities* for pattern concatenation and alternation? i.e., what patterns p_c and p_a have the properties that, for all patterns p,

(a) $p \,\widehat{}\, p_c = p \,\widehat{}\, p_c\, p = p$
(b) $p \mid p_a = p_a \mid p = p$

3.8 Show using the definitions of Section 3.2.3 that for all patterns p_1, p_2, and p_3,

(a) $(p_1 \,\widehat{}\, p_2) \,\widehat{}\, p_3 = p_1 \,\widehat{}\, (p_2 \,\widehat{}\, p_3)$
(b) $(p_1 \mid p_2) \mid p_3 = p_1 \mid (p_2 \mid p_3)$
(c) $(p_1 \mid p_2) \,\widehat{}\, p_3 = (p_1 \mid p_3) \,\widehat{}\, (p_2 \mid p_3)$

Also, show by giving counter-examples that the following are not valid in general:

(d) $p_1 \,\widehat{}\, (p_2 \mid p_3) = (p_1 \,\widehat{}\, p_2) \mid (p_1 \,\widehat{}\, p_3)$
(e) $(p_1 \,\widehat{}\, p_2) \mid p_3 = (p_1 \mid p_3) \,\widehat{}\, (p_2 \mid p_3)$
(f) $p_1 \mid (p_2 \,\widehat{}\, p_3) = (p_1 \mid p_2) \,\widehat{}\, (p_1 \mid p_3)$

3.9 Define a pattern operation $not(p)$ that succeeds if p fails and fails if p succeeds. Then, describe the effects of pattern operations defined as follows:

(a) $test(p) = not(not(p))$
(b) $and(p_1, p_2) = test(p_1) \,\widehat{}\, p_2$
(c) $butnot(p_1, p_2) = not(p_2) \,\widehat{}\, p_1$

Is $and(p_1, not(p_2)) = butnot(p_1, p_2)$?

*3.10 Show that $\cong$ is an equivalence relation.

*3.11 If $\mathbf{A'}\cong\mathbf{A}$ and $\mathbf{B'}\cong\mathbf{B}$, show that

    (a) $\mathbf{A'}\times\mathbf{B'}\cong\mathbf{A}\times\mathbf{B}$
    (b) $\mathbf{A'}+\mathbf{B'}\cong\mathbf{A}+\mathbf{B}$
    (c) $\mathbf{A'}\rightarrow\mathbf{B'}\cong\mathbf{A}\rightarrow\mathbf{B}$

*3.12 Given that $\mathbf{A}$, $\mathbf{B}$, and $\mathbf{C}$ are any sets, $\mathbf{0}$ is the empty set, and $\mathbf{1}$ is any singleton set, show that

    (a) $\mathbf{A}\times\mathbf{1}\cong\mathbf{A}$
    (b) $\mathbf{A}\times\mathbf{0}\cong\mathbf{0}$
    (c) $(\mathbf{A}\times\mathbf{B})\times\mathbf{C}\cong\mathbf{A}\times(\mathbf{B}\times\mathbf{C})$
    (d) $\mathbf{A}+\mathbf{0}\cong\mathbf{A}$
    (e) $(\mathbf{A}+\mathbf{B})+\mathbf{C}\cong\mathbf{A}+(\mathbf{B}+\mathbf{C})$
    (f) $\mathbf{A}\rightarrow\mathbf{1}\cong\mathbf{1}$
    (g) $\mathbf{1}\rightarrow\mathbf{B}\cong\mathbf{B}$
    (h) $(\mathbf{A}+\mathbf{B})\rightarrow\mathbf{C}\cong(\mathbf{A}\rightarrow\mathbf{C})\times(\mathbf{B}\rightarrow\mathbf{C})$

*3.13 Show that $(\mathbf{A}\times\mathbf{B})+(\mathbf{A}\times\mathbf{C})\cong\mathbf{A}\times(\mathbf{B}+\mathbf{C})$ and relate this to the treatment of record types in PASCAL.

*3.14 Show that $(\mathbf{A}\times\mathbf{B})\rightarrow\mathbf{C}\cong\mathbf{A}\rightarrow(\mathbf{B}\rightarrow\mathbf{C})$ and relate this to the treatment of multidimensional arrays in PASCAL.

*3.15 The *powerset* $\mathcal{P}(\mathbf{D})$ of a set $\mathbf{D}$ is the set of all subsets of $\mathbf{D}$, including the empty subset and $\mathbf{D}$ itself. Show that $\mathcal{P}(\mathbf{D})\cong\mathbf{D}\rightarrow\{false,true\}$. Compare types **set of** T and **array** [T] **of** *Boolean* in PASCAL.

*3.16 Show that $\mathbf{D^*}\cong\sum_i\mathbf{D}^i$.

*3.17 Show that the set of (parsed) binary numerals, as described by abstract syntax

    N binary numerals

    $N ::= 0 \mid 1 \mid N0 \mid N1$

is isomorphic to the domain defined by equation

    $Nml=\mathbf{1}+\mathbf{1}+Nml+Nml$

where $\mathbf{1}$ is any singleton set. Show that it is possible to define a general correspondence between abstract syntax notation and "polynomial" domain equations (i.e., in which only operations $\times$ and $+$ are used).

*3.18 (Universality)

    (a)   Show that for all sets $\mathbf{A}$ and $\mathbf{B}$, $\mathbf{A}\times\mathbf{B}=\{(a,b) \mid a\in\mathbf{A},b\in\mathbf{B}\}$ and its projection functions $p_\mathbf{A}(a,b)=a$ and $p_\mathbf{B}(a,b)=b$ have the following property: for any set **D** and any functions $f : \mathbf{D} \rightarrow \mathbf{A}$ and $g : \mathbf{D} \rightarrow \mathbf{B}$, there exists a unique function $\theta: \mathbf{D} \rightarrow \mathbf{A} \times \mathbf{B}$ such that $f(d)=p_A(\theta(d))$ and $g(d)=p_B(\theta(d))$ for all $d \in \mathbf{D}$.

(b) Conversely, show that if **P** is a domain and $p_1 : \mathbf{P} \rightarrow \mathbf{A}$ and $p_2 : \mathbf{P} \rightarrow \mathbf{B}$ are functions that have the above property, then $\mathbf{P} \cong \mathbf{A} \times \mathbf{B}$.

The significance of these results is that they show that domain construction $\mathbf{A} \times \mathbf{B}$ is the *most general* of its class of domain constructions, and is *uniquely* characterized by this property (up to isomorphism). The sum, function domain, and limit constructions have similar universal properties.

*3.19 An enthusiastic language designer proposes to improve his favorite language CATCHALL by extending the equality operation ('=') to procedures. How would you persuade him that this is unwise?

PROJECT

Design a language that would allow both hierarchical structuring of data, as in LISP, and iterative structuring of data, as in APL.

BIBLIOGRAPHIC NOTES

The four constructions discussed in this chapter were first applied to programming language examples in McCarthy [3.6]; see also Hoare [3.4], Scott [3.7], Strachey [3.12], and Lehmann and Smyth [3.5]. The model of patterns in Section 3.2.3 is due to Gimpel [3.2]. The discussion of approximations, limits, and continuity in Section 3.3.2 is based on work of Scott [3.7–3.10]. For a detailed and rigorous presentation of Scott's theory of computation, see a book by Stoy [3.11]. For the project, see Gull and Jenkins [3.3] and Burge [3.1].

3.1 Burge, W. H. *ISWIM, a Mixture of APL and LISP*, Research Report RC 6967, IBM, Yorktown Heights, N.Y. (1978).

3.2 Gimpel, J. F.: "A theory of discrete patterns and their implementation in SNOBOL4", *Comm. ACM*, **16** (2), 91–100 (1973).

3.3 Gull, W. E. and M. A. Jenkins. "Recursive data structures in APL", *Comm. ACM*, **22** (2), 79–96 (1979).

3.4 Hoare, C. A. R. "Notes on data structuring", in *Structured Programming* (by O.-J. Dahl, E. W. Dijkstra, and C. A. R. Hoare), pp. 83–174, Academic Press, London (1972).

3.5 Lehmann, D. J. and M. B. Smyth. "Algebraic specification of data types: a synthetic approach", *Math. Systems Theory*, **14** (to appear).

3.6 McCarthy, J. "A basis for a mathematical theory of computation", in *Computer Programming and Formal Systems* (eds., P. Braffort and D. Hirschberg), pp. 33–70, North-Holland, Amsterdam (1963).

3.7 Scott, D. S. "Outline of a mathematical theory of computation", in *Proc. 4th Annual Princeton Conference on Information Sciences and Systems*, Dept. of Electrical Engineering, Princeton University (1970); also technical monograph PRG-2, Programming Research Group, University of Oxford (1970).

3.8 Scott, D. S. "Lattice theory, data types, and semantics", in *Formal Semantics of Programming Languages* (ed., R. Rustin), 2nd Courant Computer Science Symposium (1970), Prentice-Hall, Englewood Cliffs, N.J. (1972).

3.9 Scott, D. S. "Data types as lattices", *SIAM J. on Computing*, **5** (3), 522–86 (1976).

3.10 Scott, D. S. "Logic and programming languages", *Comm. ACM*, **20** (9), 634–41 (1977).

3.11 Stoy, J. E. *Denotational Semantics: The Scott–Strachey Approach to Programming Language Theory*, MIT Press, Cambridge, Mass. (1977).

3.12 Strachey, C. "The varieties of programming language", *Proc. Int. Computing Symposium*, pp. 222–33, Cini Foundation, Venice (1972); also technical monograph PRG-10, Programming Research Group, University of Oxford, England (1973).

4 STORAGE

In the preceding chapter, storage was mentioned only in connection with a *pragmatic* problem, representation of infinite domains. Because none of the operations discussed there had "destructive" effects, the use made of storage by processors could be ignored in descriptions of the *semantics*. However, when a language includes commands (such as assignments), or operations with side effects on their arguments, some concept of storage must be introduced into semantic descriptions in order to record and transmit these effects. This is the subject of the present chapter.

4.1 STORES AND LOCATIONS

To describe the effects of assignment commands on the store, we must know what a store is. Fortunately, it will not be necessary to concern ourselves with such details as the word size, data representations, and addressing mechanisms of particular computers in order to describe high-level features of languages. It will be possible to use a much simpler *logical* model of storage.

It might seem from consideration of simple assignments such as

$$n := n+1$$

that a store could be modelled logically as a set of associations between *identifiers* (such as 'n') and *storable values* (such as the numerical value of '$n+1$'). Then the effect of executing a command of the form

$$I := E$$

would be to yield a new store that differs from the old one only in that the target identifier, I, is associated with the value (relative to the old state) of the source expression, E.

However, this simple view of assignment and storage is adequate only for very limited programming languages. One difficulty is that the target of an assignment might be more complex than a simple identifier, as in

$a[i] := \cdots$

This could possibly be regarded as an abbreviation of an assignment to identifier '*a*'. But, consider PASCAL block

> **var** *p*:↑*integer*;
> **begin**
>   ⋮
>   *new*(*p*);
>   *p*↑:=···
>   ⋮
> **end**

Assignment '*p*↑:=···' illustrates that a target might not contain an identifier with which to associate a new value: this assignment updates the *anonymous* "variable" created by procedure *new*. In general, the target of an assignment is a (possibly composite) *l-expression*, and not necessarily a simple identifier. Furthermore, *l*-expressions may be used in contexts where there is no accompanying source expression, so that *l*-expressions themselves should be meaningful. But what is the "value" of an *l*-expression when it is being used as an assignment target?

Another factor that makes it difficult to regard a store as an association of *identifiers* with values is that in languages with nested blocks or recursively defined procedures it is possible to have many distinct "variables" with the *same* name. Even more problematical is that it is possible for one "variable" to have several names, so that execution of an assignment having one of them as its target also affects the values of the others, as in the following PASCAL block:

> **var** *i*:*integer*;
> **procedure** *p*(**var** *x*,*y*:*integer*);
>   **begin**
>   *x*:=···;
>   ···*y*···*i*···
>   **end**;
> **begin**
>   ⋮
>   *p*(*i*,*i*);
>   ⋮
> **end**

When the procedure is invoked using '$p(i,i)$', execution of the assignment to *x* also surreptitiously changes the values of *y* and *i*! This is a form of storage sharing known as **aliasing**.

These difficulties of semantic description may be overcome by introducing a domain of *semantic* entities, termed **locations** (or "references" or "cells") to be intermediaries between identifiers and stored values. Locations are the "logical" counterparts of machine addresses. Unlike physical machine words, locations do not have a "size", nor is it necessary to postulate a linear ordering on the locations. Indeed, all that must be assumed is that it is possible to test equality of locations. Then, a *store* is simply a finite set of associations of *locations* with *storable values*: a location is associated with the value that we want to regard as being currently **contained in** (or "stored at") that location.

To see how locations and stores may be used in semantic descriptions, consider an execution of the following PASCAL block:

```
var n:integer;
begin
  n:=0;
  while n<u do
    begin
      n:=n+1;
        ⋮
    end;
    ⋮
end
```

Execution of declaration

```
var n:integer;
```

has the effect of *allocating* some "new" (i.e., currently unused) location; let us designate this location *l*. Therefore, execution of the declaration yields a new store that records the fact that location *l* is now "in use", so that any subsequent allocations cannot claim the same location. The declaration also produces a new environment in which identifier '*n*' is bound to location *l*; that is, throughout the block (the scope of the declaration), '*n*' will denote *l*. Assignments may affect the value *contained* in *l*, but do not change the *binding* of '*n*' to *l*.

Note that allocation of new storage takes place *each time* the block containing a **var** declaration is executed. For the language FORTRAN, it is possible to *implement* all storage allocations for a program before its execution, so that if a declaration is executed more than once, the same location may in fact be used. However, the description of standard FORTRAN does not *require* this approach to implementation, so that FORTRAN programmers should *not* assume that the initial contents of locations are "left over" from previous executions of the block (unless the special SAVE statement has been used).

Execution of assignment

$$n := 0$$

initializes l. In the store resulting from this execution, the location denoted by '*n*' has become associated with the value of the source expression, literal '0'. All of the other location-value associations are, of course, unchanged.

After initialization of the location, the value of an occurrence of identifier '*n*' in expressions such as '$n < a$' and '$n + 1$' is the contents of *l* in the current store. This value is obtained by using the *environment* to determine that '*n*' is bound to location *l*, and using the *store* to determine what is currently contained in *l*. On the other hand, an occurrence of '*n*' as the *target* of

$$n := 0$$

or

$$n := n + 1$$

denotes *l* and not its contents, and the effect of executing such an assignment is to update the location to contain the value of the source expression.

In general, an occurrence of an identifier that is bound to a location may be "evaluated" in two ways: as the target of an assignment, it denotes the location; in an expression such as '$n + 1$', its value is the current contents of that location. These are known as the *l-value* and the *r-value*, respectively, of the identifier ("*l*" for *l*eft or *l*ocation, "*r*" for *r*ight or sto*r*ed). These two modes of evaluation are also applicable to more complex expressions, but some kinds of expression have *only* an *r*-value; for example, '1' and '$n + 1$' do not have *l*-values in PASCAL. An expression that does not have an *l*-value cannot appear as the target of assignment commands (and in other contexts where *l*-values are required). It is possible (though unusual) for expressions to have an *l*-value but not an *r*-value.

After execution of the block, location *l* is no longer accessible from within the program, and this is always true of locations allocated by **var** declarations in PASCAL. Processors take advantage of this by re-claiming such locations for other uses. This will be termed *disposal* of a location.

The period of time between an allocation and the subsequent disposal of a location is termed the *lifetime* of that "incarnation" of the location. Note the difference between the *scope* of an identifier binding (which is a region of program text), and the *lifetime* of a location. For locations allocated by **var** declarations in PASCAL, these concepts are closely related; in general, this need not be the case.

4.2 VARIATIONS ON ASSIGNMENT

4.2.1 Selective Updating

Consider assignments

$$a:=b;$$
$$c:=a[i]$$

in the context of declarations

var a,b:**array**[1 .. n]**of** *char*;
i:1 .. n;
c:*char*;

These assignments could be explained simply by supposing that a and b denote *single* locations which can contain arrays of characters. Then, the first assignment would update location a to contain the contents of b, and the second assignment updates c to contain the ith component of the contents of a. In both cases, the effect is to update the l-value of the target to contain the r-value of the source.

But now, consider assignment

$$a[i]:=c$$

If we want to continue to describe the effect of assignment commands as that of updating the l-value of the target to contain the r-value of the source, then we must change our view of the effect of an array declaration, because a *single* location is not decomposable. We therefore suppose that the effect of

var a:**array**[1 .. n]**of** *char*;

is to bind 'a' to an *array* of locations, each of which can contain single characters. The l-value of 'a' is then the array of locations it denotes, so that an assignment like

$$a:=b$$

must be regarded as a multiple update of each of these to contain the corresponding component of array b. The l-value of '$a[i]$' is obtained by using the r-value of 'i' to select a component location of the l-value of 'a' (i.e., the array of locations). So now our general description of assignment applies to examples like '$a[i]:=c$' as well as to '$a:=b$' and '$c:=a[i]$'.

In PASCAL, arrays, records, and files (but not sets) are *storage structures* (and not merely *data* structures) in that they may be *selectively* updated by using l-expressions like '$a[i]$'. It is evidently more efficient to selectively update a storage structure "in place" than to operate on or copy "large" data structures.

4.2.2   Other Updating Operations

Execution of an assignment of the form

$$L:=L+E$$

requires *two* evaluations of *l*-expression L, although the *r*-value of L is obtainable from its *l*-value. Because such updating operations are very common, some languages provide mechanisms that allow them to be expressed so that only a single evaluation is necessary. For example,

ADD E TO L

in COBOL, and

$$L+:=E$$

in ALGOL 68 have the effect of updating the *l*-value of L to contain the sum of the *r*-values of L and E, but the *r*-value of L is obtained from its *l*-value, rather than by a separate evaluation. Note that because evaluation of L can have side effects, the number of evaluations is, in general, a semantic (as well as a pragmatic) issue.

4.2.3   Multiple Targets

Some languages allow more than one target *l*-expression in an assignment, so that its execution can update several storage structures to contain the same *r*-value. For example, the assignment command in ALGOL 60 has the general form

$$L_1:=L_2:=\cdots:=L_n:=E$$

It is executed by evaluating the *l*-values of *l*-expressions L_1, L_2, $\cdots$, and L_n and the *r*-value of E, and then updating all of the *l*-values to contain the *r*-value.

4.2.4   Multiple Assignments

In some circumstances, it is desirable to have an assignment involving several *sources* as well as several targets. For example, three conventional assignments and an explicit temporary location are normally required to swap the contents of two locations. With a *multiple* (or "simultaneous") assignment of the form

$$L_1,L_2,\cdots,L_n:=E_1,E_2,\cdots,E_n$$

swapping of the contents of, say, x and y could be expressed more simply and clearly by

$$x,y:=y,x$$

In general, the multiple assignment command is executed by first evaluating the l-values of all the l-expressions L_i and the r-values of all the expressions E_i, and then doing all of the updatings. Note that if there were any sharing among the l-values, the order of the updatings could be significant. For example, if $i=j$ the effect of executing

$$a[i],a[j]:=x,y$$

would depend on the order of the updatings (unless the values at x and y happened to be the same).

4.2.5 Assignment Expressions

In some programming languages, assignments are *expressions* (with side effects), rather than commands. For example, in ALGOL 68

$$L:=E$$

is an expression whose value is that of L, and updates storage as a side effect. This allows assignments to be written within expressions, as in

$$\textbf{while } (n:=n+1)<a \textbf{ do} \cdots$$

Such idioms are often difficult to read because expressions are normally expected to be free of side effects.

4.3 POINTERS

We have seen that locations are a kind of semantic entity to which identifiers may be bound by executing **var** declarations and which may be composed into storage structures such as arrays. In some languages, storage locations and structures are not only *denotable* by identifiers, but also *storable* as contents of locations. Storage locations and structures that are themselves stored are known as *pointers* (or "references" or "links").

For example, the two blocks in Fig. 4.1 are equivalent in PASCAL, (except that after executing the second, the new location is still accessible via np). In the first, execution of the **var** declaration *binds* identifier 'n' to a new location. In the second, invocation of procedure *new* has the effect of updating its argument, np, to *contain* a new location. This may be depicted in a linkage diagram as follows:

np

(i)   **var** *n:integer*;
             begin
                  n:=0;
                  while *n<a* **do**
                       begin
                            n:=*n*+1;
                            ⋮
                       end;
                  ⋮
             end

(ii)   **begin**
                  new(np);
                  np↑:=0;
                  while *np*↑*<a* **do**
                       begin
                            np↑:=*np*↑+1;
                            ⋮
                       end;
                  ⋮
             end

Fig. 4.1.

L-expressions of the form

E↑

are used in PASCAL to access storage indirectly, that is to say, via a pointer value. The *l*-value of such an expression is the storage that is (pointed at by) the *r*-value of sub-expression E. Therefore, the location incremented by executing

$$np↑:=np↑+1$$

is not *np*, but the location that is (pointed at by) the contents of *np*, that is to say, the *r*-value of expression '*np*'.

A location that can contain pointers can also contain a special value denoted by the literal '**nil**' in PASCAL. This value is used mainly to terminate chains of links and it is an error to attempt to use it to access storage.

In general, storage allocated by an invocation of *new* in PASCAL may still be accessible on exit from the enclosing block, so that there is no automatic disposal. Some processors provide a procedure *dispose* so that the programmer can indicate explicitly when a location will no longer be accessed. In others, inaccessible locations are automatically searched for and disposed of whenever more storage is needed; this is known as *garbage collection*.

Programming with pointers is notoriously error-prone, and programmers often have to resort to complex linkage diagrams to understand and describe the status of storage structures because the storage subject to updating by an assignment is not identified by name. Other problems are that pointers cannot meaningfully be input or output, and that storage management is much more complex when pointers are used. Why then are pointers available in high-level programming languages? There appear to be three reasons:

(1) *Allocation and disposal*

The **var** declaration in PASCAL and analogous mechanisms in other languages allocate storage only at block entry, and this is disposed of only on block exit. Pointers allow storage to be addressed indirectly, so that it may be allocated and disposed of at arbitrary execution points.

(2) *Sharing*

If a pointer value is contained in *several* locations, then all the locations *share* access to the storage pointed at. For example, after execution of

$$p := q$$

in the context of

var $p,q:\uparrow t;$

storage $q\uparrow$ is also accessible via p. In contrast, execution of

$$new(p);$$
$$p\uparrow:=q\uparrow$$

allocates new storage and copies the contents of $q\uparrow$ into it, so that $p\uparrow$ and $q\uparrow$ may be independently updated. Therefore, when pointers are used, the degree of sharing in a complex storage structure may be controlled by the programmer.

(3) *Structural modifications*

Pointers allow storage to be partially *re-structured* without re-constructing almost the entire structure. For example, insertion of a component into a sequence or removal from a sequence of one component is quite easy when the sequence is implemented as a linked structure of "nodes" in which each node points at the successor and predecessor nodes in the structure.

It would be desirable to have language facilities that achieve these objectives without the use of pointers, at least in some restricted or specialized situations. In the meantime, programmers might be advised to use pointers only as a last resort.

4.4 STORAGE INSECURITIES

An attempt to access the contents of a location *before* its initialization is a serious programming error, because the location will contain something "left-over" from its previous incarnation. Similarly, it is an error to attempt to update or access a location that has been disposed of while it is still accessible, because the location might also be in use in a subsequent incarnation. Storage that has been prematurely disposed of (whether at the explicit request of the programmer or implicitly by a processor) is known as a *dangling reference*.

Dangling references can sometimes be prevented by careful language design. In PASCAL, for example, pointer values can be created only by procedure *new*, but in some languages it is possible to store *any* l-value as a pointer. For example, the following is illegal in PASCAL:

```
var i:integer;
    p:↑integer;
begin
    ⋮
    p:=i;
    ⋮
end
```

but its counterpart in ALGOL 68 is allowed, and has the effect of storing (a pointer to) location *i* in *p*. Note that in such a context it is the *l*-value (and not the *r*-value) of the source expression that is used. Similarly, language PL/I has a procedure ADDR that returns the *l*-value of its actual parameter as a pointer value that may then be stored. If, in such cases, the storage pointed at is automatically disposed of on exit from the block in which it was allocated, it becomes a dangling reference.

To illustrate the danger, suppose that an analogous procedure *addr* were added to PASCAL; then consider the following:

```
var p:↑integer;
procedure q;
    var i:integer;
    begin
        p:=addr(i)
    end;
```

If location i is disposed of on exit from the body of procedure q, it will be left dangling in p:

By restricting pointers to point only at storage allocated by *new*, PASCAL simplifies storage management and eliminates one source of dangling references. However, pointers may be dangling references if they are deallocated after a premature invocation of *dispose*.

Dangling references and uninitialized locations are common insecurities because they are difficult to prevent by language design and their detection by processors can be quite difficult and expensive. Some processors can take advantage of special hardware mechanisms and detect them during execution without too much inefficiency. In some cases, potential errors of this sort can be detected *before* execution by a static analysis of programs. But the most common implementation "solution" is to do nothing, thereby shifting the burden to the programmer.

4.5 TWO CASE STUDIES OF STORAGE STRUCTURING

4.5.1 Selective Updating in LISP

In Section 3.2.1 the domain of S-expressions in LISP was defined by

$$S = A + (S \times S),$$

where A is the domain of atoms. (That section should now be reviewed by readers not familiar with LISP.) This domain was satisfactory for explaining the five primitive operations of pure LISP (CONS, CAR, CDR, ATOM, and EQ), because none of these operations involved "destructive" effects.

But full LISP provides two procedures, RPLACA ("replace the CAR") and RPLACD ("replace the CDR"), that modify their arguments. To describe the effects of these procedures, the LISP *storage* structures must be described. The domain of representations for S-expressions may be defined as follows:

$$R = A + (L \times L)$$

where L is the domain of *locations* that may contain elements of R. (In fact, even atoms have modifiable sub-structures termed "property lists", but we shall not discuss this.) The value of an expression in full LISP is therefore an element of R. When literal S-expressions are evaluated or when procedure CONS is invoked, new location pairs are allocated to represent S-expression pairs. For example, the storage structure that represents S-expression

((A   B)   C)

may be depicted

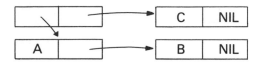

Similarly, if the value of identifier 'X' is

then the result of evaluating

(CONS   (QUOTE   A)   X)

is

Note that if

(CONS   X   X)

is evaluated, sub-structure X will be *shared*, as follows:

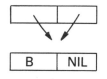

In general, elements of **R** are "unprintable"; when the value of an expression must be output, contents of locations are taken until atoms are reached.

If the value of expression E is the pair of locations (l_1, l_2), the values of

(CAR   E)   and   (CDR   E)

are the *contents* in the current store of locations l_1 and l_2, respectively.

It may be verified that with these definitions, the existence of the storage structure is "invisible" to a programmer who uses only the five primitive operations of pure LISP. But the motivation for introducing **R** was to be able to describe the effects of the selective updating operations, **RPLACA** and **RPLACD**. If the value of E_1 is the pair of locations (l_1, l_2), the value resulting from invocation

$$(RPLACA \quad E_1 \quad E_2)$$

is that of E_1, but it also has the *effect* of updating l_1 to contain the value of E_2. Similarly, the effect of

$$(RPLACD \quad E_1 \quad E_2)$$

is to update l_2 to contain the value of E_2.

For example, if the value of identifier 'Y' is

the effect of executing

$$(RPLACD \quad Y \quad Y)$$

is to make Y a "re-entrant" storage structure, in which the CAR component of Y still contains atom 'A', but the CDR component of Y contains Y itself:

Such values must be used with care because of the danger of non-termination. For example, if an attempt were made to print Y, the system would start to output the *infinite* list

$$(A \quad A \quad A \quad A \quad \cdots$$

Another danger of RPLACA and RPLACD is that they may update the contents of storage structures that are unexpectedly shared at a higher level. Despite these pitfalls, selective updating is essential for efficiency in many applications of LISP.

4.6.2 Files in PASCAL

The design of high-level facilities for using "external" storage devices such as magnetic tapes and disks has been very problematical. Such facilities must be suitable for efficient implementation on a wide variety of hardware devices, and also must be compatible with complex and varied operating and file management systems. Other problems include specification of conversion and formatting for legible input and output, and establishment of correspondences between internal and external names for files. In this section, some aspects of the facilities provided in the language PASCAL for using sequential access devices (such as magnetic tapes, card readers, and line printers) will be described.

The concept underlying file types in PASCAL is the *sequence*. This may be seen most clearly if we begin by regarding a file name 'f' as denoting a location containing a sequence $\langle x_1, x_2, \cdots, x_n \rangle$ of values. Then the following operations may be defined:

$rewrite(f)$ is equivalent to $f := \langle \rangle$

$write(f,x)$ is equivalent to $f := f^\frown \langle x \rangle$

$read(f,x)$ is equivalent to $x := first(f);\ f := rest(f)$

$eof(f)$ is equivalent to $f = \langle \rangle$

These operations can be implemented efficiently because they insert or remove components only at the ends of sequences. There is no need to copy entire sequences, as might be necessary if the operations of assignment and concatenation of sequences were available to the programmer.

However, the above operations do not prevent a programmer from alternating freely between writing to and reading from a file, and this is impractical for implementation on most external storage devices. So an additional operation, *reset*, is introduced. Reading from a file is possible only after invoking *reset*. Furthermore, it is convenient to allow a file to be "re-read"; the *read* operation above does not save the file for subsequent re-reading. This suggests that a file f should be regarded as a *pair* of sequences, $\overleftarrow{f}$ and $\overrightarrow{f}$; $\overleftarrow{f}$ is either the file being written or the subfile already read, and $\overrightarrow{f}$ is the unread subfile. (These components are not directly accessible to the programmer.) Then the file operations may be defined as follows:

$rewrite(f)$ is equivalent to $\overleftarrow{f} := \langle \rangle;\ \overrightarrow{f} := \langle \rangle$

$write(f,x)$ is equivalent to $\overleftarrow{f} := \overleftarrow{f}^\frown \langle x \rangle;\ \overrightarrow{f} := \langle \rangle$

$reset(f)$ is equivalent to $\overrightarrow{f} := \overleftarrow{f}^\frown \overrightarrow{f};\ \overleftarrow{f} := \langle \rangle$

$read(f,x)$ is equivalent to $x := first(\overrightarrow{f});\ \overleftarrow{f} := \overleftarrow{f}^\frown \langle x \rangle;$

                                                              $\overrightarrow{f} := rest(\overrightarrow{f})$

$eof(f)$ is equivalent to $\overrightarrow{f} = \langle \rangle$

Note that these definitions allow writing to a file (possibly after reading from it) without an intervening invocation of *rewrite*; some file systems would not allow this.

A further complication is introduced by the concept of the *buffer*, $f\uparrow$, of a file f. Cyclic buffer areas are an important implementation mechanism for making efficient use of external storage devices. The main motivation for making a "buffer" available to the *programmer* is to allow *selective* use and updating of file components. Suppose that the components of a file f are "large" values. If '$read(f,x)$' is used, these large values must be copied from the buffer area to x, even if x is never updated or only a "small" part of x is used. Similarly, it is often necessary to construct a "large" value component-by-component before writing it to a file. If only '$write(f,x)$' is available, this must be done in x and the resulting value copied into the actual buffer area for the file. These inefficiencies can be avoided by allowing the programmer to access directly one component, denoted $f\uparrow$, of the physical buffer area.

File operations may be defined (still without reference to the underlying implementation) as follows:

$rewrite(f)$	is equivalent to	$\vec{f}:=\langle\rangle; \overleftarrow{f}:=\langle\rangle; f\uparrow:=?$
$put(f)$	is equivalent to	$\overleftarrow{f}:=\overleftarrow{f}\cdot\langle f\uparrow\rangle; \vec{f}:=\langle\rangle; f\uparrow:=?$
$reset(f)$	is equivalent to	$\vec{f}:=\overleftarrow{f}\cap\vec{f}; \overleftarrow{f}:=\langle\rangle; f\uparrow:=first(\vec{f})$
$get(f)$	is equivalent to	$\overleftarrow{f}:=\overleftarrow{f}\cdot\langle first(\vec{f})\rangle; \vec{f}:=rest(\vec{f});$ $f\uparrow:=first(\vec{f})$
$eof(f)$	is equivalent to	$\vec{f}=\langle\rangle$

where '?' stands for an "undefined" (i.e., unpredictable) value and we define $first(\langle\rangle)$ to be '?'. Derived operations $read$ and $write$ are now definable in terms of these as follows:

$write(f,x)$	is equivalent to	$f\uparrow:=x; put(f)$
$read(f,x)$	is equivalent to	$x:=f\uparrow; get(f)$

Note that the programmer's buffer becomes "undefined" after a *put* operation, for no apparent reason. The explanation is that the programmer's buffer is implemented by using an "internal" pointer into the actual cyclic buffer area. The *put* operation is implemented by moving this internal pointer, and this action makes the contents of $f\uparrow$ unpredictable. It is unfortunate that this implementation aspect is "visible" to the programmer as an apparently unnecessary aspect of the logical model. Despite this, the treatment of sequential files in PASCAL is remarkably clean in comparison to similar facilities in most other programming languages.

EXERCISES

4.1 Is it possible in PASCAL to test equality of locations?

4.2 What are the advantages and disadvantages of the following approaches to the problem of uninitialized locations:

(a)   The programmer can be compelled to initialize new locations; for example, the syntax of the **var** declaration might be extended to include an expression whose value becomes the initial contents, as in

   var I:T=E;

(b)   New locations can be initialized by the implementation to a "dummy" value such that any attempt to use this value will be trapped by run-time tests.

(c)   New locations can be initialized by the implementation to a "neutral" value, such as zero for integer locations.

(d)   New locations can be initialized by the implementation to an "unlikely" value, such as *maxint* (the largest representable integer).

(e)   Programs can be analyzed at compile-time and possible uses of uninitialized locations detected and treated as syntactic errors.

4.3 Give an example to show that in general an ALGOL 60 assignment

$$L_1:=L_2:=\cdots:=L_n:=E$$

is not equivalent to

$$L_n:=E;$$
$$L_{n-1}:=L_n;$$
$$\vdots$$
$$L_1:=L_2$$

even when none of the expression evaluations have side effects.

4.4 (a)   Describe in detail the effect of executing PASCAL assignment

$$a[a[i]]:=a[i]+1$$

(b)   Is it always the case (in PASCAL) that the *r*-value of L after executing assignment L:=E is equal to the *r*-value of E before executing the command? *Hint*: consider the assignment in part (a).

4.5 Suggest an extension to PASCAL that would make it possible for *sets* to be selectively updated.

4.6 An enthusiastic language designer proposes to extend his favorite language CATCHALL by allowing array expressions and assignments. To simplify the implementation, he suggests that these be interpreted on a component-by-component basis; for example, in the context of

var a,b:**array**[1 .. n]**of** *real*;
       x:*real*;

assignment

$a := a*x + b$

would be interpreted as

for $i := 1$ **to** n **do**
     $a[i] := a[i]*x + b[i]$

How would you persuade him that this is unwise? *Hint*: consider assignment

$a := a*a[j] + b$

4.7 Show how analogs of LISP primitives CONS, CAR, CDR, EQ, ATOM, RPLACA, and RPLACD may be implemented in PASCAL using the types defined by

        type $ref = \uparrow sexp$;
             $sexp =$ **record case** *isatom*:*Boolean* **of**
                  true:(at:*atom*);
                  false:(car,cdr:*ref*)
             end;

Explain how this approach to representation of infinite domains has characteristics of *both* of the approaches discussed in Section 3.3.1.

4.8 Why, in PASCAL, will the following not work as the programmer probably intended?

        var f:**file of record**$\cdots$;a:*char*;$\cdots$**end**;
        begin
            $\vdots$
          with $f\uparrow$ **do**
            while not *eof*(f) **do**
            begin
               write(*output*,a);
               get(f)
            end;
            $\vdots$
        end

4.9 Some file systems allow a sequential file to be backspaced so that it may be read from back to front. Define an operation *backspace*(f) in terms of the model for PASCAL files.

4.10 Suppose that a file f is regarded as a pair of sequences, $\overleftarrow{f}$ and $\overrightarrow{f}$; then define the following operations:

        rewrite(f)   is equivalent to $\overleftarrow{f} := \langle\rangle$; $\overrightarrow{f} := \langle\rangle$

        extend(f)   is equivalent to $\overleftarrow{f} := \overleftarrow{f}\frown\langle?\rangle$; $\overrightarrow{f} := \langle\rangle$

$f\uparrow$ is equivalent to $last(\vec{f})$

$reset(f)$ is equivalent to $\vec{f}:=\vec{f}^\frown\vec{f};\ \vec{f}:=\langle\rangle$

$get(f)$ is equivalent to $\vec{f}:=\vec{f}^\frown\langle first(\vec{f})\rangle;\ \vec{f}:=rest(\vec{f})$

$eof(f)$ is equivalent to $\vec{f}=\langle\rangle$

and the following derived operations:

$write(f,x)$ is equivalent to $extend(f);\ f\uparrow:=x$

$read(f,x)$ is equivalent to $get(f);\ x:=f\uparrow$

For a programmer, how would this approach to files differ from the approach in PASCAL? Does it have any advantages?

4.11 Why is the following a reasonable definition of a domain of stores:

$$S=L\rightarrow(R+\{unused\})$$

where **L** and **R** are the domains of locations and storable values, respectively?

4.12 An enthusiastic language designer proposes to extend PASCAL by allowing recursive **type** definitions without (explicit) use of pointers, as in

```
type string=record case isnull:Boolean of
               true:();
               false:(first:char;rest:string)
           end;
```

He proposes that this facility be implemented by representing values of such types using "internal" pointers (which would not be accessible to the programmer) to storage that would be allocated dynamically, as needed. For example, if, in the context of

```
var s:string;
```

s contained string $'ABC'$, then this would be represented by

What problems will arise with this approach if both updating and selective updating of locations like s are allowed? *Hint*: consider

```
var t:string;
begin
    ⋮
    t:=s;
    s.first:='Z';
    write(t.first);
    ⋮
end
```

PROJECTS

4.1 Design extensions to PASCAL that would allow more convenient (but still efficient) text processing.

4.2 Design high-level language facilities for making efficient use of "slow" random-access storage devices, such as disks.

BIBLIOGRAPHIC NOTES

The storage model presented in this chapter is due to Scott and Strachey [4.4, 4.5, 4.6]. The model for PASCAL files presented in Section 4.5.2 is that of Hoare and Wirth [4.2]. The suggestion in Exercise 4.10 is an improvement on the idea presented in Tennent [4.7]. For Exercise 4.12, see Hoare [4.1]. For Project 4.1, see Sale [4.3].

4.1 Hoare, C. A. R. "Recursive data structures", *Int. J. Computer and Information Sciences*, **4** (2), 105–32 (1975).

4.2 Hoare, C. A. R. and N. Wirth. "An axiomatic definition of the programming language PASCAL", *Acta Informatica*, **2**, 335–55 (1973).

4.3 Sale, A. H. J. "Strings and the sequence abstraction in PASCAL", *Software Practice and Experience*, **9** (8), 671–83 (1979).

4.4 Scott, D. S. "Mathematical concepts in programming language semantics", *Proc. 1972 Spring Joint Computer Conference*, pp. 225–34, AFIPS Press, Montvale, N.J. (1972).

4.5 Scott, D. S. and C. Strachey. "Towards a mathematical semantics for computer languages", in *Proc. of the Symposium on Computers and Automata* (ed., J. Fox), pp. 19–46, Polytechnic Institute of Brooklyn Press, New York (1971); also technical monograph PRG-6, Programming Research Group, University of Oxford (1971).

4.6 Strachey, C. "The varieties of programming language", *Proc. Int. Computing Symposium*, pp. 222–33, Cini Foundation, Venice (1972); also technical monograph PRG-10, Programming Research Group, University of Oxford (1973).

4.7 Tennent, R. D. "A note on files in PASCAL", *BIT*, **17**, 362–6 (1977).

5 CONTROL

The preceding chapter was devoted primarily to the semantics of assignment commands. In this chapter, we shall study composite syntactic structures that allow effects of assignments to be combined in useful ways. These are known as *control structures*. Discussion of forms of control sequencing that require more complex semantic models (such as concurrency and sequencers like the **goto**) will be deferred to subsequent chapters.

The *null* command, which makes *no* change to the store, is expressed in PASCAL by a null token string. In order to make null commands "visible" in examples, we shall use comment '{null}'.

5.1 SEQUENTIAL COMPOSITION

Sequential composition of commands C_1 and C_2 is expressed in PASCAL by using the semicolon as a separator:

$$C_1;C_2$$

Note that the null command expresses the *identity* for sequential composition; that is, for all commands C,

$$\{null\};C \quad \text{and} \quad C;\{null\}$$

are both equivalent to C.

In some languages, sequential composition is expressed by line separation (e.g., in FORTRAN) or by textual succession of commands (e.g., in PL/I), rather than by an explicit symbol such as the semicolon. For example, the PASCAL commands

$$f:=f*i; \; i:=i+1$$

would be expressed in FORTRAN by

```
F=F*I
I=I+1
```

and in PL/I by

$$F=F*I; \ I=I+1;$$

The semicolons here terminate (rather than separate) the commands.

5.2   SELECTIVE COMPOSITION

In mathematics, selection is typically expressed as in the following example:

$$d(i,j)=\begin{cases} 0, & \text{if } i \neq j \\ 1, & \text{if } i=j. \end{cases}$$

Programming languages have *selective* control structures, such as the **if** and **case** commands in PASCAL:

> **if** E **then** C$_1$ **else** C$_2$

and   **case** E **of**$\cdots$;K$_i$:C$_i$;$\cdots$**end**

The single-alternative form of **if** construct may be regarded as an abbreviation for

> **if** E **then** C **else** {null}

Another abbreviation provided in PASCAL is to allow a list of static expressions as case labels in the **case** construction, so that the corresponding command need not be written out more than once. That is,

> **case** E **of**
> $\vdots$
> K$_i$: C;
> $\vdots$
> K$_j$: C;
> $\vdots$
> **end**

may be expressed more compactly by

> **case** E **of**
> $\vdots$
> K$_i$,K$_j$: C;
> $\vdots$
> **end**

in which command C is not duplicated.

What should be the effect of a **case** command when the selecting expression has a value that is *not* one of the specified cases? One possibility is to adopt the null command as the implicit default for all cases that are not specified explicitly, much like the single-alternative form of **if** command. But this is rather undesirable because then erroneous selecting values will not be detected. In PASCAL, such an occurrence is treated as an error which aborts program execution.

The conventional implementation for **case** commands in PASCAL systems is to select a case for execution by using the value of the selecting expression as a "subscript" into an array of commands; that is, program space must be reserved for each value in the range from the smallest to the largest of the case labels. This implementation approach is simple and fast, but, because of space requirements, unsuited to examples like

```
case i of
    1:      ···;
    13.     ···;
    245:    ···;
    1768:   ···;
    32002.  ···,
end
```

in which the case labels are "sparse".

More sophisticated implementation techniques which use search to reduce space requirements are possible. However, if implementation simplicity is an important design criterion (as in PASCAL), it would perhaps have been better to simply forbid "gaps" between cases and verify this before program execution.

Some PASCAL processors provide an extension that allows a command to be specified by the programmer for all otherwise unspecified cases, as in

```
case E of
    K₁: C₁;
      ⋮
    Kₙ: Cₙ
    others Cₙ₊₁
end
```

But a similar effect can be obtained in standard PASCAL as follows:

```
if E in [K₁,···,Kₙ] then
    case E of
        K₁: C₁;
          ⋮
        Kₙ: Cₙ
    end
else Cₙ₊₁
```

This is equivalent, provided that expression E does not have side effects.

Another abbreviation that is sometimes provided is to accept subrange notation in case labels, as in

> **case** E **of**
> $\vdots$
> $K_{i1} .. K_{i2}$: C_i;
> $\vdots$
> **end**

But then examples like

> **case** i **of**
> $-maxint .. -1$:$\cdots$;
> 0 :$\cdots$;
> $1 .. maxint$:$\cdots$
> **end**

are inappropriate if the conventional implementation of the **case** construct is used.

In some languages, the **if** construct is terminated syntactically by a "closing bracket", such as '**endif**' or '**fi**':

> **if** E
> **then** C_1
> **else** C_2
> **endif**

However, this approach to syntax would make a *nested* sequence of selections clumsy to express because of the accumulation of closing brackets, as in:

> **if** E_1 **then** C_1
> **else if** E_2 **then** C_2
> **else if** $\cdots$
> $\vdots$
> **else if** E_n **then** C_n
> **else** C_{n+1}
> **endif**$\cdots$**endif endif endif**

Therefore, such languages generalize the **if** form so that a sequence of tests may be expressed with a single construct, as follows:

> **if** E_1 **then** C_1
> **elsif** E_2 **then** C_2
> **elsif** $\cdots$
> $\vdots$
> **elsif** E_n **then** C_n
> **else** C_{n+1}
> **endif**

Expressions E_i are evaluated for $i=1,2,\cdots$ until a *true* value is obtained. Then the corresponding C_i is executed, or C_{n+1} if none are *true*.

5.3 ITERATIVE COMPOSITION

Iterative notations such as

$$\sum_{i \in S} \cdots i \cdots$$

are common in mathematics, and these concepts have been adapted to programming languages. We shall distinguish between *definite* iterations, for which the number of repetitions is determined *before* any of the executions of the iterated construct (though not necessarily before program execution), and *indefinite* iterations, for which the number of repetitions is not predetermined. Note that this is similar to the distinction between definite integration

$$\int_a^b \cdots x \cdots dx$$

and indefinite integration

$$\int \cdots x \cdots dx.$$

5.3.1 Definite Iteration

The simplest approach to determining the number of repetitions is to provide *no* means to terminate the iteration. For example, the construct

> **loop**
> C
> **end**

might express the (potentially) infinite repetition of C. This is analogous to a definite integral like

$$\int_0^\infty \cdots x \cdots dx.$$

Some *additional* language mechanism (such as a sequencer) would be used to avoid non-terminating executions.

The other approach is to determine the number of iterations by evaluating expressions. This can be made more convenient by allowing the programmer to access the iteration count from within the iterated construct with a "control variable", analogous to iteration index 'i' in

$$\sum_{i \in S} \cdots i \cdots$$

Furthermore, the "counting" may be made more flexible by allowing both lower and upper count limits and, possibly, an increment to be specified. The PASCAL constructs of this kind have the forms

> **for** $I := E_1$ **to** E_2 **do** C

and

> **for** $I := E_1$ **downto** E_2 **do** C

The "counting" can be over programmer-defined enumerations, character values, and Boolean values, as well as integers. Although the increments are restricted to those obtained by single uses of *succ* or *pred*, these are the most useful by far, and somewhat simpler to describe and implement than arbitrary increments.

5.3.2 Indefinite Iteration

The indefinite iteration constructs in PASCAL are

> **while** E **do** C

and > **repeat** C **until** E

The termination test is done either before or after each execution of C. The construct

> **loop**
> C_1
> **while** E:
> C_2
> **repeat**

has been proposed as a generalization of these. It allows the termination condition to be tested in the "middle" of the loop body. Note that the effect of the **while** form in PASCAL may be obtained by making C_1 the null command, and an effect similar to that of the **repeat** form by making C_2 the null command.

An even more flexible approach would be to allow *several* termination tests, as in

> **loop**
> C_1
>   **when** E_1 **exit**
> C_2
>   **when** E_2 **exit**
> $\vdots$
>   **when** E_n **exit**
> C_{n+1}
> **repeat**

But then, after the iteration terminated, there would be no way to tell which of the tests caused the termination without re-evaluating them. Therefore, it would be desirable to allow specification of some computation after any successful termination test, as in

> **loop**
> C_1
>   **when** E_1 **do** C_1' **exit**
> C_2
>   **when** E_2 **do** C_2' **exit**
> $\vdots$
>   **when** E_n **do** C_n' **exit**
> C_{n+1}
> **repeat**

However, the syntax of this construct is rather too intricate for it to be recommended. In Chapter 10, we shall discuss a more flexible and syntactically simpler approach to multiple exits using sequencers.

An interesting special case of the use of more than one termination condition sometimes arises. Consider PASCAL iteration

> **while** $(i \leq n)$ **and** $(a[i] \neq x)$ **do** $i := i + 1$

in the context of declaration

> **var** a : **array**$[1..n]$**of** t;

With most PASCAL processors, evaluation of the composite test is in error when $i=n+1$ because the subscript in '$a[i]$' is out of range.

This problem is avoided if expression

$$E_1 \text{ and } E_2$$

is evaluated *sequentially*, that is to say, if E_2 is only evaluated when the value of E_1 is *true*. When the value of E_1 is *false*, the result is *false* and E_2 is not evaluated at all. In the example, the erroneous subscripting operation is then avoided. Similarly, for expression

$$E_1 \text{ or } E_2$$

E_2 is evaluated only if the value of E_1 is *false*.

Another possible approach is to augment the syntax of the **while** and **repeat** constructs to allow *several* tests as immediate constituents, as in

> **while** E_1 **andthen** E_2 **andthen**$\cdots$**andthen** E_n **do** C

and   **repeat** C **until** E_1 **orelse** E_2 **orelse**$\cdots$**orelse** E_n

and to test them sequentially. For the **while** form, expressions E_i would be evaluated in order until one has the value *false* (and for the **repeat** form, until one has the value *true*); otherwise, command C would be executed. Note that 'andthen' and 'orelse' here are separators which are components of the iterative constructs, rather than operators forming composite Boolean expressions.

5.3.3 Iteration in ALGOL 68

Many other iteration constructs are possible, combining in various ways the concepts discussed in the preceding sub-sections. As an example of a relatively complex iteration mechanism, we shall discuss the construct in ALGOL 68. In its most elaborate form, it is

> **for** I **from** E_1 **by** E_2 **to** E_3 **while** E_4 **do** C **od**

Its meaning should be clear from the syntax if it is noted that expressions E_1, E_2, and E_3 are integer-valued and are evaluated only once, and the scope of I is E_4 and C.

In its complete form, as above, the construct is rather complex, but portions of it may optionally be omitted as follows:

(a) if "**for** I" is omitted, the iteration count is not accessible in E_4 or C;
(b) if "**from** E_1" is omitted, the default initial value of I is one;
(c) if "**by** E_2" is omitted, the default increment for I is one;
(d) if "**to** E_3" is omitted, the default limiting value for I is infinity;
(e) if "**while** E_4" is omitted, no termination condition is tested.

Thus the only part of the construct that is never omitted is

do C **od**

In effect, there are thirty-two iterative constructs wrapped into one. This approach is quite different from that of PASCAL, which provides a *small* number of *distinctive* iterative constructions.

One difficulty with the approach in ALGOL 68 is that in general an iteration might be terminated by either the iteration count limit being exceeded or the **while** condition failing, and there is no convenient way of knowing without re-testing the condition. Another is that some simple and useful forms of iteration (such as the **repeat** in PASCAL) are not conveniently expressible.

*5.3.4 Semantics of Iterations

We have so far been rather vague about the semantics of iterations, relying on the reader's programming experience. But the question arises: how can the semantics of a construction like

while E **do** C

be specified? In many language descriptions this is achieved by *translating* the iteration into an equivalent form that uses the **goto** sequencer, such as

```
   begin
1: if E then
      begin
         C;
         goto 1
      end
   end
```

Although this may be how the **while** loop is actually *implemented*, it does not solve the problem of *semantic* description, because it is quite difficult to describe the semantics of labels and sequencers such as the **goto**. Therefore, the translation approach is conceptually quite unsatisfactory. The reason that the **while** loop is available in programming languages is to provide a semantically *simple* means of expressing a common pattern of control sequencing, so that it is rather inappropriate to describe its effect to the programmer in terms of semantically more complex linguistic devices such as labels and sequencers.

Another approach that has been used, particularly for languages without sequencers, is to specify that the effect of

while E **do** C

is to be equivalent to

> **if** E th̃en
> **begin**
>   C;   (5.1)
>   **while** E **do** C
> **end**

Again, we would certainly expect this equivalence to be true of the semantics of these control structures, but it is not quite adequate as a *definition* of the **while** form because its meaning is given in terms of *itself*, and not in terms of the meanings of its immediate constituents, E and C, alone.

This problem may be solved by a method that is closely analogous to the limit construction for recursively defined domains discussed in Section 3.1.5. Let C_0 be any command whose execution *never* terminates. For example, C_0 might be

> **while** $0<1$ **do** {null}

Then, define commands C_{i+1} for $i \geq 0$ to be

> **if** E **then**
> **begin**
>   C;
> C_i
> **end**

C_{i+1} is just command (5.1) with the "recursive" occurrence of the **while** loop replaced by C_i. In general, each of the C_i is a command whose effect is exactly that of the **while** loop, provided that less than i iterations are sufficient. Therefore, the meanings of all the C_i are *approximations* to the intended meaning of

> **while** E **do** C

in the sense that whenever they provide any information at all, the same information would be obtained by executing the **while** loop. Furthermore, the sequence of meanings of C_0, C_1, C_2,··· is a sequence of better and better approximations to the intended meaning of the **while** loop, in that they represent the effect of more and more computation. Consequently, it is appropriate to *define* the meaning of the **while** loop as the *limit* of this sequence of approximate meanings, making use of the concepts discussed in Section 3.3.2. It can be proved that this limit is equal to the meaning of command (5.1).

Note that each C_{i+1} was defined using only the meanings of immediate constituents E and C of the **while** loop, the "simple" control structures ';' and 'if', and C_i. It is evident by simple induction on i that all of the approximate meanings and therefore their limit really depend *only* on the meanings of E and C, the immediate constituents of the **while** loop. The use of selection and sequencing control structures and the initial command, C_0, is just a convenient way of expressing the approximate meanings.

5.4 EXPRESSION CONTROL STRUCTURES

Most of the examples of control structures in the preceding sections have been *commands*; however, most of the concepts discussed also arise with *expressions*. For example, ALGOL 68 has a composite expression form

$$E_1 ; E_2$$

whose value is that of E_2, evaluated *after* evaluation of E_1 (for its side effect only; the *value* of E_1 is simply discarded). For example, the following is an expression in ALGOL 68:

$$a := a * a;$$
$$b := b * b;$$
$$a + b$$

(Recall that assignments are *expressions* in ALGOL 68.)

An example of a selection expression is the conditional expression of ALGOL 60:

if E **then** E **else** E

Some languages (such as ALGOL 68) also have **case** expressions.

Iterative expressions are rather rare in programming languages, though they are quite common in mathematics. An example is the "implied DO" of FORTRAN input and output commands. For example,

$$(A(I), I = 1, N)$$

is equivalent to

$$A(1), A(2), \cdots, A(N)$$

It would be possible to have a fairly general iterative expression of the form

for $I = E$ **to** E **op** O **on** E

where O is a binary operator. For example,

for $i = a$ **to** b **op**+**on** $\cdots i \cdots$

would be the analog of

$$\sum_{i=a}^{b} \cdots i \cdots$$

5.5 NON-DETERMINATE SELECTION

The description of a language does not have to *fully* specify the result of a computation. It is possible and sometimes desirable to allow implementations to have some degrees of freedom. Language features whose computational results are only partially specified will be termed ***non-determinate*** (or "non-deterministic").

There are several motivations for non-determinacy. One is to allow processors on different machines to use whatever approach is most efficient for each computer, even if results may differ somewhat, as with arithmetic operations on "real" (i.e., floating-point) numbers. Another reason is to allow a programmer to make explicit in his program the fact that there may be several equally acceptable computational paths to a solution, or possibly several acceptable solutions. An important example of non-determinacy that will be discussed in Chapter 11 arises with concurrent (parallel) processing, when the relative speeds of the processors are not determined.

The effect of interpreting a non-determinate construct may be described in terms of a (non-empty) set of *possible* "results", say, values or stores. A *processor* has the freedom to produce *any* element of the set; on the other hand, a *programmer* has the responsibility to ensure that *every* element of the set would be acceptable to him. Program correctness is especially important with non-determinacy, because results of program executions may not be reproducible. This makes conventional debugging extremely difficult and unreliable.

The simplest non-determinate control structure allows a choice of interpreting *either* of two expressions or commands. This might be expressed by

$$E_1 \mid E_2 \qquad \text{or} \qquad C_1 \mid C_2$$

The set of possible values or stores resulting from interpretation of these constructs would be the *union* of the sets of possible results of the immediate constituents. However, there seems to be no good reason to provide this particular form of non-determinacy in a programming language.

A more useful control structure is non-determinate sequencing of commands, which might be expressed by

$$C_1, C_2$$

The commands are to be executed in sequence, but the order of execution is not determined. This is equivalent to

$$C_1; C_2 \mid C_2; C_1$$

and could be used wherever conventional sequencing would be unnecessarily over-specific.

The following control structure which uses non-determinate selection has been proposed:

$$\textbf{if } E_1 \rightarrow C_1$$
$$\mid E_2 \rightarrow C_2$$
$$\vdots$$
$$\mid E_n \rightarrow C_n$$
$$\textbf{end}$$

The implementation is expected to select for execution any of the commands C_i whose "guard" E_i evaluates to *true*. If none are *true*, the computation is in error; if more than one is, the computation may have more than one possible result. For example, the effect of executing

$$\textbf{if } a[i] \leq a[j] \rightarrow m := i$$
$$\mid a[i] \geq a[j] \rightarrow m := j$$
$$\textbf{end}$$

is to set m to the index of the smaller of $a[i]$ and $a[j]$. Note the symmetry of the construction: if $a[i] = a[j]$, either of the assignments may be executed, yielding different but presumably equally acceptable results.

Similarly, the following is an *iteration* that uses non-determinate selection:

$$\textbf{loop } E_1 \rightarrow C_1$$
$$\mid E_2 \rightarrow C_2$$
$$\vdots$$
$$\mid E_n \rightarrow C_n$$
$$\textbf{end}$$

An implementation is expected to execute any of the commands whose guard evaluates to *true*, and then repeat this until none of the guards are *true*. As before, if more than one guard is *true*, the implementation has a choice of which computational path to pursue.

The kind of non-determinacy that has been discussed so far in this section has been termed *demonic* non-determinacy. A programmer must assume that the implementation will always make the *worst* possible choice at every branch point; otherwise, he could not be certain that the program would *always* execute correctly. For example, the following is *not* suitable for setting i to an arbitrary non-negative integer, because it is possible for an implementation to *always* choose the first guarded command, so that the computation never terminates:

$$i := 0, b := true;$$
$$\textbf{loop } b \rightarrow i := i + 1$$
$$\mid b \rightarrow b := false$$
$$\textbf{end}$$

Another kind of non-determinacy, which might be termed *oracular* non-determinacy, requires a processor to try whenever possible to avoid any "bad" choices, that is to say, branches leading to errors, failure, non-termination, or other kinds of computational disaster. The processor may be thought of as consulting an oracle to guide its choice of computational path into a "safe" branch. Of course, this is really implemented by following *all* possible computational paths until a successful one, if any, is found. This is achieved either by using separate processors in parallel, or by sharing one processor among the alternative branches. Note that such sharing must be *fair* in that computation must not be restricted exclusively to any single branch (unless all of the other branches have already failed), in case it becomes an *infinite* computation that should be avoided. Oracular non-determinacy is more convenient for the programmer than the demonic variety, but is much harder to implement.

EXERCISES

5.1 Some languages have **case** constructions that select by *position*. For example, in the following, if the value of expression E is integer *i*, then command C_i is selected:

> **case** E **of**
> C_1;
> C_2;
>   ⋮
> C_n
> **end**

What disadvantages does this approach have in comparison with the case construction in PASCAL?

5.2 The **case** command in PASCAL may be thought of as a way of indexing into a (one-dimensional) *array* of commands. Design a *multi-dimensional* generalization of the **case** command.

5.3 Show how to get the effect of the PASCAL form

> **repeat**
>   C
> **until** E

in ALGOL 68.

5.4 In mathematics, the value of

$$\sum_{i \in S} \cdots i \cdots$$

is zero when S is the empty set. In PASCAL, command

> **for** I:=E_1 **to** E_2 **do** C

has no effect (except for side effects of the evaluations) if the value of E_1 is greater than that of E_2. What general principle governs these conventions? If the value of E_1 is greater than that of E_2, what should be the values of iterative expression

> **for** I=E_1 **to** E_2 **op** O **on** E_3

when O is **'and'**, **'or'**, and **'*'**? What about **'−'** and **'/'**?

5.5 How might the iterative construction in ALGOL 68 be extended so that it could be used as an expression?

5.6 Show how to get the effect of

> **for** I:=E_1 **to** E_2 **do** C

in PASCAL without using **for** or **goto**. *Hint*: consider

> **for** i:=m **to** n **do**$\cdots$

in the context of declarations

> **var** m:*integer*;
> i:$1..n$;

5.7 In ALGOL 60, the increments and limit values of the **for** iteration form may be real numbers. What problems can arise from this?

5.8 Why do some PASCAL processors prevent the count identifier for a **for** construct from being updated during execution of the iteration body?

5.9 Design facilities that would allow commands such as the following to be expressed more compactly:

(a) **if** $a[1]=x{\rightarrow}i:=1$
     $\mid$ $a[2]=x{\rightarrow}i:=2$
     $\vdots$
     $\mid$ $a[n]=x{\rightarrow}i:=n$
     end

(b) **loop** $a[1]=x{\rightarrow}b[1]:=b[1]+1$; $next(x)$
     $\mid$ $a[2]=x{\rightarrow}b[2]:=b[2]+1$; $next(x)$
     $\vdots$
     $\mid$ $a[n]=x{\rightarrow}b[n]:=b[n]+1$; $next(x)$
     end

where $next(x)$ updates x. The control structures are those described in Section 5.5.

5.10 Is there any need for *selective* control structures whose tests are evaluated sequentially, as in the following?

> **if** $i{>}n$ **orelse** $a[i]{\neq}x$ **then**$\cdots$**else**$\cdots$

*5.11   Describe the semantics of

(a)   **repeat** C **until** E   (PASCAL)
(b)   **loop** C **while** E:C′ **repeat**   (Section 5.3.2)
(c)   **loop**$\cdots|E_i{\rightarrow}C_i|\cdots$**end**   (non-determinate)

as limits of sequences of approximate meanings.

PROJECT

Do a critical study of the iterative construct in the programming language ALGOL 60.

BIBLIOGRAPHIC NOTES

The **loop**$\cdots$**while**$\cdots$**repeat** construct was proposed by O.-J. Dahl and discussed by Knuth [5.2]. The non-determinate control structures of Section 5.5 were described by Dijkstra [5.1].

5.1   Dijkstra, E. W. *A Discipline of Programming*, Prentice-Hall, Englewood Cliffs, N.J. (1976).

5.2   Knuth, D. E. "Structured programming with **goto** statements", *Computing Surveys*, **6** (4), 261–301 (1974).

6 BINDING

It may be recalled that distinctions were made in Section 2.3 between *binding* (of identifiers) and *updating* (of storage), between *environments* (which associate identifiers with the values they denote) and *stores* (which associate locations with the values they contain), between *definitions* (which yield new environments) and *commands* (which yield new stores), and between scope (of identifier bindings) and *lifetime* (of incarnations of locations). Programmers generally feel more at ease with the assignment-related concepts discussed in the preceding two chapters (updating, locations, stores, commands, lifetime) because of their familiarity with the properties of storage devices. But binding and related notions are equally or even more important in programming languages, particularly when *large* programs must be written.

Unlike assignment-related notions, which are features distinctive to programming languages, the terminology and concepts related to identifier binding are derived from mathematical notations. For example, the symbol 'x' in

$$\int_a^b \sin^2(x)\ dx$$

is conventionally known as a **bound** variable, and the expression '$\sin^2(x)$' occurring in it is known as the **scope** of the binding. The same terminology and concepts arise in programming languages.

In the present chapter, attention is focussed on *where* binding occurs in programs. In the first section, two kinds of identifier occurrences will be distinguished, and the subsequent section will survey the various approaches to binding taken in programming languages. In the final section, the concept of a *free* identifier is introduced.

6.1 BINDING OCCURRENCES AND APPLIED OCCURRENCES

Consider the PASCAL definition

$$\textbf{const } i = -j;$$

It contains two identifier occurrences. The occurrence of 'i' is a ***binding*** occurrence: the identifier is being defined, and merely stands for itself. The occurrence of 'j' is an ***applied*** occurrence: it is being used rather than defined, and must have been defined elsewhere. In every form of definition in PASCAL, there is a binding occurrence of the identifier being defined by that definition. Applied occurrences of identifiers are typically in expressions, where the identifier is used to symbolize the value with which it is associated in the current environment.

Note that an occurrence of an identifier as the left-hand side of an assignment is an applied and not a binding occurrence. For example, in

> **var** i : *integer*;
> **begin**
> $i := 0$;
>   ⋮
> $i := i + 1$;
>   ⋮
> **end**

the occurrence of 'i' in the declaration is the *only* binding occurrence. At that point, the identifier is bound to a storage location. All of the other occurrences of 'i' are applied occurrences, where the identifier denotes that same storage location. The assignment has the effect of updating the location, but does not change the binding of identifier 'i' to that location.

Usually, the meaning of an applied identifier occurrence is established at a unique and explicit binding occurrence of that identifier. This may be depicted by drawing an arrow in the program text from the applied occurrence to its (circled) binding occurrence, as in

> **type** ⓘ = $0 .. 31$;
> **var** ⓘ : t ;
> **begin**
> $i := 0$;
>   ⋮
> $i := i + 1$;
>   ⋮
> **end**

Note that if programmers could use such arrows in programs, the identifiers themselves would in principle be redundant.

6.2 APPROACHES TO BINDING

6.2.1 Syntactic Bindings

An important property of a programming language is the ease with which a program reader can *find* binding occurrences in programs, for it is at binding occurrences that identifiers acquire their meaning. This is easiest if binding occurrences are determined by the syntax of the language, in which case the binding may be termed *syntactic*. Table 6.1 gives the productions of the abstract syntax of PASCAL (from Appendix B) with all of the syntactically determined binding occurrences of identifiers and label numerals indicated by circled symbols Ⓘ and Ⓝ.

The binding occurrences in definitions, parameters, and **record** type

---

L ::= I|L.I|L[E]|E↑

E ::= B|I|OE|EOE|I(···,E,···)|L.I|L[E]|E↑
|[···,E,···,E..E,···]|(E)

K ::= B|I|OK

T ::= I|(···,Ⓘ,···)|K..K|↑I|**set of** T
|**array**[T]**of** T|**file of** T|**record**···;Ⓘ:T;···**end**
|**record**···;Ⓘ:T;···**case** Ⓘ:I **of**···;K:(···;Ⓘ:T;···);···**end**

Q ::= I:I|**var** I:I
|**procedure** I(···;Q;···)|**function** I(···;Q;···):I

P ::= Ⓘ:I|**var** Ⓘ:I
|**procedure** Ⓘ (···;Q;···)|**function** Ⓘ (···;Q;···):I

D ::= **const** Ⓘ=K;|**type** Ⓘ=T;|**var** Ⓘ:T;
|**procedure** Ⓘ (···;P;···);C;|**function** Ⓘ (···;P;···):I;C;

S ::= **goto** N

C ::= |L:=E|I|I(···,E,···)|C;C
|**if** E **then** C|**if** E **then** C **else** C
|**case** E **of**···;K:C;···**end**
|**while** E **do** C|**repeat** C **until** E
|**for** I:=E **to** E **do** C|**for** I:=E **downto** E **do** C
|Ⓝ:C|S
|**with** L **do** C|···D···**begin** C **end**|**begin** C **end**

M ::= **program** Ⓘ(···,I,···);C.

Table 6.1 Binding Identifier Occurrences in PASCAL

expressions are predictable and easy to locate. Others, such as command labels and enumerated constant identifiers, though syntactically determined, may be "buried" in large type expressions or commands where binding occurrences are not expected, and these are often less easy to find.

6.2.2 Nested Bindings

In PASCAL, a programmer is allowed to *re*-define identifiers. For example, in

> **const** $i=3$;
> ⋮
> ⋮ {here $i=3$}
> ⋮
>
> **procedure** p;
>   **const** $i=4$;
>   **begin** {p}
>   ⋮
>   ⋮ {here $i=4$}
>   ⋮
>   **end**; {p}
> **begin**
>   ⋮
>   ⋮ {here $i=3$}
>   ⋮
> **end**

the **procedure** definition contains a ***nested*** binding of 'i'. Note that this creates a "hole" in the scope of the outer binding. The scope of a binding in PASCAL excludes any *nested* scopes of the same identifier.

It might seem desirable to *forbid* nested bindings for the sake of program readability. Yet almost every programming language allows such re-definition. The reason appears to be that this allows a programmer of an "inner" scope to ignore any non-local identifier bindings that are not actually inherited and used in the local scope. If nested bindings were forbidden, he would have to keep in mind *all* of the identifiers that were bound non-locally, or be forced to examine the whole context of that inner scope before introducing any local names. This is so undesirable that nested bindings are tolerated, but as a matter of good programming style, they should be avoided as much as possible. Language processors could help programmers by pointing out nested bindings in program listings with warning messages, and by making it easy to systematically change identifiers in order to remove inadvertent name clashes.

6.2.3 Implicit Bindings

Not all identifier bindings in PASCAL may be attributed to explicit binding occurrences of those identifiers. Execution of command

> **with** L **do** C

involves binding the field names of the type of L to the corresponding components of the l-value of L. For example, in

> **var** x : **record**$\cdots$;i:$\cdots$;$\cdots$**end**;
> **begin**
> $\vdots$
> **with** x **do**$\cdots i \cdots$;
> $\vdots$
> **end**

applied occurrences of 'i' in the **with** command denote the 'i' component of x. This is an example of what may be termed *implicit* binding, in that at the program point where the identifier is bound, there is no explicit occurrence of it.

If, in

> **with** L **do** C

command C is "large", possibly itself containing implicit bindings, it may become quite difficult for a program reader to find the binding points for applied identifier occurrences, particularly since all other identifier bindings in PASCAL are in procedure headings. Programmers should use this construction only with "small" commands C. This problem with the **with** command in PASCAL would not have arisen if the construct had required programmers to make explicit the bound field names, as in

> **with** $(\cdots,I_i,\cdots)$=L **do**
> $\cdots I_i \cdots$

Processors for languages with implicit binding could improve program readability by making implicitly bound identifiers manifest in program listings. This could be done by inserting "comments" that specify the bound identifiers (and their types) at the points where they are implicitly bound.

6.2.4 Default Bindings

In PASCAL, any applied identifier occurrence that is *not* in the scope of any binding occurrence of that identifier and is not a pre-defined ("standard") identifier, is in error. However, in some languages (including FORTRAN and PL/I), any applied identifier occurrences that are not *explicitly* bound are assumed to be bound by *default* in some way.

Default bindings are intended to be a convenience to the program *writer*; however, there is the significant disadvantage that the program text contains less information for program *readers*, including language processors. Therefore time can be wasted in trying to locate an explicit binding occurrence for an identifier that is actually bound by default. Furthermore, languages with default binding are very susceptible to errors arising from trivial misspellings: a misspelled identifier or keyword will be bound by default. It can be extremely difficult for programmers to find such errors, or even to be aware that they have occurred, unless the program's output is evidently incorrect. The minor "convenience" of being allowed to omit an explicit binding is often paid for by more difficult debugging, incorrect results, or disaster.

Programmers should bind explicitly all identifiers used in their programs, even if the language in use allows default binding, and processors of such languages could help by making any default bindings manifest in program listings with added "comments" or warning messages.

6.2.5 Overloaded Identifiers

Normally, an identifier does not denote more than one semantic entity in any context. But in some languages it is possible for a programmer to *overload* an identifier, that is to say, to bind it to more than one meaning. Of course, the value of an applied occurrence of such an identifier would then be ambiguous, so that the context of the applied occurrence must be used to resolve the ambiguity.

An example of overloading in PASCAL is the treatment of **function** names. Within the body of a **function** definition, the identifier denotes a location for returning a value in some *l*-expression contexts, and the procedure itself in other contexts. For example, identifier '*f*' is overloaded in

> **function** $f(n : integer) : integer$;
> **begin**
>   **if** $n=0$ **then** $f:=1$ **else** $f:=n*f(n-1)$
> **end**

Some other languages make more extensive use of overloading. For example, PL/I allows several procedures to have the same name. The types of the actual parameters of an invocation are used to select the appropriate procedure. This allows conceptually similar procedures on distinct domains to have the same name, just as literal operators like '+' and '*' may be used with both *integer* and *real* operands. Overloaded procedure names and operators are sometimes termed "generic".

6.2.6 Pseudo-identifiers

Let us suppose that PASCAL were to allow (as do many other languages) use of symbol 'return' for exiting from a procedure body:

> **procedure** I($\cdots$;P;$\cdots$);
> $\vdots$
> **begin**
> $\vdots$
> **return**
> $\vdots$
> **end**;

Although 'return' is evidently not a programmer-defined identifier, its meaning does depend on the context in which it is used. In such a language, procedure definitions may be regarded as (implicitly) *binding* symbol 'return'. Furthermore, the usual rules of *scope* would apply. The scope of such a binding would be the procedure body, excluding any nested scopes of 'return'. For example, in

> **procedure** *p*;
>   **procedure** *q*;
>   **begin** $\lfloor q \rfloor$
> $\vdots$
>   **return**
> $\vdots$
>   **end**; {*q*}
>   **begin** {*p*}
> $\vdots$
>   **return**
> $\vdots$
>   **end**; {*p*}

the first occurrence of 'return' is for exiting from procedure *q*, and the second is for exiting from *p*, which is a scope with a "hole" in it.

    Symbols such as 'return' that have the binding and scope properties of identifiers but are not chosen by the programmer will be termed ***pseudo-***

identifiers. The main disadvantage of pseudo-identifiers is that, unlike normal identifiers, a scope hole cannot be avoided by a systematic change of identifier. For example, in the program fragment above, there would be no way to exit procedure p as a whole from within the body of procedure q.

6.2.7 Other Variations on Binding

In some languages an identifier occurrence may be both binding *and* applied. For example, in PL/I an identifier can be declared to be 'EXTERNAL', as in

DECLARE (I) EXTERNAL···;

The identifier occurrence in such a declaration is an applied occurrence because the meaning of the identifier must be obtained from the "external" environment; but, it is also a binding occurrence with respect to the "internal" or local context.

Another variant is to have more than one binding occurrence associated with a single binding. For example, to allow use of procedure identifiers *before* their actual definitions, PASCAL permits a **forward** "declaration" for the procedure name, as in

> **procedure** I(···;P;···); **forward**;
> ⋮
>   {use of I allowed here}
> ⋮
> **procedure** I; C;
> ⋮

where both uses of I stand for the same identifier. Both of these binding occurrences of the procedure name are associated with the *same* binding. Note that the parameter list must be omitted in the actual definition of the procedure.

Finally, it is possible for an identifier occurrence to be *neither* binding nor applied, that is to say, unnecessary. For example, the following illustrates the syntax required by some PASCAL processors for specifying procedural parameters:

> **function** *integral*(**function** *f*(*x:real*) : *real*;
>   *a,b,eps:real*) : *real*;
>   **begin** ··· **end**;

The occurrence of identifier '*x*' in parameter specifier '*x:real*' is neither binding nor applied. The role of the specifier is to indicate the type and kind of parameter expected by procedural arguments f to *integral*; identifier 'x' is irrelevant and could in principle be omitted.

6.3 FREE IDENTIFIERS

An identifier is said to be *free* in (or "non-local" to, or "global" to) a construct if it has an applied occurrence in the construct that is not bound in the construct. These are known as the *free occurrences* of the identifier in the construct. For example, in PASCAL block

> **var** $z:t$;
> **begin**
> $z := x$;
> $x := y$;
> $y := z$
> **end**

(a) 'i' is not free, because it has no occurrences in the block;
(b) 'z' is not free, because both of its applied occurrences in the block are in the scope of a binding occurrence in the block;
(c) 't', 'x', and 'y' are free, because they have applied occurrences that are not bound in the block.

The free occurrences of identifiers in a construct may be thought of as having "binding arrows" that go outside the construct, as in

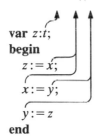

A construct must be interpreted relative to an environment which determines what is denoted by each of the free identifiers of the construct.

Note that freedom of an identifier and of identifier occurrences depends on the construct under consideration. For example, identifier 'z' is free in expression 'z' and free in command '$z := x$' but not free in block

var z : t;
begin
    $z := x$;
      $\vdots$
end

because all of its applied occurrences are "captured" by the declaration. Also, note that it is possible for a free identifier of a construct to have binding occurrences as well as applied occurrences in the construct; some of the latter must be outside the scopes of all of the former.

EXERCISES

6.1 Which of the identifier occurrences in the following are binding and which are applied?

$$\int_{a}^{b} \sin(x) + (\int_{x}^{c} \cos(y) \ dy) \ dx$$

If possible, draw binding arrows from applied identifier occurrences to the occurrence that binds them. What are the free identifiers of this expression?

6.2 Why might a PASCAL programmer want to use a procedure name before its definition, and therefore need a **forward** declaration?

6.3 What is the disadvantage to program readers of not having the parameter list in the actual definition of a **forward**-declared procedure in PASCAL? Are formal parameter identifiers needed in **forward** "declarations"?

6.4 In PL/I, definitions may appear *anywhere* in a block, and not necessarily before the body of the block. What are the advantages and disadvantages of this flexibility?

6.5 Give an example showing that an identifier which is free in a construct may have binding occurrences in the construct.

6.6 An enthusiastic language designer proposes to extend his favorite language CATCHALL by allowing parameter list definitions of the form

> **param** I=($\cdots$;P;$\cdots$);

where P is a formal parameter. For example,

> **param** p=(i:*integer*; **var** x:*real*);
> $\vdots$
> **procedure** $q(p)$; **begin**$\cdots i \cdots x \cdots$**end**;
> **procedure** $r(p)$; **begin**$\cdots i \cdots x \cdots$**end**;

would then be equivalent to

> **procedure** $q(i$:*integer*; **var** x:*real*);
>   **begin**$\cdots i \cdots x \cdots$**end**;
> **procedure** $r(i$:*integer*; **var** x:*real*);
>   **begin**$\cdots i \cdots x \cdots$**end**;

Why should he be discouraged?

7 PROCEDURAL ABSTRACTION

Procedural abstraction is provided in PASCAL by its **procedure** and **function** definition forms. The basic components of a procedural abstraction mechanism are:

(a) a formal parameter part (possibly empty) which contains binding occurrences of the formal parameter identifiers, and
(b) a body: a construct whose interpretation is deferred until the resulting procedure is invoked (by being supplied with appropriate arguments).

For example, in

> **procedure** *inc*(**var** *i:integer*);
>   **begin** *i*:=*i*+1 **end**;

the formal parameter part is

> (**var** *i:integer*)

in which '*i*' has a binding occurrence, and the body is command

> **begin** *i*:=*i*+1 **end**

In this chapter, the *body* component of procedural definitions and abstracts will be discussed in detail; issues relating to *parameters* will be considered in the following chapter.

7.1 COMMAND PROCEDURES

A **procedure** definition in PASCAL has the syntactic form

> **procedure** I(···;P;···); C;

To focus attention on abstraction-related aspects, it is convenient to regard this as if it had the form

$$I = \mathbf{procedure}(\cdots;P;\cdots);\ C;$$

where abstract

$$\mathbf{procedure}(\cdots;P;\cdots);\ C$$

is an expression whose value is a *command procedure*. This means that (a) the body, C, of the abstract defining it is a command, and that (b) the procedure it defines is invoked by executing an invocation that is itself a command. For example, the value of the abstract implicit in

$$\mathbf{procedure}\ inc(\mathbf{var}\ i{:}t);$$
$$\mathbf{begin}\ i{:}=i+1\ \mathbf{end};$$

may be invoked by a command such as

$$inc(n)$$

What then *is* a command procedure, as a semantic object? Consider the "incrementing" procedure defined above. Its effect when invoked is to increment the integer contained in its argument (a location). This means that the procedure may be regarded abstractly as a *function* mapping a location (its *explicit* argument) and a store (its *implicit* argument) to a new store. The new store is like the old one except that the integer in the location has been incremented.

In general, a command procedure in PASCAL (and most other languages) may be modelled by a function that maps a sequence of argument values and a store into a new store. The explicit arguments are obtained by evaluating the actual parameters of an invocation, and the implicit argument is the state of the store just after these evaluations. The store yielded by executing an invocation is the new store obtained by applying the procedure to its arguments.

Now we may describe precisely what procedure is defined by an abstract of the form

$$\mathbf{procedure}(\cdots;P;\cdots);\ C$$

The value of the abstract is the command procedure that, when applied to a sequence of argument values and a store, yields the store obtained by executing the command C relative to the supplied store. Note that by using mathematical functions to model *what* procedures do, we have been able to "abstract" away from *how* these functions happen to be described by particular **procedure** definitions.

But, an important question must still be answered: what *environment* is used for executing C? In other words, what do identifiers denote in C?

Consider abstract

> **procedure**(**var** *i*:*t*);
>   **var** *temp*:*t*;
>   **begin**
>   *temp*:=*i*+*k*;
>   *i*:=*temp*
>   **end**

Identifier '*temp*' is bound *locally* within the body, so that there is no question about what it denotes there. Identifier '*i*' is a *formal parameter* of the abstract; parameter binding will be discussed in the next chapter, but it is evident that in this case '*i*' must be bound to the *l*-value of the actual parameter of the invocation. Finally, there are identifiers '*k*' and '*t*', which are *free* identifiers of the abstract. Where are free identifiers of abstracts or procedure definitions bound? This question is addressed in the next section.

7.2 FREE IDENTIFIERS OF ABSTRACTS

7.2.1 Static Binding

In PASCAL, free identifier occurrences are bound in the environment of the *abstract*. This is known as **static** binding, because the binding occurrence is determined "statically", that is to say, without executing the program; furthermore, the binding occurrence does not change during program execution.

For example, consider definitions

> **const** *k*=3;
> **type** *t*=0..99;
> **procedure** *inc*(**var** *i*:*t*);
>   **begin** *i*:=*i*+*k* **end**;

The free identifiers of the **procedure** definition are, as before, '*k*' and '*t*'. The abstract is evaluated in an environment in which '*k*' denotes 3 and '*t*' denotes the subrange from 0 to 99. Therefore, in a language using static binding (such as PASCAL), these are the meanings of the free occurrences of these identifiers in the abstract, no matter what the environment of any *invocation* of the procedure. This may be depicted by binding arrows as follows:

> **const** *k*=3;
> **type** *t*=0..99;
> **procedure** *inc*(**var** *i*:*t*);
>   **begin** *i*:=*i*+*k* **end**;

Note that free identifier 'k' would be bound in the same way even if it denoted a location, rather than a number, as in

type t=0..99;
var k:t;
procedure inc(**var** i:t);
    begin i:=$i+k$ **end**;

In this case the store resulting from an invocation of the procedure depends on the contents in the store (at the time of invocation) of location k allocated in the declaration, but *not* on the meaning of identifier 'k' in the environment of the invocation. In other words, the procedure has a *store* as an implicit argument, but the *environment* for the definition body is determined once and for all when the procedure is defined (except for parameter bindings).

7.2.2 Dynamic Binding

Another approach to free identifiers of abstracts is used in LISP and APL. In these languages, free identifier occurrences of abstracts are bound in the environments of *invocations* of the procedure. Consider the same **procedure** definition as the previous example, but now suppose that the procedure is invoked from an environment in which 'k' has a different meaning:

procedure inc(**var** i:t);
    begin i:=$i+k$ **end**
    $\vdots$
procedure q;
    const k=5;
    var n:t;
    begin
        $\vdots$
        inc(n);
        $\vdots$
    end;

If the environment of the *invocation* were used to determine the meanings of free identifiers of the **procedure** definition, then this invocation of the procedure would increment its argument by 5. Other invocations might have other effects on their arguments, depending on the environments of those invocations.

This approach is known as ***dynamic*** binding, because binding occurrences of free identifiers of abstracts can change during program execution. In languages that use dynamic binding, procedures are functions not only of the stores, but also of the environments of their invocations.

In languages like LISP and APL that are normally implemented by interpreters rather than compilers, dynamic binding is somewhat easier to implement than static binding. But its disadvantages are quite severe. With dynamic binding it is much more difficult for program readers to determine where identifier occurrences are bound and for language processors to verify type compatibility and identifier binding before program execution.

An even more serious disadvantage of dynamic binding is the vulnerability of identifiers accessible in the environment of an invocation. For example, consider the following:

> **var** n,k,t;
> **begin**
> ⋮
> $p(n)$;
> ⋮
> **end**

In PASCAL and in any language with static binding, execution of the invocation could not affect the contents of k because 'k' is not an actual parameter and the definition of procedure p is not in the scope of the declaration of 'k'. Therefore, the contents of this location cannot be modified or even examined by p. But in a language with *dynamic* binding, k may be accidentally or maliciously accessed or modified by p if 'k' is a free identifier of the definition of p, and there is little that the programmer of the invocation can do to prevent this! With dynamic binding, locally defined or private information is vulnerable to errors or breaches of privacy in *other* program components, and this is quite unacceptable in large systems.

7.3 EXPRESSION PROCEDURES

By analogy with the properties of *command* procedures, it might be expected that (a) an *expression procedure* would be invoked by evaluating an invocation *expression*, and that (b) the body of an abstract defining an expression procedure would be an expression. The first of these holds in PASCAL and in most programming languages, and in some languages so does the second. For example, the syntax of a "statement function" definition in FORTRAN is

$$I(\cdots,P,\cdots)=E$$

where the body to the right of the '=' symbol is an expression. However, in PASCAL (b) apparently does not hold, because the syntax for the **function** definition is

function I($\cdots$;P;$\cdots$):I; C;

where the body is a *command*. But conceptually the body of a **function** definition in PASCAL *is* an expression, because it is executed to yield a value. There is a special convention involving the name of the procedure that allows an execution of command C to yield a value.

Let us defer consideration of this somewhat confusing convention for the moment and regard

function ($\cdots$;P;$\cdots$):I; E

with expression E as its body as the general form of an expression procedure abstract. Then, the semantics of expression procedure invocation and abstraction may be described by analogy with the treatment of *command* procedures as follows:

(a)   An expression procedure may be regarded as a (mathematical) function mapping a sequence of (explicit) argument values and a store (the implicit argument) into a value and a new store.

(b)   An invocation expression invokes an expression procedure by applying it to the values of the actual parameter expressions and the current state of the store.

(c)   The value and the store yielded by evaluating an invocation expression are those returned by the expression procedure invoked.

(d)   The value of abstract

function($\cdots$;P;$\cdots$):I; E

is the expression procedure that, when applied to a sequence of values and a store, yields the value and the store obtained by evaluating E relative to the supplied store.

The environment for the evaluation of E in (d) is established along the same lines as the environment for execution of the body of a command procedure abstract. In a language that uses static binding, free identifiers are bound in the environment of the abstract itself, and not the invocations. In a language that uses dynamic binding, expression procedures are also functionally dependent on the invocation environment.

For example, if abstract

function(**var** *a*,*b*:*integer*):*integer*;
   begin
      a:=*sqr*(*a*);
      b:=*sqr*(*b*)
   result *a*+*b*

is evaluated in an environment in which free identifiers '*integer*' and '*sqr*' have their standard meanings, then the expression procedure defined by this abstract will return as its value the sum of the squares of the contents in the current store of its (explicit) arguments, and it will also have the side effect of squaring the contents of these locations. (To avoid the side effect, the "value" parameter form may be used.) In a language that uses dynamic binding, the value and effect of the invocation would also depend on the meanings of *'integer'* and *'sqr'* in the environment of the invocation.

Let us now survey the conventions employed in programming languages for returning values when the bodies of expression procedure abstracts are *commands* (syntactically). In PASCAL and ALGOL 60, a location is allocated when an expression procedure is invoked. If the name of the procedure is used as an assignment target in the body of the abstract, it denotes this location, and its contents after executing the body becomes the value returned by the procedure. In contexts other than as assignment targets, the procedure name denotes the procedure itself (recursively), so that the location for the return value is effectively "write-only".

There are two ways this overloading might have been avoided: (a) use a pseudo-identifier like **result** (rather than the name of the procedure) to denote the location for the return value, or (b) allow the programmer to name the location, as in

> **function** $f(n:t)result:t$;
> **begin**
> $\vdots$
> $result: = \cdots$;
> $\vdots$
> **end**;

Another approach is to avoid a special location and use a sequencer. For example, sequencer

> RETURN(E)

is used in PL/I to transfer control to the end of the abstract (and then back to the invocation expression) with the value of E.

It should be pointed out that none of these conventions has essentially to do with procedural abstraction: all could equally well be adapted for use in *arbitrary* expressions whenever it is desired to precede sub-expression evaluation with sub-command execution, as in expression form

> **begin** C **result** E

Generally, language designers have restricted such constructs or conventions to expression procedure abstracts or definitions in order to limit sources of side effects.

7.4 THE PRINCIPLE OF ABSTRACTION AND selector DEFINITIONS

We have seen that, aside from some minor syntactic idiosyncracies, the two kinds of procedure in PASCAL are very closely analogous: a ––––– procedure, where "–––––" is either "command" or "expression", is invoked by a ––––– invocation and defined by an abstract whose body is (at least conceptually), a –––––. The question now arises: can these concepts be applied to *other* kinds of "–––––"? The answer is yes: *any* semantically meaningful syntactic class "–––––" can in principle be used as the body of a form of abstract, and the resulting ––––– procedure may be invoked in an invocation that is a –––––. This is known as the ***principle of abstraction***. Of course, this is not to suggest that all such procedures are necessarily useful or desirable in programming languages, but it is important for a language designer to be aware that they are *possible*.

A simple first application of the principle of abstraction is the concept of abstraction from *l-expressions*. It may be recalled that an expression is an *l*-expression if it has an *l*-value and so may be used as the target of assignments. So, let us consider ***l-expression procedures***, which must be defined by abstracts whose bodies are *l*-expressions and must be invoked by invocations which are *l*-expressions.

A possible PASCAL-like syntax for definitions of such procedures is

> **selector** $I(\cdots;P;\cdots):I;$
> $\quad L;$

By analogy with ordinary expression procedures, such a procedure returns the *l*-value of L, where the evaluation is relative to the environment of the definition (extended by parameter bindings) and a store from the invocation. For example, consider

> **type** $stack = $ **record**
> $\qquad\qquad\quad a$:**array**$[1..n]$**of** $t;$
> $\qquad\qquad\quad p$:$0..n$
> $\qquad\quad$ **end**
> $\vdots$
> **selector** $top($**var** s:$stack$)$:t;$
> $\quad s.a[s.p];$
> $\vdots$

The **selector** definition defines an *l*-expression procedure *top* that may be invoked in an *l*-expression as follows:

> $top(d):=\cdots$

where *d* is of type *stack*. This procedure allows the "top of a stack" to be *updated* (as well as fetched). This may be compared to use of the built-in selector notation

$$L\uparrow$$

in PASCAL when the value of L is a file.

Further applications of the principle of abstraction with other syntactic classes will be discussed in subsequent chapters.

EXERCISES

7.1 Give outlines of programs in which

(a) two occurrences of the same **procedure** definition define distinct (i.e., non-equivalent) procedures, and

(b) a single occurrence of a **procedure** definition is interpreted more than once and the two interpretations define distinct procedures.

Assume that the programming language uses static binding.

7.2 In a language with dynamic binding, where is a free identifier of a procedure definition bound if it does not have a binding occurrence in the context of the invocation?

7.3 What should be the *r*-value of an invocation of an *l*-expression procedure?

7.4 What restrictions must be imposed on **selector** definitions if locations allocated by local declarations in the body are disposed of on exit from it?

7.5 Compare *l*-expression procedures to ordinary expression procedures which return pointer values.

7.6 Is it accurate to describe a language with dynamic binding as one in which an applied identifier occurrence is always bound by the *most recent* interpretation of a binding of that identifier?

7.7 Is it accurate to describe a language with static binding as one in which an applied identifier occurrence is always bound by the *most recent* interpretation of a statically enclosing binding of that identifier? *Hint:* consider the occurrence of '*b*' in the definition of '*outputb*' in the following PASCAL block:

```
procedure p(b : Boolean; procedure q);
  procedure outputb;
    begin write (b) end;
  begin {p}
    if b then p (false, outputb) else
    begin
      outputb;
      q
    end
  end; {p}
procedure dummy;
  begin {null} end; {dummy}
begin p(true, dummy) end
```

BIBLIOGRAPHIC NOTES

Abstraction principles have long been important in set theory and logic [7.1, 7.2]. The principle of abstraction for programming languages described here was suggested by Tennent [7.3].

7.1 Church, A. *The Calculi of Lambda Conversion*, Princeton Univ. Press, Princeton, N.J. (1941).

7.2 Quine, W. V. *Set Theory and its Logic*, Harvard Univ. Press, Cambridge, Mass. (1963).

7.3 Tennent, R. D. "Language design methods based on semantic principles", *Acta Informatica*, **8**, 97–112 (1977).

8 PARAMETERS

The basic concepts involved in parameterization are very straightforward: when a programmer-defined procedure is invoked, the body of its definition is interpreted in an environment which binds the formal parameter identifiers to values which are in some way associated with the corresponding *actual* parameters of the invocation. The great variety of parameter mechanisms in programming languages arises primarily from the many answers possible to two questions: *when* and *how* are the actual parameters of an invocation evaluated?

8.1 PARAMETERS IN PASCAL

The language PASCAL has four formal parameter forms:

(a) $I:I'$
(b)   **var** $I:I'$
(c)   **procedure** $I(\cdots;Q_i;\cdots)$
(d)   **function** $I(\cdots;Q_i;\cdots):I'$

In these, I is the bound formal parameter identifier and I' is an applied occurrence of a type identifier. (For some processors, the list $(\cdots;Q_i;\cdots)$ of formal parameter specifiers is omitted.)

In PASCAL, actual parameters are always evaluated *before* the procedure is invoked, but different modes of evaluation are used for the various forms of formal parameter. With the *value* parameter form (a), the formal parameter identifier is bound to new storage that is initialized to the r-value of the actual parameter. Therefore, assignments in the procedure body having the formal identifier as their target update the "private" storage, rather than the l-value of the actual parameter.

For the **var** parameter form, the actual parameter must be an

117

l-expression, and the formal parameter identifier is bound to its *l*-value. This means that assignments having the formal identifier as target update the *l*-value of the actual parameter.

For a **procedure** or **function** parameter, the actual parameter must be the name of a command or expression procedure, respectively, and the formal parameter identifier is bound to that procedure.

Type compatibility constraints for parameters in PASCAL will be discussed in Chapter 12.

8.2   NAME PARAMETERS IN ALGOL 60

The *name* parameter mechanism is described in the ALGOL 60 Report as follows:

> The effect of [a procedure invocation] will be equivalent to the effect of performing the following operations on the program at the time of execution of the procedure [invocation]:
>
> Any formal [name parameter identifier] is replaced, throughout the procedure body, by the corresponding actual parameter, after enclosing the latter in parentheses if it is an expression but not [an *l*-expression]. Possible conflicts between identifiers inserted through this process and other identifiers already present within the procedure body will be avoided by suitable systematic changes of the formal or local identifiers involved.
>
> Finally, the procedure body, modified as above, is inserted in place of the procedure [invocation] and executed. If the procedure is called from a place outside the scope of any [free identifier] of the procedure body, the conflicts between the identifiers inserted through this process of body replacement and the identifiers whose declarations are valid at the place of the procedure statement will be avoided through suitable systematic changes of the latter identifiers.

This algorithm is evidently not a denotational semantic description; that is, it does not specify the meaning of invocations in terms of the meanings of their immediate constituents. In particular, in order to carry out the substitutions, it is necessary to know *how* a procedure is defined.

To illustrate the substitution process, consider PASCAL **procedure** definition

```
procedure square(var i:integer);
   var t:integer;
   begin
     t:=sqr(i);
     i:=t
   end;
```

Now suppose that formal parameter '**var** *i:integer*' were to be treated as a name parameter. Then the description above says that an invocation such as

$$square(a[j])$$

is to have the effect of

```
var t:integer;
begin
  t:=sqr(a[j]);
  a[j]:=t
end
```

provided that '*integer*' and '*sqr*', the free identifiers of the procedure definition, have the same meaning in this environment.

Note that each use of a formal name parameter in the definition body results in an evaluation of the corresponding actual parameter expression *during* interpretation of the procedure body. This can be very inefficient and may have surprising effects because even the *l*-value of the identifier can change dynamically.

An example that illustrates the power of name parameters is

```
function sum(a,b:integer; var i:integer; f:real):real;
   var s:real;
   begin
     s:=0;
     for i:=a to b do
       s:=s+f;
     sum:=s
   end;
```

If '*f*' were a name parameter, then in the context of

```
var j:1 .. n;
    p,q:array[1 .. n]of real;
```

invocation

$$sum(1,n,j,p[j]*q[j])$$

would determine the inner product of "vectors" p and q, much like

$$\sum_{j=1}^{n} p_j \times q_j.$$

Of course it would be clearer and no less convenient to express this using a **function** parameter as follows:

> **function** *sum(a,b:integer*; **function** *f(i:integer):real):real*;
>   **var** *s:real*;
>   *i:integer*;
>   **begin**
>   *s:=0*;
>   **for** *i:=a* **to** *b* **do**
>   *s:=s+f(i)*;
>   *sum:=s*
>   **end**;

A typical invocation might then be

> *sum(1,n,***function***(j:integer):real*; *p[j]*q[j])*

where abstract

> **function***(j:integer):real*; *p[j]*q[j]*

has been used as an actual parameter to express an "anonymous" procedure.

Another use for name parameters is to allow a programmer to define a procedure that can choose to avoid evaluating an actual parameter. For example, the procedure defined by

> **function** *andthen(x,y:Boolean):Boolean*;
>   **begin**
>   **if** *x* **then** *andthen:=y* **else** *andthen:=false*
>   **end**;

would provide the sequential conjunction of Section 5.3.2 if 'y' were a name parameter.

To see the reasons for the two kinds of "systematic change of identifiers" mentioned in the rules quoted above, consider invocation

> *square(t)*

in the context of

> **var** *t:integer*;
> **function** *sqr(x:integer):integer*;
>   **begin** *sqr:=* $\cdots$ **end**;

Without changes of identifiers the invocation would be replaced by

> **var** t:*integer*;
> **begin**
> $t := sqr(t)$;
> $t := t$
> **end**

which is unsatisfactory for two reasons.

(a)   There is a conflict between the occurrence of 't' in the actual parameter and local identifier 't' of the **procedure** definition body into which the actual parameter is being substituted.

(b)   There is a conflict between the occurrence of 'sqr' in the **procedure** definition body and local identifier 'sqr' of the context into which the body is being substituted.

The given rules solve these problems by requiring

(a)   replacement of all occurrences of 't' in the body of the **procedure** definition by any other identifier that is *not* free in the actual parameter, and

(b)   replacement of all occurrences of 'sqr' in the context of the invocation by any other identifier that is *not* free in the modified body of the **procedure** definition.

For example, the result might be

> **var** t:*integer*;
> **function** $newsqr(x:integer):integer$;
>   **begin** $newsqr := \cdots$ **end**;
>   ⋮
>   **var** $newt$:*integer*;
>   **begin**
> $newt := sqr(t)$;
> $t := newt$
>   **end**;
>   ⋮

where all occurrences of 'sqr' in the ellipses are to be replaced by '$newsqr$'.

There is a much simpler way to describe the semantics of name parameters. An actual name parameter may be treated in the same way as an abstract with a null parameter list. The formal parameter identifier would then be bound to a *procedure* which would be invoked whenever the identifier was evaluated.

For example,

$$square(a[j])$$

may be regarded as if it were

$$square(\ \textbf{selector}{:}integer;\ a[j]\ )$$

The actual parameter of *square* is abstract

$$\textbf{selector}{:}integer;\ a[j]$$

which defines an *l*-expression procedure (see Section 7.4) with no (explicit) arguments. In this way, the meaning of a procedure invocation involving name parameters can be explained solely in terms of the meanings of its immediate constituents without knowing how the procedure is defined.

8.3 OTHER PARAMETER MECHANISMS

PL/I and many FORTRAN processors use a parameter mechanism which combines the effects of the value and **var** forms in PASCAL: the formal parameter identifier is bound to the *l*-value of the actual parameter *if* this is an *l*-expression which has the same type as the formal parameter, and to new storage that is initialized to the *r*-value of the actual parameter otherwise. However, note that any mismatch between formal and actual parameters can lead to unexpected results.

In some implementations of FORTRAN, it is more efficient or convenient to use another approach. A formal parameter identifier is bound to new storage which is initialized to the *r*-value of the actual parameter (i.e., like value parameters in PASCAL), but *after* execution of the procedure body the *l*-value of the actual parameter (if it is an *l*-expression) is then updated by the final contents of the new storage. This is known as the *value-result* (or "copy-restore") parameter mechanism.

Actual parameters can also be evaluated before program execution if they are static or type expressions. This possibility will be discussed in Chapter 12. Another approach is to allow an actual parameter to be omitted. The corresponding formal parameter identifier would then be bound to a "default" value specified either by the programmer in the procedure definition, or by the language. A few additional parameter mechanisms will be discussed in the exercises.

8.4 PARAMETER LISTS

Procedures often have more than one (explicit) parameter. This is usually expressed, as in PASCAL, by allowing *lists* of formal and actual parameters. The correspondences between the formal and actual parameters are established by their respective positions in these lists.

If a parameter list is long, such positional correspondence tends to be error-prone and difficult to read, and some languages allow actual parameter expressions to be labelled by the corresponding formal parameter identifier, as in:

> **function** *integral*(**function** $f(x:real):real$; $a,b,eps:real):real$;
>   **begin**
> $\vdots$
>   *integral*: $= \cdots$;
>   **end**;
>   **begin**
> $\vdots$
>   *integral*(*a*: -1.0, *b*: 1.0, *eps*: $1E-8$, *f*: *fct*)
> $\vdots$
>   **end**

Note that the order of the actual parameters need not be the same as the order of the formal parameters.

Procedures may have a *null* list of formal parameters. In PASCAL and many other languages, such a procedure is invoked by using the name of the procedure by itself. But in some languages it is necessary to distinguish between an invocation with a null actual parameter list and a reference to the procedure itself (or to an identifier bound by default). In FORTRAN, for example, if F is an expression procedure with no formal parameters, it must be invoked by expression 'F()'.

EXERCISES

8.1 When may storage allocated for a value parameter be disposed of in PASCAL without creating dangling references?

8.2 Why do the substitution rules for name parameters require enclosing of actual parameter expressions in parentheses?

8.3 Would substitution rules like those for name parameters be simpler for a language that uses *dynamic* binding for free identifiers of abstracts?

8.4   Devise an example to show that the value-result parameter mechanism is *not* equivalent to the **var** parameter mechanism in PASCAL. Assume that the *l*-value of the actual parameter is evaluated *before* invoking the procedure.

8.5   Is it possible in PASCAL to access a location via both an identifier and a pointer in the same context?

8.6   Define a context in PASCAL such that the three occurrences of identifier '*f*' in

$$f:=g(f,f)$$

have different meanings.

8.7   Consider definitions

```
type matrix=array[1..n,1..n]of real;
    ⋮
procedure transpose(var a:matrix; b:matrix);
    var i,j:1..n;
    begin
      for i:=1 to n do
        for j:=1 to n do
          a[i,j]:=b[j,i]
    end;
```

(a)   Suppose that the PL/I parameter mechanism were used for *a* and *b*; would invocation

transpose(q,q)

have the effect that the programmer probably intended?

(b)   Why do PL/I programmers sometimes enclose actual parameter expressions in parentheses?

(c)   Many PASCAL programmers use a **var** parameter instead of a value parameter to avoid unnecessary copying of "large" structures. Why is this a dangerous practice?

8.8   Consider definition

```
procedure swap(var x,y:integer);
    var z:integer;
    begin
      z:=x; x:=y; y:=z
    end;
```

and suppose that '*x*' and '*y*' were name parameters.

(a)   If $a[1]=2$, $a[2]=5$, and $i=1$, what would be the effect of '*swap(a[i],i)*'

(b)   What would be the effect of '*swap(i,a[i])*' in the same circumstances?

(c)   In the context of definitions

```
type ind=1..n;
var a:array[ind]of integer;
function min(i:ind):ind;
   var m,j:ind;
   begin
     m:=i;
     for j:=i+1 to n do
       if a[j]<a[m] then m:=j;
     min:=m
   end;
```

the following is intended to sort array *a* by selecting successive minima:

```
for i:=1 to n −1 do
   swap(a[i],a[min(i)])
```

What would in fact be the overall effect on *a*? Explain.

8.9   A book on the design of correct programs claims that in PASCAL

   while E do C

is equivalent to an invocation of the procedure defined by

```
procedure whiledo(e:Boolean; procedure c);
   begin
     if e then
     begin c; whiledo(e,c) end
   end;
```

Why is this incorrect? Suggest a suitable correction to the **procedure** definition.

8.10   The *result* parameter mechanism in ALGOL W may be described as follows: the formal parameter identifier is bound to (uninitialized) new storage; *after* execution of the procedure body, the *l*-value of the actual parameter (which must be an *l*-expression) is updated to the final contents of the new storage. Give examples to show that in general this is not equivalent to either the **var** parameter in PASCAL or the name parameter in ALGOL 60.

8.11   The *lazy evaluation* parameter mechanism defers evaluation of the actual parameter until the value of the formal parameter is first needed. When (and if) this evaluation takes place, the resulting value is saved for any subsequent evaluations of the formal parameter. Under what conditions would this be equivalent to the name parameter mechanism? What advantage does it have over the name parameter?

PROJECTS

8.1   Pre-defined procedures *read* and *write* in PASCAL illustrate the convenience of variable-length actual parameter lists. Design extensions to PASCAL that would allow programmer-defined procedures to have variable-length parameter lists.

8.2   Devise syntactic (i.e., statically verifiable) constraints that would be sufficient to ensure that a **var** parameter could be implemented like a value-result parameter and the implementation would always produce correct results.

8.3   Devise syntactic constraints that would be sufficient to ensure that a value parameter could be implemented like a **var** parameter and the implementation would always produce correct results.

8.4   Devise syntactic constraints that would be sufficient to ensure that an expression procedure cannot have side effects on storage.

BIBLIOGRAPHIC NOTES

The history of attempts to give a correct definition of substitution between contexts is traced in Church [8.1, pp. 289–90]. The parameter mechanism called "lazy evaluation" by Henderson and Morris [8.2] was invented by Wadsworth [8.4], who termed it "call by need". For projects 8.2 and 8.3, see Hoare [8.3].

8.1   Church, A. *Introduction to Logic*, Vol. 1, Princeton Univ. Press, Princeton, N.J. (1956).

8.2   Henderson, P. and J. H. Morris. "A lazy evaluator", *Conf. Record of the 3rd ACM Symposium on Principles of Programming Languages*, 95–103, ACM, New York (1976).

8.3   Hoare, C. A. R. "Procedures and parameters: an axiomatic approach", in *Symposium on Semantics of Algorithmic Languages* (ed., E. Engeler), *Lecture Notes in Mathematics*, **188**, 102–16, Springer, Berlin (1971).

8.4   Wadsworth, C. P. *Semantics and Pragmatics of the Lambda-calculus*, D.Phil. thesis, University of Oxford (1971).

9 DEFINITIONS AND BLOCKS

The basic concepts underlying definitions and blocks are illustrated by the simple PASCAL block

> **const** $i = -j$;
> **begin**
>   *write(i)*
> **end**

The occurrence of identifier 'i' on the left-hand side of the definition is a binding occurrence. The effect of interpreting the definition is to create a new environment that binds identifier 'i' to the value of expression '$-j$' for execution of command '*write(i)*'.

In this chapter, we shall be studying the relationships between definitions and parameters, the interpretation of recursive definitions, various block constructions, composite definitions, and definition procedures.

9.1 THE PRINCIPLE OF CORRESPONDENCE

Compare the following two PASCAL fragments:

(a)
> **var** i : *integer*;
> **begin**
> $i := -j$;
>   *write(i)*
> **end**

(b)
> **procedure** $p(i : integer)$;
> **begin**
>   *write(i)*
> **end**;
> **begin**
> $p(-j)$
> **end**

In (a), identifier 'i' is declared by a **var** declaration. Therefore, it is bound to a new storage location and command '$write(i)$' is executed in the scope of this binding, after the location is initialized by the value of expression '$-j$'.

In (b), a procedure p is defined and then immediately invoked. Because its formal parameter is a value parameter, identifier 'i' will be bound to a new storage location. Then '$write(i)$' will be executed in the scope of this binding after the location is initialized by the value of actual parameter '$-j$'.

It is evident that the two fragments are equivalent. This is not a coincidence; in general, for *any* identifiers I_1 and I_2, expression E, and command C,

> **var** $I_1 : I_2$;
> **begin**
> $I_1 := E$;
>   C
> **end**

and

> **procedure** $I_0(I_1 : I_2)$;
>   **begin**
>   C
>   **end**;
> **begin**
> $I_0(E)$
> **end**

are equivalent in PASCAL (provided that procedure name I_0 is chosen to be any identifier that is not free in C or E). Note that

(i)   the declared identifier and its type specification in fragment (a) correspond respectively to the formal parameter identifier and its type specification in (b);

(ii) the body of the block (except for the initializing assignment) in (a) corresponds to the body of the procedure in (b); and

(iii) the initializing expression in (a) corresponds to the actual parameter in (b).

If an initializing expression were part of the **var** declaration in PASCAL, the correspondences would be even more direct:

$$\begin{array}{ll}
\textbf{var } I_1 : I_2 = E; & \textbf{procedure } I_0(I_1 : I_2); \\
\textbf{begin} & \textbf{begin} \\
\quad C & \quad C \\
\textbf{end} & \textbf{end;} \\
& \textbf{begin } I_0(E) \textbf{ end}
\end{array}$$

Similar equivalences and correspondences can be established for other forms of parameters and definitions. For example, in ALGOL 68, blocks

$$\begin{array}{ll}
\textbf{begin} & \textbf{begin} \\
\quad T\ I_1 = E; & \quad \textbf{proc } I_0 = (T\ I_1)\textbf{void}:\ C; \\
\quad C & \quad I_0(E) \quad . \\
\textbf{end} & \textbf{end}
\end{array}$$

are equivalent (provided that procedure name I_0 is not free in E or C). For example,

    begin
       int $i = -j$;
       write(i)
    end

is equivalent to

    begin
       proc $p = ($**int** $i)$**void**: *write*(i);
       $p(-j)$
    end

The parameter mechanism here binds 'i' directly to the value of the actual parameter; that is, 'i' denotes an integer, rather than an integer-containing location, and is *not* subject to assignments. Similarly, definition

    int $i = -j$

binds 'i' directly to the value of the right-hand side expression '$-j$'. This is just like a **const** definition in PASCAL, but without the restriction that the expression be statically evaluable.

It is not surprising that programming languages have such correspondences: the underlying semantic notions for both parameter and definition
mechanisms are simply *expression evaluation* (of an actual parameter or the
right-hand side of a definition) and *identifier binding* (of a formal parameter
or the left-hand side of a definition.) Therefore all the discussion of parameters in Chapter 8 is also applicable to definitions. For any parameter
mechanism, an analogous definition mechanism is possible, and *vice versa*.
This is known as the ***principle of correspondence***.

Like the principle of abstraction, the principle of correspondence can be
useful to a language designer by pointing out possible inconsistencies and
deficiencies. For example, in PASCAL there is no definition mechanism that
is the exact analog of the **var** parameter mechanism. (We have already seen
that the **var** declaration corresponds fairly closely to the value parameter.)
The closest is the rather specialized **with** construction which can only be used
for binding record field names to the corresponding components of a record.
Otherwise, if it is desired to establish a local name for storage in a PASCAL
program, this must be done by defining a procedure with a **var** parameter,
and this may be inconvenient or inefficient.

As another example, construct

    loc int $I := E$

in ALGOL 68 is a declaration that binds I to new storage and initializes it to
the value of E, so that it is similar to the value parameter and the **var**
declaration in PASCAL. But there is no analogous *parameter* mechanism in
ALGOL 68. An equivalent effect can be achieved either by using an additional local declaration within the procedure, as in

$$
\begin{aligned}
&\textbf{proc } I_0 \\
&\quad = (\textbf{int } I')\textbf{void:} \\
&\quad\quad \textbf{begin} \\
&\quad\quad\quad \textbf{loc int } I := I'; \\
&\quad\quad\quad \vdots \\
&\quad\quad \textbf{end;} \\
&\quad \vdots \\
&I_0(E)
\end{aligned}
$$

or by putting the storage allocation in the *actual* parameter, as follows:

proc I_0
   = (**ref int** I)**void**:
      begin
         $\vdots$
      end;
  $\vdots$
I_0(**loc int** := E)

But neither of these is as convenient or as efficient as the value parameter in PASCAL.

We shall see other applications of the principle of correspondence in later chapters.

9.2 RECURSIVE DEFINITIONS

9.2.1 Basic Concepts

A form of definition will be termed *recursive* if free occurrences of the defined identifier on its right-hand side are to denote the value it defines; i.e., the scope of the binding includes the definition. For example, all **procedure** definitions are interpreted recursively in PASCAL, so that in a definition of the form

      procedure $I(\cdots;P;\cdots)$; C

free occurrences of I denote the procedure value it defines. Some languages (such as FORTRAN) do not provide recursive definition forms in order to simplify implementation.

If a **procedure** definition were not interpreted recursively, then the usual rules of scope would apply to occurrences of the name of the procedure in its definition. For example, in a language with static binding, these occurrences would be bound in the environment external to the **procedure** definition, like other free identifiers. This non-recursive interpretation of **procedure** definitions is useful in some circumstances, and some programming languages allow a programmer to specify whether a recursive or a non-recursive interpretation is intended.

*9.2.2 Semantics of Recursive Definitions

Let D stand for definition

> **procedure** I;
>   **begin** C **end**;

If D is to be interpreted *recursively*, then its meaning may be specified as discussed in Chapter 7, but with the following crucial difference: the environment for executing C must already include a binding of I to the procedure being defined. The circularity here may be avoided by a limit construction, as in Sections 3.3.2 and 5.3.4.

A convenient way of constructing a sequence of better and better approximations to the meaning of D (interpreted recursively) is suggested by the requirement that D be equivalent to

> **procedure** I;
>   D   (1)
>   **begin** C **end**;

Let D_0 be any definition that defines I to be a parameter-less procedure whose invocations *never* terminate. For example, D_0 might be

> **procedure** I;
>   **begin**
>   **while** $0<1$ **do** {null}
>   **end**;

Then, for $i\geq0$, let D_{i+1} be definition

> **procedure** I;
> D_i
>   **begin** C **end**;

Note that each D_{i+1} can be interpreted non-recursively (as in Chapter 7), because any free occurrences of I in C will be bound by the *local* definition D_i. Also, notice that D_{i+1} is definition (1) above, with D replaced by D_i.

It is evident that the meanings of D_0, D_1, D_2, $\cdots$ are better and better approximations to the intended meaning of D. Each D_i defines a procedure which fails to terminate if the depth of self-activation reaches i, but has the same effect as the procedure defined by D whenever its invocation terminates. The meaning of D interpreted recursively may therefore be specified as being the *limit* of this sequence of approximate meanings.

9.3 THE PRINCIPLE OF QUALIFICATION

The principle of correspondence establishes the relationship between *parameters* of abstracts and *definitions*. Similarly, there is a relationship between the *bodies* of abstracts and the *bodies* of blocks, that is to say, the constructs prefixed or "qualified" by definitions. For example, command C in procedure definition

> **procedure** $p(I : I')$;
> **begin**
>   C
> **end**;

corresponds to command C in block

> **var** $I : I'$;
> **begin**
>   C
> **end**

In both cases, C is qualified by a local binding of I to new storage.

The principle of abstraction tells us that the body of an abstract does not have to be a command: it can in principle be in *any* semantically meaningful syntactic class. So, it may be concluded that the body of a *block* may similarly be in any meaningful syntactic class. This is known as the **principle of qualification**.

In a conventional *command* block in PASCAL

> D
> **begin**
>   C
> **end**

command C is the block body. An example of an *expression* block is the form

> **begin**
>   D;
>   E
> **end**

in ALGOL 68. It is also possible to have *definition* blocks; this is one of the definition structures that will be discussed in Section 9.5.

9.4   OTHER FORMS OF BLOCK

The blocks that have been described so far have consisted of a block body composed with a definition part, as in

> D
> **begin** C **end**

In this section, some other block-like constructions in programming languages will be described.

One example is command

> **with** L **do** C

in PASCAL, in which there are no *explicit* definitions. Nonetheless, command C is executed in the scope of implicit bindings of identifiers to storage.

Another example of a block-like construction is the **for** iteration in some languages (including ALGOL W and ALGOL 68). The body is repeatedly executed in an environment in which the count identifier is *bound* to an integer. In PASCAL, the identifier must already denote a location which is *updated* before every execution of the body. The advantages of the block approach are that (a) the identifier can easily be protected against assignments to it during execution of the body; (b) there is no need to specify a value for the identifier after termination of the iteration; and (c) the programmer does not have to make a separate declaration of the identifier.

In ALGOL 68 there is a block-like *selective* construct that is used for discriminating values of expressions having **union** types. For example, if identifier '*ic*' has type **union(int,char)**, then the following construction will select execution of C_1 if the current value of '*ic*' is an integer, and C_2 if it is a character:

> **case** *ic* **of**
>   (**int** *i*): C_1,
>   (**char** *c*): C_2
> **esac**

Furthermore, execution of either C_1 or C_2 will be qualified by a binding of either '*i*' or '*c*', respectively, to this value.

Finally, a labelled command creates a local binding of the label, so that the part of the program qualified by such a binding is a form of block. Labels and their scope will be discussed in Chapter 10.

9.5 DEFINITION STRUCTURES

In general, a block in PASCAL consists of a block body prefixed by a *sequence* of definitions:

$$D_1$$
$$D_2$$
$$\vdots$$
$$D_n$$
begin
  C
end

We shall see that it is desirable to treat the definition part of the block

$$D_1$$
$$D_2$$
$$\vdots$$
$$D_n$$

as a *definition structure* whose immediate constituents are definitions D_1, D_2, $\cdots, D_n$.

By making a small adjustment in our view of the meaning of a definition, we can treat both simple definitions and structured definitions like this as being in the same syntactic class. From now on, we shall regard a definition as binding *any* number of identifiers. The syntactic class of definitions will then include both the simple definitions considered earlier, which bind *single* identifiers, and definition structures (such as the definition sequence in PASCAL) which may bind *many*. This is analogous to the way that the syntactic class of *commands* includes both simple commands (such as the assignment) and control structures (such as sequential composition $C_1 ; C_2$).

Our task now is to consider how the meanings of definition structures might be composed out of the meanings of simpler constituents.

9.5.1 Definition Structuring in PASCAL

The basic scope rule in PASCAL is that the scope of an identifier defined in a block is the whole block, including all the definitions in the block (but excluding, as usual, nested scopes of the same identifier). But, this simple rule must be hedged and qualified in some respects.

It is unreasonable to require **const** definitions to be interpreted recursively. For example,

> **const** $i=i$;

should be syntactically invalid. One way to prevent such circularities is to require applied occurrences of defined identifiers to *follow* their definitions. This is also convenient for language processors. But this requirement excludes useful circular definitions such as

> **type** *node*= **record**
>   *info* : *integer*;
>   *link* : ↑*node*
>   **end**;

and

> **procedure** *p*;
> **begin** ⋯ *p*; ⋯ **end**;

On the other hand, a definition such as

> **type** *sequence*=**record case** *isnull* : *Boolean* **of**
>   *true* : ();
>   *false* : (*first* : *t*; *rest* : *sequence*)
>   **end**

should be illegal, for the pragmatic reasons discussed in Section 3.3.1.

When all of these pragmatic considerations and special cases are taken into account, the definition composition mechanism in PASCAL is quite complex and difficult to describe accurately. In the following sub-sections, we shall study a number of systematic ways of composing definitions out of simpler constituents.

9.5.2 Mutually Recursive Definitions

If a simple definition D is interpreted recursively, then the scope of the binding includes D. There is an obvious generalization of this to *several* definitions. Definitions $D_1, D_2, \cdots, D_n$ are said to be *mutually recursive* if the scope of any of the identifiers they bind includes *all* of the D_i. For example, each of the following **procedure** definitions contains applied occurrences of both of the defined identifiers, '*p*' and '*q*':

```
procedure p;
    begin···p···q···end;
procedure q;
    begin···p···q···end;
```

9.5.3 Sequential Definitions

A "definition before use" requirement may be achieved by structuring definitions *sequentially*, so that each constituent definition is interpreted in the scope of the *preceding* definitions.

For example, suppose that

```
const i=j;
      j=−i;
```

is interpreted as a sequential definition structure. Then, if '*j*' denotes 3 in the original environment, the effect of the definition sequence is to bind '*i*' to 3 and then '*j*' to −3.

9.5.4 Simultaneous Definitions

Another definition composition mechanism is suggested by the principle of correspondence; consider block

```
procedure I0(I1 : I1'; I2 : I2');
    begin C end;
begin
    I0(E1,E2)
end
```

in PASCAL. If we allow initialized **var** declarations and I_0 is not free in C, E_1, or E_2, then the above would be equivalent to

```
var I1 : I1'=E1;
    I2 : I2'=E2;
begin
    C
end
```

if *both* expressions E_1 and E_2 were evaluated in the *original* environment. Therefore, E_2 should not be in the scope of the binding of I_1 set up by the first definition. This composition mechanism will be termed *simultaneous* definition.

9.5.5 Definition Blocks

In all of the definition structures considered so far, the names bound in any of the constituent definitions are also bound in the resulting environment. Another way of composing definitions is to have one definition qualify *only* the other. This is the ***definition block*** mentioned in Section 9.3 as an application of the principle of qualification.

Let us extend PASCAL to include such a construct, expressed in the form

> **private**
> D_1
> **within**
> D_2

The environment it produces is obtained by adding the bindings of D_2 to the original environment; however, the environment used for interpreting D_2 is obtained from the original environment by adding the bindings of D_1.

For example, definition block

> **private**
> **var** *a* : *integer* = *seed* **mod** *d*;
> **within**
> **procedure** *draw*(**var** *x* : *real*);
> **begin**
> *a* := *a*∗*m* **mod** *d*;
> *x* := *a*/*d*
> **end**;

defines a procedure for generating random numbers. Storage location *a* is allocated before the procedure is defined and is then accessible *only* from the procedure definition, because the scope of the first definition is restricted to the second definition. Therefore this definition structure is different from the conventional

> **var** *a* : *integer*;
> **procedure** *draw*(**var** *x* : *real*);
> **begin** ⋯ **end**;

Here, the scope of '*a*' would also include the "users" of procedure *draw*, and this would not be desirable. On the other hand, it would not be possible to place the declaration of '*a*' within the procedure definition, as follows:

procedure *draw*(**var** *x* : *real*);
   var *a* : *integer*;
   begin ⋯ **end**;

because then a new location would be allocated for each *invocation* of the
procedure.

9.5.6 Commands in Definitions

Some languages allow initializing expressions in declarations. For example,
the ALGOL 68 declaration

loc T I := E

has the effect of making the value of E the initial contents of the new storage
to which identifier I is bound. However, for "large" storage structures, it
would be more appropriate to initialize *selectively*. For example, a file in
PASCAL is initialized by applying procedure *rewrite* to it, rather than by
assignment of an empty file.

One way that such command-oriented initialization can be provided in
definitions is to introduce a structure that composes a definition with a
command. For example, suppose that PASCAL were extended to include a
definition structure

D
initial
   C
end

Command C is executed relative to the new environment (and new store)
created by interpreting definition D. Then a file declaration might be composed with an initialization as follows:

var *f* : **file of** *integer*;
initial *rewrite*(*f*) **end**

Note that this definition structure is syntactically similar to the command block

D
begin
   C
end

in that the immediate constituents are also a definition and a command; however, the block is a form of *command*, and the identifier bindings of D are *local* to it, whereas the initializing definition structure creates identifier bindings for qualification of constructs which are external to it.

In some applications it is also desirable to allow a programmer to specify a *finalization* in a definition; that is to say, computation that is to occur *after* interpretation of the construct qualified by the definition. For example, the following definition structure would check whether the file is non-empty after its use:

> **var** f : **file of** *integer*;
> **initial** *rewrite*(f) **end**
> **final**
>   **if not** *eof*(f) **then** *leftover*(f)
> **end**

9.5.7 Discussion

We have seen in the preceding sub-sections that there are several ways of usefully combining simple definitions and commands into definition structures. The composition principles are of course applicable to composite forms as well as to simple ones. For example,

> **private**
>   **const** $m = 32$;
>   **var** a : **array**[$1 .. m$]**of** *char*;
> p : $0 .. m$;
>   **initial** $p := 0$ **end**
>   **final if** $p \neq 0$ **then** *error* **end**
> **within**
>   **procedure** *push*;
>   **begin** $p := p + 1$ **end**;
>   **procedure** *pop*;
>   **begin** $p := p - 1$ **end**;
>   **selector** *top* : *char*;
> $a[p]$;

is a definition structure that defines procedures for using a (bounded) "stack" of characters. A sequence of simple definitions composed with initialization and finalization commands is private to a set of mutually recursive procedure definitions.

Note that in a PASCAL program it would be difficult to bring together these closely related definitions and commands, because of rules on definition ordering and the absence of initialization and finalization mechanisms in definitions. Furthermore, PASCAL does not provide a way to make definitions private to other definitions, so that the representation of the stack (*a* and *p*) would typically be accessible to the part of the program that *uses* the stack procedures *push*, *pop*, and *top*. This would be a serious breach of the principles of program modularity. It would allow the stack discipline to be violated by direct access to the representation. Also, it would be unsafe to modify the representation for the stack without examining all of the code that uses it.

Surprisingly, no widely used programming language has incorporated these notions of definition structuring, though they were developed as long ago as the early 1960s. The usual approach has been to try to find a single "universal" definition structuring mechanism. This is as futile and pointless as trying to find a single "universal" control structure or data structure or parameter mechanism. It is perhaps unnecessary for a language to incorporate *all* of the definition structuring mechanisms discussed here, but it is evident that some, such as private definitions, are definitely lacking in all current languages.

9.6 DEFINITION PROCEDURES AND class DEFINITIONS

According to the principle of abstraction (Section 7.4), it is possible to have procedures whose bodies and invocations are *definitions*. In the language SIMULA, these are known as *classes*.

The general form of a **class** definition in a PASCAL-like notation might be

> **class** I($\cdots$; P$_i$; $\cdots$);
> D
> **end**;

Here is a small example:

> **class** *random*(*seed* : *integer*);
>   **private**
>   **var** *a* : *integer*;
>   **initial** *a* := *seed* **mod** *d* **end**
>   **within**
>   **procedure** *draw*(**var** *x* : *real*);
>   **begin**
>   *a* := *a*m* **mod** *d*;
>   *x* := *a/d*
>   **end**
> **end**;

The effect of an invocation of this definition procedure, say

  random(*i*)

would be to allocate and initialize a new location and bind identifier '*draw*' to a procedure for generating successive elements of a random number sequence.

An invocation of a class is itself a form of definition and could be used wherever a definition can appear, such as in the definition part of a block, as in

    random(*i*); {create a random number generator}
    begin
     ⋮
     draw(*r*); {update *r* to the next random number}
     ⋮
    end

In SIMULA, this is known as **block prefixing**.

A disadvantage of this notation for class invocation is that it does not permit more than one invocation of any class in the same context, because this would bind identifiers more than once. A simple solution to this problem is to allow class invocations and applied occurrences of the identifiers which they bind to be **qualified** by an additional identifier, as in

    p.random(*i*); {create a random number generator *p*}
    q.random(*j*); {create a random number generator *q*}
    begin
     ⋮
     p.draw(*r*); {update *r* to the next random number from *p*}
     ⋮
     q.draw(*r*); {update *r* to the next random number from *q*}
     ⋮
    end

The qualifying identifiers '*p*' and '*q*' distinguish between the two **instances** of class *random* used in the block.

Such qualification has another important benefit. Note that the binding created by an invocation of *random* is an implicit one (Section 6.2.3), in that identifier '*draw*' which is bound by it is not explicit in the text at that point.

But if applied occurrences of '*draw*' are qualified, as in the above, then the corresponding binding points may easily be found at the binding occurrence of the qualifying identifier ('*p*' or '*q*' in the example).

For these reasons, it is desirable to use the following syntax for invocation of a class I:

$$I'.I(\cdots,E,\cdots)$$

where I' becomes the name of an instance of the class. Any of the identifiers I_i defined by the body of the class would then be accessible in the scope of this invocation by a qualified reference of the form

$$I'.I_i$$

Definition procedures are extremely useful for structuring large programs because they allow definitions to appear in one context and be used in other contexts. Unfortunately, SIMULA is the only widely available programming language that provides classes. In most other languages, the concept must be simulated or approximated.

In PASCAL, the definition of *random* could be simulated as follows:

```
procedure random(seed : integer;
                  procedure inner(procedure draw(var x : real)));
  var a : integer;
  procedure draw(var x : real);
    begin
      a := a*m mod d;
      x := a/d
    end;
  begin
    a := seed mod d;
    inner(draw)
  end;
```

Parameter '*inner*' represents the computation that uses an instance of *random*, when given access to a generating procedure '*draw*'.

An invocation of class *random* and use of that instance of the class may then be simulated as follows:

procedure *use*(**procedure** *draw*(**var** *x* : *real*));
   begin
     ⋮
     draw(*r*);   {update *r* to the next random number}
     ⋮
   end;
   begin
     random(*i*,*use*)   {create a random number generator}
   end

Note that this simulation of class definition and invocation involves only *local* transformations. In particular, a **class** definition can be transformed without knowing how its instances are used, and each of its uses can be transformed without knowing its definition. The simulation therefore retains the modularity of the original, but of course is neither as convenient nor as readable.

EXERCISES

9.1 Devise syntax and describe the semantics of definition forms that would correspond (in the sense of the principle of correspondence) to (a) name parameters (as in ALGOL 60); (b) PL/I parameters; and (c) value-result parameters.

9.2 What procedure would be defined by

    function *eof*(*f* : *text*) : *Boolean*;
      begin
        if *eof*(*f*) **then** *eof*:= *true* **else** *eof*:=*f*↑ = ′@′
      end;

if the definition were interpreted (a) recursively; and (b) non-recursively?

9.3 In an environment in which '*i*' denotes 2 and '*j*' denotes 3, what would be the effect of **const** definitions

    i=*j*;
and
    j=−*i*;

if they were composed (a) sequentially; (b) simultaneously; (c) with the first private to the second; and (d) as in PASCAL?

9.4 In PASCAL, definitions in a block must occur in the order

> **const**
> **type**
> **var**
> **procedure** and **function**

Suggest reasons why this order might have been imposed and comment on the success and desirability of this rule.

9.5 In PASCAL, command blocks

> D **begin** C **end**

may only appear as the bodies of entire programs or procedures. In most other languages, such blocks may be used in *any* command context. What are the advantages and disadvantages of the approach in PASCAL?

9.6 The storage for an *own* declaration in ALGOL 60 is allocated and initialized just once, *before* program execution, rather than *each* time the declaration is interpreted; however, the *scope* of the binding created by an **own** declaration is the same as for an ordinary declaration. In a PASCAL-like notation, we might express this form of declaration as follows:

> **own** I : T = K;

where the value of static expression K is used to initialize the storage. (In ALGOL 60, only a default initialization is possible.) For example, the following definition is similar to the random number generator of Section 9.5.5:

> **procedure** *draw*(**var** *x* : *real*);
>   **own** *a* : *integer=seed*;
>   **begin**
>   *a*:= *a∗m* **mod** *d*;
>   *x*:= *a/d*
>   **end**;

In general, what disadvantages does this approach have in comparison with the definition block approach described in Section 9.5.5?

9.7 Use the simulation method suggested at the end of Section 9.6 to transform into strict PASCAL an example in which more than one instance of a class is used in some context.

9.8 It would be feasible for a language to provide blocks in which the definition part *follows* the block body, as in the following PASCAL-like command block:

> **begin**
> C
> **where**
> D
> **end**

The block body C is to be executed in the environment obtained by first interpreting definition D. Discuss the advantages and disadvantages of such constructs.

PROJECT

Explore the feasibility and usefulness of interpreting **class** definitions *recursively*.

BIBLIOGRAPHIC NOTES

Most of the concepts discussed in this chapter are due to Landin [9.1] and Strachey [9.3]. The interpretation of SIMULA classes as definition procedures was given in Tennent [9.4], and the simulation of classes by procedures is from Reynolds [9.2].

9.1 Landin, P. J. "The next 700 programming languages", *Comm. ACM*, **9** (3), 157–64 (1966).

9.2 Reynolds, J. C. "Syntactic control of interference", *Conf. Record of the 5th ACM Symposium on Principles of Programming Languages*, pp. 39–46, ACM, New York (1978).

9.3 Strachey, C. *Fundamental Concepts in Programming Languages*, lecture notes for the International Summer School in Computer Programming, Copenhagen (1967).

9.4 Tennent, R. D. "Language design methods based on semantic principles", *Acta Informatica*, **8**, 97–112 (1977).

10 JUMPS

In preceding chapters it was convenient to assume that evaluation of an expression *always* produces a value, that execution of a command *always* produces a new store, and that interpretation of a definition *always* produces a new environment. These assumptions are unrealistic for non-trivial programming languages.

One problem is that executing an iteration or invoking a recursively defined procedure may result in a *non-terminating* (i.e., infinite) computation and never produce a final value or store or environment. A second problem is that a computation may be "trapped" and aborted because of an error such as an array index being out of range. Finally, control may "jump" out of or into a construct because of language features like the **goto** sequencer.

Because their effects are "global", non-termination and abortion can easily be treated as special cases. For example, interpretation of

$$E_1 + E_2$$

can be described as yielding the sum of the values of E_1 and E_2 *if* both of these interpretations terminate without error, and otherwise, as either non-terminating or erroneous. By always "propagating" errors and non-termination in this way, the correct result for an incorrect or non-terminating program will be specified. For convenience, we shall continue to describe expression interpretation as "evaluation", even when it is possible that no value will be produced.

It is more difficult to cope with control jumps. The first section of this chapter introduces the concept of *continuations*, which will be used in subsequent sections to discuss the semantics of sequencers, labels, sequencer procedures, coroutines in SIMULA, and backtracking in SNOBOL4.

10.1 CONTINUATIONS

The *continuation* for some computation is whatever comes after it, expressed as a function of the results expected for that computation. For example, the result expected for a command execution is a new store. Consequently, the continuation for a command execution is the computation that follows it, as a function of the store resulting from that execution (if it terminates without error, of course).

For example, consider an execution of a composite command of the form

$$C_1; C_2$$

The continuation for the execution of C_1 starts with an execution of C_2 relative to the store resulting from the execution of C_1. The execution of C_2 inherits the continuation of the whole construct as its continuation.

The continuation for an expression evaluation depends on the value and the store that results from that evaluation. For example, in an execution of a command of the form

if E **then** C_1 **else** C_2

the continuation for the evaluation of expression E starts by using the resulting truth value to select execution of either C_1 or C_2. The execution selected inherits the continuation of the whole construct as its continuation.

As another example, consider the iterative construct

    loop
      C_1
    while E:
      C_2
    repeat

described in Section 5.3.2. The continuation for an execution of C_1 starts with an evaluation of E relative to the resulting store. The continuation for this evaluation starts by using the resulting value to select either the execution of C_2 or the continuation of the whole construct. Finally, the continuation for an execution of C_2 starts with a re-execution of C_1.

Similarly, the continuation for interpreting a *definition* is a computation that is functionally dependent on the environment and store the definition produces. For example, in an execution of a PASCAL block of the form

    D
    begin
      C
    end

the continuation for the interpretation of D starts with an execution of C relative to the resulting environment and store.

The semantics of a language that has no sequencers or other jumping mechanisms can be described without mentioning continuations. In the following sections it will be demonstrated that when jumps *are* possible, languages can be conveniently described denotationally using continuations.

10.2 SEQUENCERS

Consider the familiar sequencer

goto N

in PASCAL. We want to describe its effect in terms of the meaning of N, its only immediate constituent. Let us assume that a label denotes a command continuation, that of continuing at the program point labelled. For example, in block

begin
 ⋮
  13: $x:=x+1$;
 ⋮
end

label '13' would denote the continuation that starts with an execution of '$x:=x+1$' and then follows the continuation of this command in the program. Note that the semantic notion of continuation is an appropriate *abstraction* from the syntactic notion of "program point": two distinct program points may represent the same continuation. For example, the two labels in

  12:{null}; 13: $x:=x+1$;⋯

are attached to distinct program points, but denote the same continuation, because they are semantically indistinguishable.

The effect of executing **goto** N can now be described as that of "following" the continuation denoted by N, using the current state of the store. Note that the "normal" (contextually determined) continuation for the sequencer is ignored. For example, in

  goto N; C

the "normal" continuation for the **goto** (which starts by executing C) would be ignored. The characteristic property of sequencers is that they always ignore their contextually determined continuation and follow some other continuation, that is to say, they always cause "jumps".

The **goto** sequencer has two properties not shared by all sequencers. (a) The continuation followed by executing a **goto** is obtained by evaluating an explicit *destination* expression that is an immediate constituent of the sequencer. (b) This continuation is a *command* continuation. There are sequencers in programming languages that have different properties. For example, sequencer

RETURN(E)

in PL/I is used within definitions of expression procedures to terminate their execution. The continuation that is followed as the result of interpreting this sequencer is an *expression* continuation because it depends on a value (the value of expression E) as well as on the store. Furthermore, the continuation that is followed is not the result of evaluating an explicit expression supplied by the programmer. The continuation is implicit in the environment component of the state with respect to which the sequencer is executed.

There are many examples of sequencers that follow command continuations but, unlike the **goto**, do not have explicit destinations. One is RETURN in command procedure definitions in PL/I or FORTRAN. Another is **break** in the language BCPL; this causes termination of the smallest enclosing iteration. However, these cannot be used to return from or exit out of *nested* procedure definitions or iterations.

10.3 LABELS

The familiar **goto** sequencer has been much criticized by some programming theorists. However, the semantic description of the **goto** construct itself simply involves following a command continuation and is no more complex than that of other sequencers, such as RETURN(E). This suggests that some of the criticism of the **goto** might be more appropriately directed against the treatment of *labels* in programming languages, that is, on how the continuations for **goto**s are determined.

Some languages (including FORTRAN, COBOL, and PL/I), allow label values (i.e., command continuations) to be *stored*. The value of the destination expression of a **goto** can then depend on the dynamic history of the computation. This is often detrimental to program readability.

In most languages which have been designed more recently, only *identifiers* (or numerals acting as identifiers) can express label values. This still allows the possibility of label *parameters* to procedures, as in ALGOL 60 or FORTRAN. An example in PASCAL-like notation would be

```
procedure p(···; label lbl;···);
  begin
      ⋮
      goto lbl;
      ⋮
  end;
```

Here the destination of the sequencer depends on the value of the actual parameter corresponding to '*lbl*' in the invocation of the procedure.

In PASCAL, label values are denotable *only* by the numeral that occurs at the destination itself. This makes the destination of every **goto** very evident to program readers.

There is also considerable variation possible in the *scope* rules for labels, that is to say, the language conventions regarding *where* applied occurrences of labels may appear. An obvious constraint on labels is that it must not be possible to jump into a block or procedure body before it has been entered (unless some default bindings are assumed for the parameters or locally defined identifiers). In FORTRAN, ALGOL 60 and PASCAL, this restriction is enforced by letting the scope of a label binding be the innermost block or procedure body that contains that binding occurrence.

The scopes of labels (or their usability) can be restricted further in order to prevent jumping into the subcommands of iterative or selective control structures. In PASCAL, a label is not usable *throughout* its scope; the usable part of a label's scope is the command sequence in which it is bound. In addition, if this compound command is the body of a block, the label is also usable in any procedure definitions in that block. This rule permits jumps within and out of command sequences, as in

```
begin
    ⋮
    goto 13;
    ⋮
13: ···
    ⋮
    begin
        ⋮
        goto 13;
        ⋮
    end;
    ⋮
end
```

as well as exits from procedure definitions in a block to the "outer level" of that block, as in

> **label** 13;
> **procedure** p;
>   **begin**
> $\vdots$
>   **goto** 13;
> $\vdots$
>   **end**;
> **begin**
> $\vdots$
> 13: $\cdots$
> $\vdots$
> **end**

but it does not allow jumps *into* control structures. For example, the following is illegal:

> **begin**
> $\vdots$
>   **goto** 10;
> $\vdots$
>   **while** E **do**
>   **begin**
> $\vdots$
>   10: C;
> $\vdots$
>   **end**;
> $\vdots$
> **end**

because the label used as the destination of the **goto** is outside the usable part of its scope.

It is possible and perhaps desirable to restrict label scopes even further. If the scope (or usability) of the label binding in a labelled command

> N: C

were this command itself, then **goto** N could only be used for re-executing a command that contains it. It might then be appropriate to change the syntax of the sequencer to, for example,

redo N

to emphasize its specialized use.

Suppose that command label N in

N: C

were interpreted as being the name of the *continuation* of this command (instead of the continuation that starts with an execution of C). If, as above, the scope (or usability) of this label binding were restricted to C, then **goto** N could be used only to exit out of commands that contain it. In this case it would be appropriate to change the syntax of the sequencer to something like

leave N

These sequencing disciplines may be simulated in standard PASCAL by using labels only immediately after **begins** or immediately before **ends** of **begin** ⋯ **end** constructs, as in

begin N:
  C_1;
  C_2;
  ⋮
  C_n
end

or

begin
  C_1;
  C_2;
  ⋮
  C_n;
N: **end**

A jump to N can only occur from within one of the commands C_i because of the usability constraints, and would always have the effect of repeating or exiting from the whole construct. With these kinds of restrictions on label scope or usability, the **goto** (and other sequencers with the same semantics) are similar in effect to sequencers such as **break** or RETURN, but are more flexible because they have explicit destinations.

10.4 SEQUENCER PROCEDURES

The "normal" continuation for a command, expression, or definition procedure is the continuation of the *invocation* of the procedure. A *sequencer
procedure* would be one that *cannot* return to its invocation; that is, both the
invocation and the body of such a procedure would effectively be
sequencers, that is to say, phrases that ignore their "normal" continuations.
This is another illustration of the principle of abstraction.

Consider, for example, definitions of the form

> **exit** I($\cdots$;P;$\cdots$); C;

which are syntactically similar to conventional **procedure** definitions. However, an invocation of an **exit** procedure would return to the end of the block
in which it is defined, rather than to its invocation. Thus, in

> **exit** *error*(*n*:*integer*);
>   **begin**
>   *write*('ERROR',*n*)
>   **end**;
> **begin**
> $\vdots$
>   *error*(21);
> $\vdots$
> **end**

any invocation of sequencer procedure *error* will result in output of an error
message followed by immediate termination of the entire block, regardless
of the continuation of the invocation.

It is possible to simulate this in PASCAL as follows:

> **label** 999;
> **procedure** *error*(*n*:*integer*);
>   **begin**
>   *write*('ERROR',*n*);
>   **goto** 999
>   **end**;
> **begin**
> $\vdots$
>   *error*(21);
> $\vdots$
> 999:**end**

However, use of a distinctive syntactic form for exit procedures would make their role more evident to program readers, and might permit a more efficient implementation.

In a language with sequencer procedure definitions, it would also be useful to allow procedures (of all kinds) to have sequencer procedure *parameters*. (Recall the principle of correspondence.) This would allow "exception handlers" for a procedure to be specified at its invocations. Some languages (including PL/I and ADA) achieve this in an ad hoc way: they use dynamic binding (Section 7.2.2) for exception handler names.

10.5 COROUTINE SEQUENCING IN SIMULA

It is sometimes desirable to have a programmer-defined procedure *suspend* its execution and transfer control to another context in such a way that subsequently it can be *re-activated* and will continue executing from the point of suspension. This is termed *coroutine* sequencing, because it allows each of several program parts to regard the others as its "subroutines".

In languages with storable label values, coroutine sequencing may be implemented by saving a continuation in a label-valued location before jumping to another context. For example, if a programmer adopts the convention that I_1 and I_2 denote label-valued locations that always contain the resumption continuation for coroutines c_1 and c_2, respectively, then suspension of c_1 and re-activation of c_2 may be expressed by

$$\vdots$$
$$I_1 := N;$$
goto I_2;
$$N: \cdots$$
$$\vdots$$

because label N denotes the resumption continuation for c_1.

But such use of storable label values and **goto**s is not very convenient or clear or efficient. In this section we shall describe the specialized coroutine facilities in SIMULA. For convenience, PASCAL-like syntax will be used.

Suppose that a **coroutine** definition resembles a **class** definition, except that the last **initial** part of its body may contain occurrences of a pseudo-identifier 'detach', as in

```
coroutine  I(···;Pᵢ;···);
   D
   initial
      ⋮
      detach;
      ⋮
      detach;
      ⋮
   end
end;
```

Interpretation of the body of a **coroutine** definition begins when it is invoked, but suspends when a **detach** is executed. Computation in the coroutine body is resumed when it is re-activated by use of a standard procedure, *call*, as in the following:

```
coroutine c;
   ⋮
   initial
      ⋮
      detach
      ⋮
   end
end;
⋮
p.c;              {invocation}
begin
   ⋮
   call(p);       {re-activation}
   ⋮
   call(p);       {re-activation}
   ⋮
end
```

Note that although they are syntactically different, the effects of '**detach**' and '*call(p)*' are quite similar: each saves its own "normal" continuation and then follows a previously saved continuation for the other context. They differ only in whether the destination is explicit (*call*) or implicit (**detach**).

A coroutine allowing node-by-node "inorder" traversal of binary trees will illustrate the use of coroutine sequencing. See Fig. 10.1. Parameter *root* is a pointer to the root node of a binary tree. Locations *current* and *more* are for communicating information between the traversing coroutine and its "user".

Execution of the **initial** part of the **coroutine** definition will set *more* to *true* and *current* to the contents of the *key* field of the "leftmost" node of the tree by using recursively defined procedure *traverse*. However, if the tree is empty (i.e., *root=***nil**), the value of *more* is set to *false*. The coroutine then suspends itself by executing **detach**, and control returns to the point of invocation of the class. A subsequent *call* of the coroutine resumes its execution from the point where it has most recently suspended itself.

```
type ptr=↑node;
     node=record
                key:integer;
                left,right:ptr
            end;
     ⋮
coroutine inorder(root:ptr);
   var current:integer;
       more:Boolean;
   initial
      procedure traverse(ref:ptr);
         begin {traverse}
            if ref ≠ nil then
            begin
                traverse(ref↑.left);
                current:=ref↑.key;
                detach;
                traverse(ref↑.right)
            end
         end; {traverse}
      begin
          more:=true;
          traverse(root);
          more:=false;
          detach
      end {begin}
   end {initial}
end; {inorder}
```

Figure 10.1

Here is how an instance of *inorder* might be created in a block prefix and then used:

```
i.inorder(root);
begin
  while i.more do
  begin
    write(i.current);
    call(i)
  end
end
```

Each execution of '*call*(*i*)' causes execution of this block to be suspended and control to follow the continuation of the most recently executed **detach** in the coroutine. This re-activation either updates *i.current* to the "next" key value in the tree, or changes *i.more* to *false* if the whole tree has been traversed.

Of course, a *complete* traversal such as the above could be programmed just as simply without using coroutine sequencing. To illustrate the usefulness of the *node-by-node* traversal obtainable with the coroutine, consider the problem of testing the equivalence of two binary search trees, that is to say, testing whether they represent the same sorted sequence of keys. Because trees may be equivalent without having the same structure, this is quite inconvenient to program efficiently without using coroutine sequencing.

Here is how this problem could be solved using an *inorder* instance for each tree:

```
var equiv:Boolean;
i1.inorder(root1);
i2.inorder(root2);
begin
  equiv:=true;
  while equiv and i1.more and i2.more do
    if i1.current=i2.current
      then begin call(i1); call(i2) end
      else equiv:=false;
  if i1.more or i2.more then equiv:=false;
    ⋮
end
```

In more complex examples, it is often convenient for a coroutine to resume another without the intermediate step of relinquishing control to the context where they were originally created. In SIMULA, this may be achieved by executing '**resume** *p*' in a coroutine. The effect is equivalent to executing '**detach**', followed immediately by a *call* of *p* in the "parent". For example, the following is the outline of the definition of a game-playing coroutine class:

```
var "game state";
coroutine player(var "opponent");
  var "private move-making data";
  initial
    "initialization";
    detach;
    loop
       ⋮
      "make move";
      resume "opponent";
      if "game over" then detach;
       ⋮
    end {loop}
  end {initial}
end; {player}
```

Each *player* instance resumes its opponent after making its move. When the game is over, a player detaches to the parent. This example illustrates clearly the *symmetry* of coroutine sequencing.

10.6 BACKTRACK SEQUENCING IN SNOBOL4

Backtracking algorithms search for solutions by repeatedly making a choice among alternatives and, if the desired solution is not subsequently found, backing up and "undoing" that choice in order to explore another alternative. Such algorithms are often programmed by using recursively defined procedures having the general form

```
var "solution";
  procedure solve;
  "local definitions"
  begin
    for "each possible choice" do
      if "the choice is feasible" then
        begin
          "record choice";
          if "solution complete"
            then "exit"
            else solve;
          "undo choice"
        end;
    {no more alternatives here; return to a higher level}
  end;
```

The pattern matching operation in SNOBOL is implemented by a similar backtracking approach. This is because a pattern formed by alternation may match in more than one way, and any matching that follows the first possible match may have to be "undone" in order to explore another of the possible matches. For many patterns, this property of the implementation need not be known by the programmer, and the relatively simple model of Section 3.2.3 is sufficient. However, some patterns in SNOBOL have *side effects* during the match, and these require that account be taken of the *sequencing* of pattern matching. For example, if the value of E_1 is a pattern p, then the value of expression

$$E_1 \ \$ \ E_2$$

is a pattern that matches like p and, whenever such a match succeeds, also has the side effect of immediately updating the *l*-value of E_2 to be the substring of the subject that is matched by p.

10.6.1 An Example

To illustrate control sequencing during pattern matching, consider matching pattern

$$('BE'|'B') ('ET'|'AD')$$

against subject 'BET' at position 0. We know from our previous discussions that the result will be a successful match up to position 3. This result is actually computed as follows. First, 'BE' matches up to position 2. Then, attempts are made to match 'ET' and then 'AD' at this position. But both of these fail, so the matching process backs up to try the most recent unexplored alternative, which is pattern $'B'$ at position 0 of the subject. This succeeds up to position 1, and now $'ET'$ matches up to position 3. If subsequent matching causes further backing up, the second alternative, $'AD'$, will be tried at position 1 but this will fail, and the matching process will then back up to try an even earlier alternative, if any.

*10.6.2 Semantic Description

Such jumps to and fro between pattern components may be described in general by assuming that application of a pattern has *two* possible continuations. One, termed the **subsequent**, is to be followed whenever a match is (initially) successful. The second, termed the **alternate**, is followed if the match fails. Thus, if the null string is used as a pattern, the subsequent will always be followed, whereas the value of 'FAIL' in SNOBOL is a pattern that always follows the alternate.

It then turns out that both alternation and concatenation of patterns are just forms of sequential composition, much like the sequential composition of commands expressed by

$$C_1 ; C_2$$

Alternation is sequential composition with respect to alternate continuations, and concatenation is sequential composition with respect to subsequent continuations. This explains why the patterns denoted in SNOBOL by 'NULL' and 'FAIL' are to pattern concatenation and alternation what the null command is to command composition, that is to say, the identity of the associated operation.

If two patterns p_1 and p_2 are composed by *alternation*, the result is a pattern that matches like p_1, but has as its alternate a match of pattern p_2 at the *same* position in the subject string. For example, in pattern

$$'BE' | 'B'$$

the alternate for $'BE'$ is a match of $'B'$ at the same position in the subject string. The alternate of the whole pattern is inherited by p_2 as its alternate. Therefore, if neither p_1 nor p_2 is successful, control will back up by following this "external" alternate. The subsequent continuation of the whole pattern is also inherited by both p_1 and p_2 as their subsequents, so that it will be followed after a successful match by *either* of them.

If two patterns p_1 and p_2 are *concatenated*, the result is a pattern that matches like p_1 and has p_2 as its subsequent. For example, with pattern

$$('BE' | 'B') \ ('ET' | 'AD')$$

a match using $'ET'|'AD'$ is the subsequent for $'BE'|'B'$. The subsequent continuation of the whole pattern is inherited by p_2 as its subsequent, so that it will be followed after successful matches by *both* p_1 and then p_2. Similarly, the alternate continuation of the whole pattern is inherited by p_1 as its alternate.

To specify the alternate continuation for p_2 when patterns p_1 and p_2 are concatenated, we must consider what kinds of continuations subsequents and alternates are. An alternate is simply a conventional command continuation; that is, an alternate depends only on the state of the store when it is followed. This means that side effects to the store during pattern matching are *not* undone. A subsequent continuation is more like an expression continuation in that it also requires a value: the position in the subject up to which previous patterns have matched. Furthermore, a subsequent also needs an alternate continuation to fall back to if it fails. In our example, after pattern component $'BE'$ matches, the subsequent match has $'B'$ (and then *its* alternate) to fall back to.

Therefore, if p_1 and p_2 are concatenated, the alternate continuation for p_2 is that supplied by p_1 when it followed its subsequent. This means that if backtracking is necessary during the match of p_2, unexplored alternatives in p_1 will be tried before resorting to the alternate for the whole concatenated pattern. This occurs in the example; the alternate that is followed when pattern $'ET'|'AD'$ fails (after the initial success of $'BE'$) is a match with $'B'$ at position 0 of the subject.

In summary, language facilities for backtrack sequencing may be described in terms of two continuations, one, like the subsequent, for "forward" sequencing, and a second, like the alternate, for "backing up".

EXERCISES

10.1 Devise a sequencer that has an explicit destination (like **goto**) but follows an *expression* continuation (like RETURN(E)). Also suggest suitable labelling conventions for use with this sequencer.

10.2 The following iterative construct has been suggested:

> **loop until** I_1 **or** I_2 **or**$\cdots$**or** I_n:
> $\quad C_0$
> **repeat**
> **then**
> $\quad I_1{:}C_1;$
> $\quad I_2{:}C_2;$
> $\quad \vdots \quad \vdots$
> $\quad I_n{:}C_n$
> **end**

It is executed by repeatedly executing C_0 until a free occurrence of any I_i is executed. Control then transfers immediately to C_i, and then follows the continuation of the whole construct. Show how to simulate the effect of this using **exit** procedures.

10.3 Would you recommend that **exit** definitions be interpreted recursively or non-recursively? Why?

10.4 Design a form of sequencer procedure that follows an expression continuation.

10.5 Show how to simulate in PASCAL the effects of **label** parameters and **exit** parameters.

10.6 Why would it be incorrect to regard the "usable" part of the scope of a label in PASCAL as being its entire scope?

10.7 Built-in operations (such as '**div**') do not allow a programmer to provide an "exception handler" for recovery from an error condition (such as for attempted division by zero). What are the advantages and disadvantages of the following design approaches to this problem:

(a) The language can use dynamic binding for the names of **exit** procedures, so that error handlers can be defined in the contexts where the operation is used.

(b) The language can provide predefined procedures that are equivalent to primitive operations but have additional **exit** parameters, such as

    function *xdiv(i,j:integer*; **exit** *zerodivide*):*integer*;
        begin
            if *j*=0 **then** *zerodivide* **else** *xdiv*:=*i* **div** *j*
        end;

A programmer can then supply an error handler as an explicit additional argument.

10.8 The effect of executing to the end of the body of a **coroutine** definition was not specified in Section 10.5. What are some possibilities? Discuss their advantages and disadvantages.

PROJECTS

10.1 Design language facilities for defining and using coroutines that return values when they "detach". (These have been termed "streams", or "generators", or "iterators".)

10.2 Investigate the use of sequencer procedures and sequencer structures (i.e., selective sequencers, sequencer blocks, sequential composition of a command with a sequencer, and so on) as replacements for conventional selective and iterative command structures.

BIBLIOGRAPHIC NOTES

The use of continuations for modelling jumps is due to Strachey and Wadsworth [10.6] and F. L. Morris [10.5]. Sequencer procedures similar to the **exit** mechanism were described by Landin [10.4] (who termed them "program points") and Clint and Hoare [10.2] (who termed them "label procedures"). The binary tree example for coroutines was suggested by Dahl and Hoare [10.3]. The semantics of backtracking is based on Tennent [10.7]. For project 10.2, see Back [10.1].

10.1 Back, R. J. R. "Exception Handling with Multi-exit Statements", in *Programmiersprachen und Programmentwicklung* (ed. H. J. Hoffman), 6. Fachtagung des Fachausschusses Programmiersprachen der GI, Darmstadt, Informatik-Fachberichte **25**, Springer, Berlin–Heidelberg (1980); also Report IW 125, Mathematical Centre, Amsterdam (1979).

10.2 Clint, M. and C. A. R. Hoare. "Program proving: jumps and functions", *Acta Informatica*, **1**, 214–24 (1972).

10.3 Dahl, O.-J., and C. A. R. Hoare. "Hierarchical program structures", in *Structured Programming* (O.-J. Dahl, E. W. Dijkstra, and C. A. R. Hoare), 175–220, Academic Press, London (1972).

10.4 Landin, P. J. "The next 700 programming languages", *Comm. ACM*, **9** (3), 157–64 (1966).

10.5 Morris, F. L. "The next 700 formal language descriptions", typescript, University of Essex, Colchester (1970).

10.6 Strachey, C., and C. P. Wadsworth. *Continuations, a Mathematical Semantics for Handling Full Jumps*, technical monograph PRG–11, Programming Research Group, University of Oxford (1974).

10.7 Tennent, R. D. *Mathematical Semantics and Design of Programming Languages*, Ph.D. thesis and technical report 59, Computer Science, University of Toronto (1973).

11 CONCURRENT PROCESSES

This chapter discusses linguistic facilities that allow or require *concurrent* (or "parallel") processing. There are two motivations for such facilities. The more obvious is that they may permit more efficient use of systems with multiple *processors*. In most computer systems, peripheral devices contain processing units that operate relatively independently of the central processor. This allows overlapping of lengthy input or output operations with "internal" computations. There are also specialized computer systems known as array processors that contain an array of identical arithmetic processing units. Whenever such a multiple processor configuration is available, it may be possible to reduce execution time and to make more effective use of hardware resources by giving programmers control over the processors by means of appropriate facilities in a programming language.

The other motivation for concurrent programming facilities is that they allow programs to be structured as autonomous (but possibly interacting) *processes*, even if they are actually implemented on a single processing device. Programs organized as interacting processes are particularly useful for operating systems, real-time control systems, simulation studies, and combinatorial search applications.

In this chapter, the issues underlying concurrent programming facilities will be discussed, using typical language features for illustration. We shall not attempt to describe all of the linguistic mechanisms that have been proposed or implemented.

11.1 INTERFERING PROCESSES

Consider extending PASCAL by allowing composite commands of the form

$$C_1 \| C_2$$

The intention is to allow an implementation to execute commands C_1 and C_2 concurrently, either using separate processors or by interleaving the executions on a single processor. What would be appropriate as the semantic description of this construct?

Consider the following simple example:

```
var i : integer;
begin
    ⋮
    begin i := 1 ‖ i := 2 end;
    ⋮
end;
```

This example involves **interfering** processes, that is to say, processes that share access to storage updated by at least one of them. In this case, the shared storage is location i.

If it were possible for these two processes *simultaneously* to update i, its final contents would be unpredictable. For example, if integers were represented in binary form, the final value might be 0 or 3, as well as 1 or 2. Of course, this cannot happen in actual computers, so that it is reasonable to assume that implementations of concurrency ensure that primitive operations of interfering processes get **indivisible** access to shared storage. That is, if "simultaneous" access is attempted by primitive operations in two processes, the implementation must delay one of these until the other process has completed its operation. If concurrency is implemented by interleaving on a single processor, then the interleaving must not be "finer-grained" than the primitive operations.

So let us assume that updating a shared storage location is in fact an indivisible operation. What then will be the value of i after executing '$i := 1$' and '$i := 2$' concurrently? Evidently, this depends on which of the updatings is done last, that is, on the relative execution speeds of the two processes.

In general, specifying *the* result of executing two processes concurrently would require exact and detailed knowledge of their execution times for all possible data. But this is completely infeasible for any but the simplest programs. Consider, for example, the problem of trying to specify the response time of a human operator at an interactive terminal, or the time needed to carry out a mechanical action in an input or output device. Execution times are far too dependent on implementation, data, algorithm, and hardware to play an important role in semantic descriptions.

The only reasonable alternative is to let the execution speed of a concurrent process be *indeterminate* (Section 5.5). Then the *possible* results of executing

$$C_1 \| C_2$$

are the stores resulting from *any* of the interleavings of the sequences of indivisible primitive operations of C_1 and C_2. For example, the result of executing '$i:=1 \parallel i:=2$' is to set i to either 1 or 2.

Note that

begin $i:=0; i:=i+1$ **end**

has the same overall effect on the store as '$i:=1$', but in the presence of concurrency, these commands are *not* semantically equivalent. For example, one of the possible results of executing

begin $i:=0; i:=i+1$ **end** $\parallel i:=2$

is to set i to 3 because of the interleaving

$i:=0;$
$i:=2;$
$i:=i+1$

When concurrency is possible, the semantics of commands must in general be expressed as sequences of indivisible primitive operations that can be interleaved by operations of other processes, rather than as overall store transformations.

When uncontrolled interference is possible, programming is extremely difficult because it is so hard to abstract from the level of primitive operations. In all but trivial examples, there will be a very large number of possible results and a programmer must verify that all of these are correct. Furthermore, he cannot rely on test runs to check a program's correctness exhaustively, nor can he expect to be able to duplicate erroneous executions for debugging.

For these reasons, concurrency that involves *unrestricted* interference is of very little practical interest except at the hardware level. In the following sections we shall discuss concurrent composition without interference, or with controlled forms of interference.

11.2 NON-INTERFERING PROCESSES

In the preceding section, constituents C_1 and C_2 in a concurrent command of the form

$C_1 \parallel C_2$

were allowed to be arbitrary commands, and this created serious difficulties if they interfered with one another. Let us therefore suppose that C_1 and C_2 are ***non-interfering***, that is to say, no storage updated by either is referred to or updated by the other. Then the effect of

$$C_1 \| C_2$$

is determinate. *All* interleavings of the two sequences of primitive operations (including sequential execution of C_1 and C_2 in either order) will have the same overall effect on the store because each constituent only modifies locations that are inaccessible to the other. The effect of the composite is therefore uniquely determined by the usual meanings of its immediate constituents, and it is not necessary to decompose these meanings into sequences of primitive actions. Non-interference is a rather severe constraint, but it greatly simplifies the semantics of concurrent composition.

As an illustration of non-interfering processes, the following is an excerpt from a program for processing a file using a procedure *update* concurrently with input and output operations:

```
        ⋮
      while not eof(input) do
        begin
          output↑ := buffer;
          buffer := input↑;
          begin get(input)
          ‖     update(buffer)
          ‖     put(output)
          end
        end;
        ⋮
```

The three processes access disjoint parts of the store, so that their concurrent composition is equivalent to any of their sequential compositions, but might be executed more rapidly.

11.3 COOPERATING PROCESSES

It is possible to relax the requirement of strict non-interference if the language provides some facility that allows a programmer to specify that *arbitrary* (i.e., *non*-primitive) operations on shared resources are to be executed indivisibly. Then, concurrent processes can **cooperate** to prevent undesirable interference.

For example, suppose that concurrent processes wish to cooperate in accumulating a *count* of some sort. At various times each process p_i will want to increment the shared counter as follows:

$$count := count + ni$$

However, without some means of specifying the *indivisibility* of these incrementing assignments, some of the increments can be lost during interleavings of more primitive operations, as in the following:

> evaluation of '*count+ni*' in process p_i;
> evaluation of '*count+nj*' in process p_j;
> assignment to '*count*' in process p_i;
> assignment to '*count*' in process p_j

Many facilities have been proposed for specifying indivisibility of operations. We will describe one that is used in several system programming languages, including CONCURRENT PASCAL, MODULA, and PASCAL PLUS. The basic principle is to specify the operations as procedures which operate on storage that the implementation makes available to at most *one* process at any time. For example, a shared counter might be described as follows:

```
monitor
    var count : integer;
    initial count := 0 end
within
    procedure increment(n : integer);
        begin count := count+n end;
    function total : integer;
        begin total := count end;
begin
    begin ··· increment(ni); ··· end
    ||begin ··· increment(nj); ··· end;
    write('TOTAL COUNT =   ', total);
    ⋮
end
```

The composite definition form

monitor D_1 **within** D_2

is syntactically and semantically similar to the definition block discussed in Section 9.5.5. But, the implementation must *also* ensure that at any time at most *one* process is executing any of the procedures defined in D_2. If a process attempts to invoke such a procedure, it will be suspended until no other process has control of the monitor. This removes from the set of possible results of the concurrent processes any that arise from interleavings of the primitive operations of the procedures. In effect, the procedures defined in D_2 become *indivisible* operations.

Note that programmers should attempt to minimize the time spent executing indivisible procedures, because during this time other processes may be forced to wait. A dangerous situation known as *deadlock* must certainly be avoided. Consider, for example, the following program fragment involving two mutually defined monitors:

```
monitor
  var "resource1";
within
  procedure p1;
    begin ··· p2; ··· end;
  ⋮
monitor
  var "resource2";
within
  procedure p2;
    begin ··· p1; ··· end;
```

A procedure in each monitor invokes a procedure in the other monitor. The danger is that if concurrent processes invoke the two procedures, they may be suspended when they attempt to access the other resource. The two processes will then wait indefinitely and are said to be deadlocked. Some implementations of monitors attempt to prevent such situations by allowing a monitor procedure to access *only* its own resources. In general, however, programmers have the responsibility of avoiding deadlocks.

11.4 SYNCHRONIZED PROCESSES

In many applications, it is necessary for a programmer to control the *order* as well as the degree of interleaving of operations of concurrent processes. For example, suppose that it is desired to define a procedure *synchronize* with which n processes may synchronize their executions. A process that invokes *synchronize* is to be suspended until all n of the processes have done so.

Many approaches to process synchronization have been proposed. We will describe one which works well with monitors. It is based on a mechanism known as a **condition** on which a process can suspend itself and *wait* until the condition is *signalled* by some other process.

The following is a monitor that uses a condition to provide the synchronization facility described above:

```
monitor
    var count : 0..n;
        all : condition;
    initial count:= 0 end
within
    procedure synchronize;
        begin
            count:= count+1;
            if count < n
                then wait(all)
                else count:= 0;
            signal(all)
        end;
```

Execution of operation

$$wait(c)$$

on a condition c within a monitor procedure results in suspension of the executing process and release of its exclusive access to the resource. Operation

$$signal(c)$$

causes one process that may be waiting on condition c to *immediately* re-claim exclusive access to the resources of the monitor and continue processing from where it suspended itself. (If no processes are waiting on condition c, '*signal(c)*' has no effect.) In the example, *all* represents the condition that all of the processes have invoked *synchronize*.

In general, more than one process may be waiting on a condition. An implementation must then choose which one of these to re-activate when that condition is signalled. If an arbitrary choice is made, there is a danger that one of these processes may be delayed indefinitely in favor of other processes. This is known as **starvation** (or "indefinite overtaking"). A simple scheduling policy that avoids this is always to re-activate the longest-waiting process.

In some applications, it is convenient to have more flexibility over scheduling. Many of the languages that provide monitors and conditions extend the *wait* operation to accept an optional argument specifying the *priority* of the suspended process. The processes waiting on the condition may then be sorted by the implementation with respect to these priorities, and the one with the greatest priority when the condition is signalled will be selected for re-activation. This facility is particularly useful in operating-system applications.

Note that the correctness of programs that use conditions (or other synchronization mechanisms) depends on the implementation being *fair* in the way processing resources are shared among concurrent processes. For example, if $n=2$ and concurrent command

$$synchronize \parallel synchronize$$

were implemented as if it were

$$synchronize \; ; \; synchronize$$

then the condition on which the first process is waiting would never be signalled, so that the execution would never terminate. However if neither process is indefinitely denied processing, then the execution terminates.

11.5 COMMUNICATING PROCESSES

Suppose that one process (the *producer*) wishes to **communicate** information to a concurrently executing process (the *consumer*). One way to avoid undesirable interference is to set up a "mailbox" in a monitor as follows:

```
monitor
    var mailbox : record case empty : Boolean of
                    true : ();
                    false : (contents : t)
                 end;
        filled, cleared : condition;
    initial mailbox.empty := true end
within
    procedure produce(x : t);
        begin
            mailbox.empty := false;
            mailbox.contents := x;
            signal(filled);
            if not mailbox.empty then wait(cleared)
        end;
    procedure consume(var y : t);
        begin
            if mailbox.empty then wait(filled);
            y := mailbox.contents;
            mailbox.empty := true;
            signal(cleared)
        end;
```

Condition *filled* is used to delay the consumer until there is a communication available. Similarly, condition *cleared* delays the producer until the communication it has just placed in the mailbox is consumed. (In practice, it would be necessary to buffer the communication, in order to smooth out temporary speed variations between the processes.)

Communication between concurrent processes (or "message-passing") is sufficiently important that it is convenient to have specialized high-level notation for it. The following illustrates one approach:

```
begin producer : begin  ···  send(consumer, x); ···  end
   || consumer : begin  ···  receive(producer, y); ···  end
end
```

Operation

$$send(I,E)$$

is a kind of "output" of the *r*-value of E to the process labelled I, much like '*write*(I,E)' in PASCAL. Similarly, operation

$$receive(I,L)$$

is an "input" from the process labelled I into the *l*-value of L, much like '*read*(I,L)'. Such communication may be *synchronized* by having a process wait when it is ready to send or receive until the process it names is also ready.

These communication primitives may also be used to implement our example of *cooperating* processes if the non-determinate control structures of Section 5.5 are generalized to allow a *receive* operation as a guard, as in the following:

```
begin
    counter : var count : integer;
                 n : integer;
             begin
             count := 0;
             loop receive(p1,n) → count := count+n
                 |   receive(p2,n) → count := count+n
             end;
             write('TOTAL COUNT =    ', count)
             end
    || p1 : begin  ··· send(counter, n1); ···  end
    || p2 : begin  ··· send(counter, n2); ···  end
end
```

A *receive* operation as a guard is satisfied if the process named is ready to send. If more than one such guard is satisfied, then an arbitrary (and not necessarily fair) choice is made of which communication to receive, and other sending processes must wait. In the example above, this ensures the indivisibility of the assignments to '*count*'. If no guard is satisfied but at least one of the processes named in a guard is still executing, the process waits. When none of the guards of an iteration is satisfied and all the processes named in the guards have terminated, the iteration terminates. Thus, in the example above, termination of *p1* and *p2* results in output of the final value of *count*, followed by termination of process *counter*.

This kind of synchronized internal input–output is a very flexible programming tool. However, it remains to be seen whether such communication primitives are efficiently implementable and effectively usable in practice.

EXERCISES

11.1   What are the possible results of executing the following?

```
var i : integer;
    b : Boolean;
begin
  i:= 0;  b:= true;
  begin
    b:= false
  ‖ while b do i:= i+1
  end;
  write(i)
end
```

11.2   Comment on the following attempt to implement cooperative counting *without* using a monitor:

```
private
  var count : integer;
      inuse : Boolean;
  initial count:− 0; inuse:= false end
within
  procedure increment(n : integer);
    begin
      while inuse do {null};
      inuse:= true;
      count:= count+n;
      inuse:= false
    end;
    ⋮
```

11.3   Conditions may be replaced in a language by commands of the form

await E

where expression E has type *Boolean*. If the value of E is *false*, then its effect is to suspend the executing process for an indeterminate (but finite) period of time. Then, the expression is tested again, and this repeats until the expression evaluates to *true*. When the process is suspended, it releases its control over the monitor, and must re-claim this to re-evaluate the expression.

For example, procedure *consume* in the "mailbox" example of Section 11.5 could be defined as follows:

```
procedure consume(var y : t);
  begin
    await not mailbox.empty;
    y:= mailbox.contents;
    mailbox.empty:= true
  end;
```

What are the advantages and disadvantages of this approach to synchronization? *Hint*: Is the following a correct definition of procedure *synchronize* (Section 11.4):

```
procedure synchronize;
  begin
    count:= count+1;
    await count=n;
    count:= 0
  end;
```

11.4 Can an implementation allow a procedure which is defined in a monitor to invoke other procedures of the *same* monitor, or to invoke itself reentrantly?

11.5 Does the "mailbox" example of Section 11.5 work correctly if there is more than one producer or consumer process?

11.6 What problems arise in describing the semantics of concurrent composition of commands if it is possible to jump out of a concurrent process?

11.7 Show how to solve the synchronization problem of Section 11.4 using the *send* and *receive* communication primitives of Section 11.5.

PROJECTS

11.1 Devise syntactic constraints that would be sufficient to ensure that constituents C_1 and C_2 of a concurrent composition $C_1 \| C_2$ did not interfere.

11.2 Design language facilities that would allow programmers to make effective use of an array processor.

BIBLIOGRAPHIC NOTES

The material in this chapter is based primarily on papers by Hoare [11.3, 11.4, 11.5, 11.6]. Concurrent programming is discussed in books by Brinch Hansen [11.1, 11.2], Holt et al. [11.7] and Welsh and McKeag [11.10]. For projects 11.1 and 11.2, see Reynolds [11.9] and Perrott [11.8], respectively.

11.1 Brinch Hansen, P. *Operating System Principles*, Prentice-Hall, Englewood Cliffs, N.J. (1973).

11.2 Brinch Hansen, P. *The Architecture of Concurrent Programs*, Prentice-Hall, Englewood Cliffs, N.J. (1977).

11.3 Hoare, C.A.R. "Towards a theory of parallel programming," in *Operating Systems Techniques* (eds., C. A. R. Hoare and R. N. Perrott), pp. 61–71, Academic Press, New York (1972).

11.4 Hoare, C. A. R. "Parallel programming: an axiomatic approach", *Computer Languages*, **1,** 151–60 (1975); also technical report CS-394, Computer Science Dept., Stanford University, Stanford, California (1973).

11.5 Hoare, C. A. R. "Monitors: an operating system structuring concept", *Comm. ACM*, **17** (10), 549–57 (1974).

11.6 Hoare, C. A. R. "Communicating sequential processes", *Comm. ACM*, **21** (8), 666–77 (1978).

11.7 Holt, R. C., G. S. Graham, E. D. Lazowska, and M. A. Scott. *Structured Concurrent Programming with Operating System Applications*, Addison-Wesley, Reading, Mass. (1978).

11.8 Perrott, R. H. "A language for array and vector processors", *ACM Trans. Prog. Lang. and Sys.*, **1** (2), 177–95 (1979).

11.9 Reynolds, J. C. "Syntactic control of interference", *Conf. Record of the 5th ACM Symp.Principles of Programming Languages*, pp. 39–46, ACM, New York (1978).

11.10 Welsh, J. and M. McKeag. *Structured System Programming*, Prentice-Hall International, London (1980).

12 TYPES

In principle, a mathematical function may be applied only to values that are in its domain of arguments. Applying an operation to a value that is *not* in its domain of arguments will be termed a ***domain incompatibility***. Dividing by zero, adding truth values, negating a character, and reading an empty file are typical examples of domain incompatibilities.

The first section of this chapter discusses several techniques for preventing domain incompatibilities. The remainder of the chapter will then focus on the most important of these: checking the *types* of program constituents before program execution.

12.1 PREVENTING DOMAIN INCOMPATIBILITIES

12.1.1 Domain Testing

Suppose the argument for an operation might *not* be in its domain of arguments. Should this be tested for by the implementation before carrying out the operation? The alternative would be to allow the operation to act on the representation of the value, even if this does not have a *semantically* well-defined result. There are few examples of the latter approach in good PASCAL processors, but consider

```
var i:integer;
begin
  write(i div 2);
    ⋮
end
```

Most PASCAL processors will treat the value initially contained in the new location as if it were an integer, though in principle it is "undefined".

There are some advantages to treating domain incompatibilities in this way. No time or storage space has to be devoted to domain testing, so that program execution is more efficient. This approach is also more flexible in that it allows programmers to access freely and "impersonate" the data representations used by an implementation. Thus, an operation may be applied to (representations of) values to which "abstractly" it is inapplicable, and a value that is *not* in the domain of arguments of an operation may be used to "impersonate" one that is (because their representations coincide). Such flexibility may allow an expert programmer to achieve the best possible execution efficiency.

But the *disadvantages* of this approach are very severe: if a "tolerated" domain incompatibility is in fact an inadvertent error (rather than a deliberate attempt to access the representation), the program's results will almost certainly be incorrect. Even if it is evident that errors have occurred, it will then be necessary to find their causes without any guidance as to where or when domain incompatibilities (if any) have occurred. Furthermore, interpreting the output will require knowledge of the data representations adopted by that particular processor, which programmers normally do not wish to be concerned with. Debugging in such circumstances is very time consuming and frustrating! Even when a program works correctly, it may be representation-dependent, and cannot reliably be used with other processors.

So, despite the efficiency and flexibility obtainable by omitting tests for domain incompatibilities, the risks and hidden costs of this approach are unacceptable in most circumstances. Except when execution efficiency is of critical importance, it is generally desirable for an implementation to test for domain incompatibility, and thereby help to prevent incorrect or representation-dependent output.

12.1.2 Coercion

What then is to be done by an implementation when an operation and its argument are incompatible? In general, two kinds of action are possible. One is to invoke an exception that aborts execution of the program and produces an error message. The other is to "convert" the argument or the operation so that they *are* compatible. Such an implicit conversion is termed a *coercion*; the context is said to coerce the "improper" value into one that is proper, so that the computation can continue.

As an example of a coercion in PASCAL, consider assignment

$$x := i$$

in the context of

> **var** *x:real*;
>   *i:integer*;

The integer contained in *i* is not in the domain required for location *x*. To allow the computation to continue, the representation of the number is converted to floating-point form and then treated as an element of the domain of real numbers. This is reasonable because the set of integer numbers is conceptually a subset of the reals and this interpretation is almost certainly what the programmer intends. In contrast, assignment

> *i:=x*

is not allowed in PASCAL, and must be replaced by either

> $i:=trunc(x)$

which truncates the fraction, or

> $i:=round(x)$

which rounds to the nearest whole number.

The advantage of coercions is that they allow the programmer to omit explicit conversion, and some languages (such as PL/I and ALGOL 68) have very elaborate systems of coercions. However, if the domain incompatibility avoided by a coercion is in fact an *error*, the computation will be allowed to continue and possibly produce bizarre results. Programmers normally do not welcome error messages, but a message that helps in locating a bug is far more useful than meaningless output. For this reason, the introduction of coercions into programming languages should be done with considerable discretion.

When a language has both coercions *and* overloaded (Section 6.2.5) operators or procedure names, there are possibilities for ambiguity and programmer error. For example, in the context of

> **var** *x:real*;
>   *i,j:integer*;

assignment

> $x:=i+j$

might be interpreted using either real or integer addition, depending on whether the integer-to-real conversion operation were applied to the arguments or the result, respectively. A good design principle is to ensure that in any such situation the results are equivalent.

12.1.3 Type Checking

The main objective of type checking is to determine *before* program execution whether a domain incompatibility can occur. If so, error messages or code for coercion or execution-time testing may be generated; if not, execution-time domain testing may safely be omitted.

For example, in the scope of PASCAL declaration

> **var** b:*Boolean*;

expression '$-b$' has a type error because of incompatibility between the type of the operand and the type expected by the operator. If the program were executed, this would usually result in a domain incompatibility. (Of course, it is possible that the flow of control might avoid the error, or that the value actually is a number because of an insecurity.) On the other hand, expression '**not** b' is type-correct and is normally evaluated without testing whether b contains a truth value. (It may not if the implementation has insecurities.)

Replacing domain tests *during* execution (also known as "dynamic type checks") by type checks *before* execution has two main advantages. One is efficiency: a program component is typically executed many times but needs to be type-checked only once. Furthermore, type information may be used by implementations to improve efficiency in many other ways. The second advantage of type checks is that they catch minor programming errors before execution, and thereby simplify program testing and debugging. Type specifications also improve program readability by making explicit the data representations used by the programmer.

The main drawbacks of type checks are that (a) the syntax of a typed language must be more complex, and (b) restrictions must be imposed on the programmer's freedom of expression. Type checking should be used in languages to prevent domain incompatibilities whenever these disadvantages are outweighed by its benefits.

12.2 A CASE STUDY: TYPE CHECKING IN PASCAL

What are types? Different answers would be given for almost every language. In general, what can be said is that the type of a program component should be (a) reliable information about its semantic properties, yet (b) determinable syntactically, i.e., without requiring execution of the program. In this section, we shall discuss some aspects of the type system of PASCAL.

12.2.1 Indexing Types

Pre-defined types *Boolean*, *char*, and *integer*, programmer-defined enumerations, and subranges of these will be termed *indexing* types. The domains of values with which these types are associated should be evident.

(a) Type *Boolean* is associated with the domain of the two truth values, *true* and *false*.

(b) Type *char* is associated with an implementation-defined domain of characters that includes the 26 capital letters, the 10 decimal digits, and the "blank".

(c) Type *integer* is associated with the subset from $-maxint$ to $maxint$ of the integers, where $maxint$ is implementation-defined.

(d) An enumeration with n elements is associated with the domain of the first n natural numbers (or any domain isomorphic to it).

(e) If K_1 and K_2 are static expressions with values min and max, respectively, then the type expressed by

$$K_1 .. K_2$$

is associated with the subset of values from min to max.

In fact, it is convenient to regard *every* indexing type as a subrange. For example, predefined type identifier '*integer*' denotes a subrange type with bounds $-maxint$ and $maxint$.

Range limits are useful for both type checks before execution and tests during execution. Consider the following program fragment:

```
var   low:  0..10;
      med:  2..6;
      high: 8..12;
begin
   ⋮
   med:=high;
   low:=med;
   low:=high;
   ⋮
end
```

Although all of the locations may be expected to contain integers, assignment '*med*:=*high*' is erroneous because there is no overlap between the ranges of the source and target sub-expressions. Note that this kind of error may be detected before execution (though in fact few PASCAL implementations do so). On the other hand, assignment '*low*:=*med*' may be executed without any execution-time domain testing because the range of the source is completely within the range of the target. Finally, assignment '*low*:=*high*' has some overlap, but in general it is impossible to be sure before execution whether the value of the source will always be in the range of the target; thus, execution-time testing would be desirable in this case. Even so, note that the value of *high* needs to be verified with respect to only the *upper* bound of the target's range, and not the lower bound.

In general, we will say that an indexing type t is **index-compatible** with another indexing type t' if t and t' are both subranges of the same basic type (either *Boolean*, *integer*, *char*, or an enumeration). If the range of values for t does not *overlap* the range of values for t', then a syntax error message may be generated. If the range of values possible is a *subset* of the range of values expected, then no execution-time testing is needed. It is evidently to a programmer's advantage to make use of subrange types and to specify bounds that are as "tight" as possible. Subrange type expressions also improve program readability and allow processors to minimize storage use.

We shall continue to use the letter t, possibly with primes or subscripts, to symbolize unspecified types, in the same way that we have been using T to stand for type expressions. Note that type expressions must be distinguished from the types they express, in part because static expressions and programmer-defined type identifiers may occur in type expressions.

12.2.2 Set Types

If T expresses an indexing type t, then type expression

> **set of** T

Expresses the *set* type

> *set of t*

Set of types are one of the composite kinds of type in PASCAL, in that they have type components, such as t. Type *set of t* is associated with the domain of all subsets of the domain with which t is associated. (In practice, t must be associated with a domain of relatively small cardinality, and in many implementations even the size of the *elements* must be small.)

Operation

> E_1 **in** E_2

may then be type checked by requiring that the type of E_2 have the form *set of t* where the type of E_1 is index-compatible with t. The type of the whole expression is *Boolean*.

The set union operation

$$E_1 + E_2$$

may be type checked by requiring that the types of E_1 and E_2 be of the form *set of* t_1 and *set of* t_2, respectively, where t_1 and t_2 are subranges of the same basic type. The tightest lower and upper bounds that may be estimated for the result type are the lesser of the lower bounds of t_1 and t_2, and the greater of the upper bounds of t_1 and t_2, respectively. The empty set literal must be treated as a special case. Type checking of the other set operations is similar.

12.2.3 Array Types

An *array* type has the form

$$array[t_1]of\ t_2$$

where t_1 must be an indexing type. Type $array[t_1]of\ t_2$ is associated with the domain of all functions *from* the domain with which t_1 is associated *to* the domain with which t_2 is associated.

Array subscripting operations of the form

$$L[E]$$

may be type checked as follows: (a) the type of L must be of the form $array[t_1]of\ t_2$, and (b) the type of E must be index-compatible with t_1. The type of the whole expression is t_2.

Note that in PASCAL the subscript bounds for a declared array are part of the *type* of that array name. This has two significant advantages.

(a)   The index compatibility check described in Section 12.2.1 eliminates the need for many execution-time subscript bound checks, without any loss of security. Furthermore, for the tests that *are* required, the bounds are known before execution, and this will often improve the efficiency of such tests.

(b)   The storage requirements for arrays are known *before* execution, which permits a simpler and sometimes more efficient implementation than is possible in languages (such as ALGOL 60 and PL/I) that allow the declared subscript bounds for an array to have been computed *during* execution. (These are known as *dynamic* array bounds, but should not be confused with the *flexible* array bounds in ALGOL 68, which may be changed after creation of the array.)

The major *disadvantage* of the approach in PASCAL is, of course, that it does not allow the size of an array to be data-dependent. Files or pointers may be used in PASCAL when the size of a storage structure cannot be estimated before execution.

The treatment of array types in PASCAL also affects the use of procedures with array parameters. Consider the following definitions:

```
type ta=array[1..m,1..n]of real;
     tb=array[1..n,1..m]of real;
  ⋮
procedure transpose(var a:ta; b:tb);
  var i:1..m; j:1..n;
  begin
    for i:= 1 to m do
      for j:= 1 to n do
        a[i,j]:= b[j,i]
  end;
```

Procedure *transpose* updates *a* to be the matrix transpose of *b*. However, this procedure may be used only on matrices of the *particular* dimensions m and n specified in the definitions for types *ta* and *tb*. If matrices of *various* sizes are to be transposed within a single program, then several essentially similar procedure definitions must be provided by the programmer. It is evident that this is very inconvenient and error-prone.

Some PASCAL implementations allow formal parameters to be specified by type expressions of the form

$$\textbf{array}[\cdots;\ I_1..I_2:I_3;\cdots]\textbf{of}\ I_4$$

In this, I_1 and I_2 are binding occurrences of identifiers, and I_3 and I_4 are applied occurrences of type identifiers. During the execution of the procedure body, I_1 and I_2 denote the lower and upper bounds of the subscript type of the corresponding actual parameter. For example, a more general matrix transposing procedure could then be defined as follows:

```
procedure transpose
  (var a:array[m1..n1:integer; m2..n2:integer]of real;
       b:array[m3..n3:integer; m4..n4:integer]of real);
  var i,j:integer;
  begin
    if (m1−m4) and (m2=m3) and
       (n1=n4) and (n2=n3)
      then for i:= m1 to n1 do
             for j:= m2 to n2 do
               a[i,j]:= b[j,i]
      else error
  end;
```

Note that this approach allows much less type checking than in the original form of the definition. For example, in the above, it is necessary to check *during* execution that the dimensions conform for transposition. Also, it would be quite complicated to verify before execution that subscripts are in range. In the original procedure, all of these checks could easily be made before execution, thereby improving the efficiency and security of the program. Note also that the lower and upper bound identifiers $m1, n1, \cdots$ are not usable as static expressions. This is why 'i' and 'j' had to be declared to be of type *integer*. In Section 12.3, an alternative approach which does not have these disadvantages will be described.

12.2.4 Record Types

If we temporarily ignore variant parts of **record** type expressions, a *record* type is a composite of the form

$$record \ I_1{:}t_1; \ I_2{:}t_2; \cdots; \ I_n{:}t_n \ end$$

where the I_i are the field names and the t_i are the corresponding types. Such a record type is associated with the *product* of the domains with which the field types are associated.

Expression

L.I

may then be type checked by requiring that the type of L be a record type having I as a field name. Then, the type of the whole expression is the corresponding field type. This is sufficient to ensure that no testing is necessary during execution.

However, consider now a **record** type expression with a "variant" part, as in

```
type sex=(male, female);
     person=
        record
           name: string;
           case s:sex of
              male:(bearded:Boolean);
              female:(pregnant:Boolean)
        end;
```

The variant part of a record type is associated with the *sum* of the domains with which the field lists of the variants are associated. Thus, in the context of

```
        var p:person;
```

field *p.name* and the **tag field**, *p.s*, are always accessible, but field *p.bearded* is meaningful only when *p.s=male*, and field *p.pregnant* only when *p.s=female*.

These requirements cannot be enforced using the kind of type check that was adequate for records without variant parts. But it is quite inefficient to test the value of the tag field at *every* use of a variant field. It is also quite complicated or even infeasible to implement such tests because of nested variant parts, the implicit bindings of field names set up by the **with** command, and the fact that the programmer can specify that the tag field is to be omitted. For these reasons, variant parts of records are insecure in most PASCAL processors.

A simple extension to the language would often reduce the need for testing during execution. Suppose, as suggested in Section 6.2.3, that the **with** command in PASCAL were to require a listing of which field names are to be bound, as in

> **with** (*name*, *bearded*)=*p* **do**
>   **begin**
>   ···*name*···*bearded*···
>   **end**

or

> **with** (*name*, *pregnant*)=*p* **do**
>   **begin**
>   ···*name*···*pregnant*···
>   **end**

It could then be checked before execution that all of the field names listed were meaningful for the same value of the tag field. A test would be necessary during execution to ensure that the tag field of the record currently had that value, but then no *further* such testing would be required in the body of the construct for the field names listed, provided that the record itself were not updated. Another possibility is to treat the field names listed in the same way as value parameters (i.e., bind them to new storage that is initialized by the value of the corresponding field); then the record itself could be accessed and updated without affecting the security of the field names listed.

This extended **with** construct would often be used in conjunction with the **case** command, as in

case *p.s* **of**
   male: **with** (*name*, *bearded*)=*p* **do**
             begin···*name*···*bearded*···**end**;
   female: **with** (*name*, *pregnant*)=*p* **do**
             begin···*name*···*pregnant*···**end**
end

It would be convenient and more efficient to have a construct that combines these effects, as follows:

case *p.s* **of**
   male(*name*, *bearded*):
     begin···*name*···*bearded*···**end**;
   female(*name*, *pregnant*):
     begin···*name*···*pregnant*···**end**
end

Many languages have facilities similar to this. For example, the equivalent in ALGOL 68 of the above is

mode male=**struct**(**bool** *bearded*),
mode female=**struct**(**bool** *pregnant*),
mode person=**struct**(**string** *name*, **union**(**male**,**female**) *s*);
    ⋮
  case *s* **of** *p* **in**
   (**male** *m*):
     begin···*name* **of** *p*···*bearded* **of** *m*···**end**,
   (**female** *f*):
     begin···*name* **of** *p*···*pregnant* **of** *f*···**end**
  esac;
    ⋮

12.2.5 File Types

A *file* type has the form

    file of t

and, as discussed in Section 4.6.2, is associated with values of the form $(f\uparrow, \overleftarrow{f}, \overrightarrow{f})$, where $f\uparrow$ and all the components of the finite sequences $\overleftarrow{f}$ and $\overrightarrow{f}$ are in the domain with which the component type *t* is associated. Because the operations *read* and *write* are defined in terms of assignments to and from a file buffer, the component type of a file must be an ***assignable*** type. For pragmatic reasons, many PASCAL processors do not allow assignment of "large" values. The *non*-assignable types are typically files, and records or arrays with non-assignable components. For example, a file of files would not be permitted.

12.2.6 Pointer Types

A ***pointer*** type has the form

$$\uparrow t$$

and is associated with the domain of storage structures for the domain with which *t* is associated, plus the *nil* value. An expression of the form

$$E\uparrow$$

may then be type-checked by requiring that the type of E be a pointer type $\uparrow t$ (or a file type). The type of the whole expression is then *t*. However, this check cannot ensure that the value of E is not *nil*, which would be a domain incompatibility. Fortunately, this can be tested for during execution with little or no overhead in most implementations.

12.2.7 Type Equivalence

In a few contexts in PASCAL it is necessary to test whether the type of an expression is the *same* as the type of another expression or of a formal parameter. One such context is procedure invocation. The actual parameter corresponding to a **var** formal parameter must be an *l*-expression of the type specified in that formal parameter. This is because the formal parameter identifier will be bound to the *l*-value of that *l*-expression during executions of the procedure body.

For value parameters and assignments, only *assignable* types are allowed, but the compatibility requirements are relaxed to allow for *integer*-to-*real* coercion, index compatibility of subrange types, and so on. Unless one of these specific "loopholes" is applicable, the type of the source (or actual parameter) expression must be the same as the type of the target *l*-expression (or formal value parameter).

But when are two types "the same"? In some PASCAL processors, types are distinguished by their structure alone, and not by how they happen to have been expressed in the program. For example, in the context of

> **type** *t*=**record** *a:real*; *b:char* **end**;
> **var** *x*:**array**[*Boolean*]**of** *t*;
>   *y*:**array**[*Boolean*]**of record** *a:real*; *b:char* **end**;

both '*x*' and '*y*' would have type

> *array*[*Boolean*]*of record a:real; b:char end*

without regard to how it was expressed in the program. This approach is known as **structural** equivalence of types.

In most PASCAL processors, a different approach is used. Each *occurrence* in a program of a type expression (except a type identifier) is interpreted as expressing a type distinct from any other type expressed in that program, even those that are structurally similar. For example, '*x*' and '*y*' above would have different types, and the types defined by

> **type** *coordinate* = **record** *first, second:real* **end**;
>   *complex* = **record** *first, second:real* **end**;

would be distinct. Thus, in the scope of

> **var** *p:coordinate*; *z:complex*;

both '*z:−p*' and '*p:−z*' would be in error.

This approach has been termed "name" equivalence of types, but this is rather misleading. Similar effects would be obtained even if the types were anonymous. For example, '*x*' and '*y*' have the *same* type in the scope of

> **var** *x,y*:**record** *first, second:real* **end**;

and *distinct* types in the scope of

> **var** *x*:**record** *first, second:real* **end**;
>   *y*:**record** *first, second:real* **end**;

Furthermore, the assignment in

```
type t=···;
var x:t;
procedure q;
   type t=···;
   var y:t;
   begin
      ⋮
      x := y;
      ⋮
   end;
   ⋮
```

is erroneous even though the types of 'x' and 'y' happen to have the same name. This approach would be better termed **occurrence** equivalence of types, because it regards types as being the same only if they are expressed by the same occurrence of a non-trivial type expression.

The motivation for adopting occurrence equivalence is to permit the programmer to make type distinctions that are more refined than the structural differences built into the language. However, this objective is only partially achieved by using occurrence equivalence. For example, if 'z' has type *complex* and 'p' has type *coordinate* then 'z := p' is rejected, but its effect may still be achieved *selectively* by executing

$$z.first := p.first;$$
$$z.second := p.second$$

Because the *representation* of the "new" types is accessible, the intended distinction between them may be subverted by using these representation operations.

In Section 12.4 we shall discuss facilities that allow programmers to create *secure* "new" types.

12.2.8 Procedural Parameter Types

If the procedure name I in an invocation

$$I(···;E_i;···)$$

is a formal parameter identifier, type checking of actual parameters E_i requires knowledge of the types of the corresponding formal parameters of that procedure. Some PASCAL processors require or allow a *specifier* for the formal parameter to supply this information. However, some processors do not require such type specification, and as a result, are either inefficient (because they do testing during execution) or insecure (because they do not do such testing).

12.3 STATIC AND POLYMORPHIC PROCEDURES

The principle of abstraction (Section 7.4) suggests that in a language that has static expressions and type expressions (such as PASCAL), it is possible to have facilities for defining procedures by abstraction from these syntactic categories. Furthermore, the principle of correspondence (Section 9.1) suggests that in a language with **const** and **type** *definitions*, it would also be possible to have corresponding **const** and **type** *parameters*. In this section, we shall be exploring these possibilities.

12.3.1 Static Procedures

It may be recalled that a static expression is one that may be evaluated *before* execution of the program. The syntax of PASCAL permits only very simple forms of static expression, but some processors allow any expression that is composed out of literals, **const** or enumeration identifiers, operators, and pre-defined identifiers.

A *static expression procedure* would be one whose definition body and invocations are static expressions. A PASCAL-like syntax for defining such procedures could be obtained by extending the **const** form with a formal parameter list, as follows:

> **const** $I(\cdots;P;\cdots)=K$;

where K is a static expression. For example,

> **const** $sum(\textbf{const}\ n)=n*(n+1)$ **div** 2;

defines a static expression procedure which could be invoked as follows:

> **var** a:**array**$[1..sum(m)]$**of** *real*;

where 'm' must be a static expression.

A similar facility would allow programmer-defined *type expression procedures*:

> **type** $I(\cdots;P;\cdots)=T$;

Here are two examples:

> **type** $string(\textbf{const}\ n)=\textbf{array}[1..n]\textbf{of}\ char$;
> $pairof(\textbf{type}\ t)=\textbf{record}\ first,second:t\ \textbf{end}$;

These might be invoked as follows:

> **type** $card=string(80)$;
> $line=string(132)$;
> $complex=pairof(real)$;
> $rational=pairof(integer)$;

12.3.2 Polymorphic Procedures

Let us now consider the possibility of using **type** and **const** parameters in conventional (i.e., non-static) procedures. It may be recalled that procedures with array parameters (such as *transpose*) are unsatisfactory in PASCAL because they are specialized to *particular* array dimensions. Suppose that the syntax of PASCAL allowed type expressions (as well as type identifiers) in parameter specifications, as in

> **const** $m=\cdots$; $n=\cdots$;
> $\vdots$
> **procedure** *transpose*(**var** a:**array**$[1..m,1..n]$**of** *real*;
> $\qquad\qquad\qquad\qquad\quad b$:**array**$[1..n, 1..m]$**of** *real*);
>   **var** i:1..m; j: 1..n;
>   **begin**
> $\vdots$
>   **end**;

This makes it evident that the reason the procedure is over-specialized is that identifiers 'm' and 'n' are bound in the context of the *definition* of the procedure, rather than in the contexts of its invocations. Rather than use dynamic binding, these identifiers should become **const** parameters of the procedure, as follows:

> **procedure** *transpose*(**const** m,n;
> $\qquad\qquad\qquad\qquad$ **var** a:**array**$[1..m, 1..n]$**of** *real*;
> $\qquad\qquad\qquad\qquad\qquad b$:**array**$[1..n, 1..m]$**of** *real*);
>   **var** i:1..m; j:1..n;
>   **begin**
> $\vdots$
>   **end**;

Actual parameters corresponding to the formal **const** parameters must be static expressions. Then the usual type checking of the other parameters and the body would always be possible, using the values of these static expressions. If a program contained several such invocations with distinct arguments, the effect would be identical in every respect to that obtainable in PASCAL by defining several procedures, each particularized to a specific set of dimensions m and n. Thus with this approach type checking is much easier than with the alternative approach discussed in Section 12.2.3, and this would provide better execution efficiency and security. Procedures that may be used with many types of parameters are termed **polymorphic** (or "generic").

It is in fact possible to simplify the notation for invoking such polymorphic procedures. Consider the following program fragment, which contains an invocation of *transpose*:

```
const k=10; l=12;
var x:array[1..k,1..l]of real;
    y:array[1..l,1..k]of real;
begin
    ⋮
    transpose(k,l,x,y);
    ⋮
end
```

It should be evident that a processor could use a straightforward "pattern match" to deduce the values of 'k' and 'l' from just the types of the *other* actual parameters and the types of the corresponding formal parameters. This suggests allowing actual static parameters to be omitted from invocations of polymorphic procedures, as in

```
transpose(x,y)
```

The definition of *transpose* might then be changed as follows to separate the static and dynamic parts of the parameter list:

```
procedure transpose[const m,n]
                (var a:array[1..m,1..n]of real;
                     b:array[1..n,1..m]of real);
    var ···
    begin
        ⋮
    end;
```

Here is another example of a polymorphic procedure, this time using a **type** parameter as well as **const** parameters:

```
procedure maparray[const m,n; type t]
                (var a:array[m..n]of t;
                     procedure p(var x:t));
    var i:m..n;
    begin
        for i:=m to n do p(a[i])
    end;
```

This procedure applies a procedure *p* to each component of an array *a*, where the subscript bounds and the base type of the array are static parameters. An example of an invocation of *maparray* might be

```
var tapes:array[1..nt]of text;
begin
    maparray(tapes, rewrite);
    ⋮
end
```

Note that it would usually be impractical to attempt to compile code for polymorphic procedures independently of their invocations. Thus, implementation of these facilities would involve some "administrative overhead" (comparable to that for a macro-assembler). This does not seem an excessive price to pay for the benefits they would provide. A more serious disadvantage is that even the type correctness of a procedure definition having **const** or **type** parameters cannot in general be checked independently of the invocations of that procedure. This issue will be addressed in Section 12.4.6.

12.4   NEW TYPES

12.4.1   Basic Concepts

Suppose that a programmer wishes to develop a program using a domain of values that is *not* a semantic primitive of the language being used, say "stacks" of characters equipped with operations for clearing, pushing, and popping a stack, selecting the top component, and testing for emptiness. In accordance with familiar programming principles of modularity and separation of levels of abstraction, it would be desirable to separate

(a) the *implementation* part of the program, which describes the *representation* for the domain of stacks and its operations in terms of some available domain of values, from

(b) the *logical* part of the program, where stacks are used (without reference to their concrete representation).

In the logical part of the program, the following would be regarded as domain incompatibilities:

(1)   impersonation: applying a *stack* operation (such as *pop*) to an argument in some *other* domain (including the representation domain);

(2)   unauthorized access: supplying a *stack* as the argument to an operation expecting an argument in some *other* domain (including the representation domain).

A language that claims to provide a facility for creating "new" types must be able to prevent these two abuses.

PASCAL and ALGOL 68 are often described as languages that allow programmers to define "new" types, but by this criterion, they do *not*. Consider PASCAL fragment

> **type** *stack* = ···{representation type}···;
> **function** *top*(*s*:*stack*):*char*;
>   **begin**···{representation operation}···**end**;
>   ⋮

The elided type expression and procedure definition bodies describe the representation of stacks in terms of some existing domain of values. Thus they make up the implementation part of the program. However, if the PASCAL processor uses structural equivalence of types, then '*stack*' is just another name for the representation type. This means that type checking would *not* prevent impersonation of a stack by a value in the representation domain *or* unauthorized access to a stack by a representation operation. If occurrence equivalence of types is used, direct impersonation is prevented. However, there is no restriction on access to the representation of a stack. As pointed out in Section 12.2.7, this also allows component-by-component construction of an impersonating value.

So, the type checks in PASCAL and ALGOL 68 only ensure the security of the domains "built into" these languages. In the following, we discuss facilities that may be used to get the same security for programmer-defined domains.

12.4.2   Definition Procedures

Some programming languages allow invocations of definition procedures (Section 9.6) to be used as type expressions. This makes it possible for a programmer to get the effect of creating a "new" type (in the sense discussed above) by keeping the representation "private" to the operations. For example, consider the following **class** definition:

```
class stack;
   private
      var a:array[1..n]of char;
          p:0..n;
   within
      procedure clear;
         begin p:=0 end;
      procedure push;
         begin p:=p+1 end;
      procedure pop;
         begin p:=p-1 end;
      selector top:char;
         a[p];
      function empty:Boolean;
         begin empty:=p=0 end
end;
```

If class invocations were allowed as type expressions, 'stack' could then be used as follows:

```
var sa:array[1..m]of stack;
    k:1..m;
    ch:char;
begin
    ⋮
    sa[k].clear;
    sa[k].push;
    sa[k].top:=ch;
    ⋮
end
```

Type checks would ensure that the stack operations were applied *only* to stacks, and that stacks were operated upon *only* by these "authorized" operations.

So, it has been demonstrated that in some circumstances new types may be created using **class** definitions. However, this approach has a significant limitation: an operation defined in a **class** body can only access the representation of *one* instance of *that* class. For example, consider adding the following to the operations on stacks:

```
function isequalto(var s:stack):Boolean;
  var eq:Boolean;i:0..m;
  begin
    eq:=p=s.p; i:=p;
    while eq and (i>0) do
      if a[i]=s.a[i]
        then i:=i-1
        else eq:=false;
    isequalto:=eq
  end;
```

Then,

> $x.isequalto(y)$

would test whether stack instances x and y were equal. However, the references in the definition of the procedure to the *private* identifiers of the *stack* parameter s are, in principle, forbidden. Some languages permit such access within the body of the class definition itself, but this is an *ad hoc* exception. More importantly, it does not allow for *mutually dependent* types, i.e., types whose operations must access the representation of instances of more than one new type. For example, *line* and *point* in a geometry package, or *node* and *edge* in a graph package might be mutually dependent types. The following section describes an approach which does not have this limitation.

12.4.3 newtype Definitions

The following (simultaneous) definitions illustrate a more flexible approach to creating new types:

```
newtype stack=record
                a:array[1..m]of char;
                p:0..m
              end;
procedure clear(var s:stack);
  begin s.p:=0 end;
procedure push(var s:stack);
  begin s.p:=s.p+1 end;
procedure pop(var s:stack);
  begin s.p:=s.p-1 end;
selector top(var s:stack):char;
  s.a[s.p];
function empty(var s:stack):Boolean;
  begin empty:=s.p=0 end;
```

The only unusual feature is the use of keyword '**newtype**' in place of the familiar '**type**'. The remaining definitions describe the operations for the new type in terms of operations on the *representation*, which is described on the right-hand side of the **newtype** definition. The right-hand sides of these definitions constitute the *implementation* part of the program. Type checks will ensure that the representation operations are compatible with the representation type.

In the scope of these definitions (i.e., the *logical* part of the program), type *stack* is distinct from all other types, including the representation type. Type checks will then ensure that stack operations are applied only to stacks (no impersonation), and that stacks are operated upon only by stack operations (no unauthorized access).

So, this approach also defines secure new types. Furthermore, it does not have the limitations of the other approach. For example, the implementation of an equality operation on stacks may be described with the other *stack* operations as follows:

```
function equal(var s,t:stack):Boolean;
  var eq:Boolean; i:0..m;
  begin
    eq:=s.p=t.p; i:=s.p;
    while eq and (i>0) do
      if s.a[i]=t.a[i]
        then i:=i−1
        else eq:=false;
    equal:=eq
  end;
```

Mutually dependent types may be specified as well, as in

```
newtype point=···;
        line=···;
procedure intersects(var p:point; var l1,l2:line);
    {computes the point p where two non-parallel lines l1 and
        l2 intersect}
    begin···end;
    ⋮
```

Facilities similar to **newtype** definitions are provided in several recent languages, including MODULA and ADA.

12.4.4 Inheritance

It may be recalled from Section 12.2.5 that in PASCAL certain types (files and structures with file components) are *non-assignable* and do not enjoy certain "privileges". The following are allowed only if *t* is an assignable type:

(a)   assignments with expressions of type *t*,
(b)   value parameters of type *t*,
(c)   a type *file of t*.

Furthermore, array and record types are assignable only if all of their components are assignable. Similar distinctions are found in almost every practical programming language because of the inefficiency involved in copying "large" values.

    Should *new* types be assignable? It would be desirable for some (e.g., a type *complex* for manipulating complex numbers); however, for others (e.g., *stack*) it would not, even if the representation were assignable. This suggests that the programmer should be able to specify whether or not a new type is to *inherit* the assignment operation from its representation.

    We shall use definitions of the form

        newdatatype I=T;

to bind I to a new *assignable* type. The updating operation for the new type is implemented by the updating operation on the representation, so that the type expressed by T must itself be assignable. The **newtype** form creates types that do *not* inherit the assignment operation and do not enjoy the privileges of assignable types.

    For example, a new assignable type *complex* could be defined as follows:

```
newdatatype complex=record
                      realpart,imagpart:real
                    end;
procedure add(var z1:complex; z2:complex);
  begin
    z1.realpart:=z1.realpart+z2.realpart;
    z1.imagpart:=z1.imagpart+z2.imagpart
  end;
  ⋮
```

A similar approach to inheritance may be taken for *indexing* types (Section 12.2.1), a subset of the assignable types which enjoy additional privileges in PASCAL:

(a)   operations *succ*, *pred*, and *ord*,
(b)   equality and ordering relations,
(c)   use as array subscripts and set elements,
(d)   **for** iteration and **case** selection.

When it is convenient to allow inheritance of these privileges by a new type, this will be specified by a definition of the form

> **newindextype** I=T;

where the type expressed by T must be an indexing type.

For example, in a program to compute "stable marriages" from priority rankings of possible spouses, the following definitions might be used:

> **newindextype**
>   *man*=1..*n*;
> *woman*=1..*n*;
>   *rank* =1..*n*;
>   ⋮
> **var**
>   *m*:*man*; *w*:*woman*; *r*:*rank*;
>   *wmr*:**array**[*man*,*rank*]**of** *woman*;
>   *mwr*:**array**[*woman*,*rank*]**of** *man*;
>   *rmw*:**array**[*man*,*woman*]**of** *rank*;
>   *rwm*:**array**[*woman*,*man*]**of** *rank*;
>   *wife*:**array**[*man*]**of** *woman*;
>   *husb*:**array**[*woman*]**of** *man*;
>   *single*:**set of** *woman*;
> **begin**
>   ⋮
> **end**

Type checks would then help to ensure that men, women, rankings, and integers were not confused.

12.4.5   New Type Constructors

It is often useful to define new type constructors, analogous to built-in type constructors like **array**[T]**of** T and **set of** T. This is possible by allowing **newtype** definitions to have static parameters, as in

```
newtype matrix(const m,n)= ···;
selector access[const m,n]
              (var a:matrix(m,n); i:1..m; j:1..n):real;
    ··· ;
procedure transpose[const m,n]
                  (var a:matrix(m,n); var b:matrix(n,m));
    var i:1..m; j:1..n;
    begin ··· end;
procedure matmult[const n1,n2,n3]
                  (var a:matrix(n1,n2);
                   var b:matrix(n1,n3);
                   var c:matrix(n3,n2));
    var i1: 1..n1; i2: 1..n2; i3: 1..n3; x:real;
    begin ··· end;
    :
```

In some cases, it is convenient to bind parameters for the whole set of simultaneous definitions. A parameterized class definition may be used for this, as in the following:

```
class stackof(type t; const m);
    newtype stack=record
                  a:array[1..m]of t;
                  p:0..m
                  end;
    procedure clear(var s:stack);
        begin s.p:=0 end;
    procedure push(var s:stack);
        begin s.p:=s.p+1 end;
    procedure pop(var s:stack);
        begin s.p:=s.p-1 end;
    selector top(var s:stack):char;
        s.a[s.p];
    function empty(var s:stack):Boolean;
        begin empty:=s.p=0 end
end;
```

Parameters t and m are bound once and for all when the class is invoked. Here is an example of how it might be used:

```
        x.stackof(char,32);
        var q:x.stack; c:char;
        begin
          x.clear(q);
          read(c);
          while c≠'$' do
            begin
              x.push(q);
              x.top(q):=c;
              read(c)
            end;
          ⋮
        end
```

12.4.6 newtype Parameters

We saw in the preceding sections that simultaneous definitions of the form

> **newtype** I=T;
> ⋮
> **procedure** $I_i(\cdots;I_{ij}:I;\cdots)$; C_i;
> ⋮

may be used to create new types. The right-hand sides of these definitions make up the *implementation* part of the program. Type expression T describes a representation for the new type, and procedure body C_i describes an implementation of an operation for the new type in terms of operations on the representation.

In this section we will consider the possibility of using **newtype** parameters that correspond (in the sense of the principle of correspondence) to **newtype** definitions. It would then be possible to have polymorphic procedures with formal parameter lists of the form

> **(newtype** I;$\cdots$; **procedure** $I_i(\cdots;I_{ij}:I;\cdots)$;$\cdots$)

or, using the "pattern matching" discussed in Section 12.3,

> **[newtype** I]$(\cdots;$**procedure** $I_i(\cdots;I_{ij}:I;\cdots)$;$\cdots$)

Similarly, **newdatatype** and **newindextype** parameters are possible.
    Here is an example:

```
procedure maparray[newtype t]
                (var a:array[m..n]of t;
                procedure p(var x:t));
var i:m..n;
begin
   for i:=m to n do p(a[i])
end;
```

This is similar to the procedure defined in Section 12.3, but with parameter 't' specified by **newtype**, rather than **type**. The difference is that the body of the procedure definition is treated as the "logical" part of the program and is type checked independently of the representations supplied by invocations of the procedure. This means that the procedure definition can only assume properties of type *t* that are specified in its formal parameter list, i.e., an array *a* with components of type *t*, and a procedure *p* whose **var** parameter is of type *t*. This type checking ensures that the procedure will work correctly for all invocations whose actual parameters match these specifications.

A more general *maparray* procedure could be obtained by also abstracting with respect to the *subscript* type of the array and the subscript limits:

```
procedure maparray[newindextype ind; newtype t]
                (var a:array[ind]of t;
                procedure p(var x:t);
                m,n:ind);
var i:ind;
begin
   for i:=m to n do p(a[i])
end;
```

Similarly, here is the definition of a general (but inefficient) array sorting procedure:

```
procedure sort[newindextype ind; newdatatype d]
                (m,n:ind; var a:array[ind]of d;
                function lessthan(x,y:d):Boolean);
var i,j,min:ind; x:d;
begin
   for i:=m to pred(n) do
   begin
      min:=i;
      for j:=succ(i) to n do
         if lessthan(a[j],a[min]) then
            min:=j;
      x:=a[min]; a[min]:=a[i]; a[i]:=x
   end
end;
```

These facilities make it possible to define procedures that are very general, yet may be type checked independently of their applications. Consequently, they are very suitable for inclusion in procedure libraries.

EXERCISES

12.1   Describe how the **case** and **for** constructs in PASCAL should be type-checked.

12.2   In Section 12.4.4, several of the examples involving non-assignable new types used a **var** parameter in a procedure that did *not* require that the parameter be an *l*-expression. It would be desirable in such cases to be able to use a parameter form that would allow verification that the formal parameter was not used as an *l*-expression, yet would be *implemented* like the **var** form. Formal parameters of the form

   val I:T

could be used for this. For example, procedure *transpose* might then be defined as follows:

```
procedure transpose[const m,n]
               (var  a:matrix(m,n);
                val  b:matrix(n,m));
   ···;
```

What additional constraint is necessary if this is to work as expected? *Hint*: consider invocation

   transpose(*x*,*x*)

12.3   What implementation difficulties may arise with *recursive* polymorp.ic procedure definitions? What constraints would avoid the difficulties?

12.4   Would it be possible or desirable for the equality operation ('=') to be inherited along with assignment when **newdatatype** is used?

12.5   A **semitype** form of definition has been proposed. It is to have the same effect as a **newtype** definition, except that representation operations *would* be allowed to have parameters of the defined type. For example, in the scope of

```
semitype complex=record realpart,imagpart:real end;
procedure add(var z1,z2: complex);
   begin···end;
   ⋮
var z:complex;
```

'*add(x,y)*' is allowed only when '*x*' and '*y*' are declared to have type *complex*, but it *is* possible to use '*z.realpart*' and '*z.imagpart*'.

(a)   Show that impersonation may still be possible with this approach.
(b)   Suggest a constraint that would prevent impersonation.
(c)   Show how the effect of a **semitype** definition may be simulated using a **newtype** definition and a conversion operation.

*12.6   By using pointer types and recursive type definitions it is possible to define *infinitary* types in PASCAL. For example, the types defined by

> **type** *ref* = ↑*node*;
> > *node* = **record**
> > > *info*:*integer*;
> > > *link*:*ref*
> > **end**;

are infinitary. Describe how structural equivalence of such types may be tested.

*12.7   The notion of *type* was originally developed in mathematics to avoid the following inconsistency, discovered by D. Russell. Suppose that it were possible to define a set *R* whose elements are all the sets that do not contain themselves. That is,

$$R = \{S \mid S \notin S\}$$

But then, $R \in R$ implies that $R \notin R$, and $R \notin R$ implies that $R \in R$. One way to prevent this contradiction is to use type restrictions to make the definition syntactically illegal.

Show that this example may be simulated in a version of PASCAL that does not require specification of parameters of procedural parameters, but is not expressible in versions of PASCAL that require such specification. *Hint*: Use characteristic functions to simulate sets.

*12.8   In some languages (including ALGOL 68), it is possible to define procedural types. An example in a PASCAL-like notation is

> **type** *p* = **function**(*p*; *integer*):*integer*;
> **function** *f*(*g*:*p*; *n*:*integer*):*integer*;
> > **begin**
> > > **if** *n* = 0 **then** *f* := 1 **else** *f* := *n**g(*g*, *n*−1)
> > **end**;

(a)   What would be the value of '*f(f,i)*' for $i \geq 0$?
(b)   Would *f* be a different procedure if its definition were interpreted non-recursively?
(c)   Simulate Russell's example of the preceding exercise using this notation. What would happen if an attempt were made to compute the analog of $R \in R$?

PROJECTS

12.1 Design a facility that would allow a programmer to define a *subtype*, i.e., a type that is associated with some *subset* of an existing domain. The subset would be characterized by some predicate (i.e., truth-valued expression procedure) on the values of the base domain. Also, show how to simulate the effect of this using a **newtype** definition and conversion operations.

12.2 Design an extension to PASCAL that would allow declaration of arrays with dynamic (i.e., data-dependent) array bounds.

12.3 Design facilities that would allow programmer-defined coercions and operator overloading.

BIBLIOGRAPHIC NOTES

Type checking in PASCAL has been discussed by Habermann [12.1], Lecarme and Desjardins [12.3], Welsh et al. [12.13, 12.14], Wirth [12.15] and Tennent [12.12]. The material in Sections 12.3 and 12.4 is based on Hoare [12.2], Morris [12.5, 12.6], Reynolds [12.7, 12.8], Tennent [12.10, 12.11], and Milner [12.4]; however, some of the facilities described are controversial and have never (to my knowledge) been implemented. For project 12.3, see a paper by Reynolds [12.9], which is also the source of the consistency condition for coercions and overloaded operators described in Section 12.1.2.

12.1 Habermann, A. N. "Critical comments on the programming language PASCAL", *Acta Informatica*, **3**, 47–57 (1973).

12.2 Hoare, C. A. R. "Proof of correctness of data representations", *Acta Informatica*, **1**, 271–81 (1972).

12.3 Lecarme, O. and P. Desjardins. "More comments on the programming language PASCAL", *Acta Informatica*, **4**, 231–43 (1975).

12.4 Milner, R. "A theory of type polymorphism in programming", *J. Comp. Sys. Sci.*, **17**, 348–75 (1978).

12.5 Morris, J. H. *Lambda Calculus Models of Programming Languages*, Ph.D. thesis and report TR-57, Project MAC, M.I.T., Cambridge, Mass. (1968).

12.6 Morris, J. H. "Types are not sets", *Conference Record of the ACM Symposium on Principles of Programming Languages*, Boston, 120–4, ACM, New York (1973).

12.7 Reynolds, J. C. "Towards a theory of type structure", Colloque sur la programmation, *Lecture Notes in Computer Science*, **19**, 408–23, Springer, Berlin (1974).

12.8 Reynolds, J. C. "User-defined types and procedural data structures as complementary approaches to data abstraction", in *New Directions in Algorithmic Languages* 1975 (ed., S. Schuman), pp.157–68, IRIA, Rocquencourt, France (1975), also in *Programming Methodology* (ed., D. Gries), pp.309–17, Springer, New York (1978).

12.9 Reynolds, J. C. "Using category theory to design implicit conversions and generic operators", Proc. of the Aarhus Workshop on Semantics-Directed Compiler Generation, *Lecture Notes in Computer Science*, Springer, Berlin (1980).

12.10 Tennent, R. D. "Language design methods based on semantic principles", *Acta Informatica*, **8**, 97–112 (1977).

12.11 Tennent, R. D. "On a new approach to representation-independent data classes", *Acta Informatica*, **8**, 315–24 (1977).

12.12 Tennent, R. D. "Another look at type compatibility in PASCAL", *Software Practice and Experience*, **8**, 429–37 (1978).

12.13 Welsh, J. "Economic range checks in PASCAL", *Software Practice and Experience*, **8**(1), 85–97 (1978).

12.14 Welsh, J., W. J. Sneeringer and C. A. R. Hoare. "Ambiguities and insecurities in PASCAL", *Software Practice and Experience*, 7, 685–96 (1977).

12.15 Wirth, N. "An assessment of PASCAL", *IEEE Trans. Software Engineering*, **1**, 192–8 (1975).

13 FORMAL SEMANTICS

In preceding chapters the semantics of programming language constructions were described *informally*. We saw in Section 2.6 that it is desirable to have *formal* descriptions of the syntax of languages. Similarly, a formal description of the *semantics* of a programming language is a precise specification of the meanings of programs, for use by programmers, language designers and implementers, and in theoretical investigations of language properties.

The basic idea of the approach we shall describe is to define *functions* that map syntactic structures into mathematical objects (such as numbers, truth values and functions) that model their meaning. The definitions of semantic functions will be *denotational*, that is to say, structured so that the meaning of any composite phrase is expressed in terms of the meanings of its immediate constituents. In the following sections this approach will be demonstrated for several simple languages.

13.1 BINARY NUMERALS

In Section 1.3, we discussed the syntax and semantics of binary numerals. This may be formalized as shown in Table 13.1. Semantic function $\mathcal{N}$ maps every binary numeral into the number that it denotes. The three sections of the table define (a) **Nml**, the syntactic domain of binary numerals, (b) **N**, the semantic domain of natural numbers, and (c) the semantic function, $\mathcal{N}$: **Nml** $\rightarrow$ **N**, using one "equation" for each of the possible forms of binary numeral. As a visual aid, syntactic operands are enclosed by special brackets "$[\![$" and "$]\!]$".

211

13.2   A SIMPLE PROGRAMMING LANGUAGE

The same approach may be used to express formally the semantics of much more complex languages. We shall demonstrate this with a fairly simple programming language that does not have type expressions, side effects, data structures or, for the present, local bindings and jumps. The complete description (except for a concrete syntax) is given in Table 13.2. The rest of this section provides commentary on this formal description and should be read concurrently with it.

From the abstract syntax it may be seen that the forms of expression are: two literals, '0' and '1'; two unary operations ('−' and '**not**'); two binary operations ('+' and '='); global identifiers; parameter-less command procedure abstracts; and parentheses as brackets. The forms of command are: the null command; the assignment; the procedure invocation (**call**); control stuctures for sequential (';'), selective (**if**), and iterative (**while**) composition; and **begin···end** for bracketing. A program consists of a command with an

---

Abstract syntax

$$N \in \textbf{Nml} \quad \text{binary numerals}$$

$$N ::= 0 \mid 1 \mid N0 \mid N1$$

Semantic domain

$$\textbf{N} = \{zero\} + \textbf{N} \qquad \text{natural numbers}$$
$$= \{0, 1, 2, \cdots\}$$

Semantic function

$$\mathcal{N}: \textbf{Nml} \to \textbf{N}$$

$$\mathcal{N}[\![0]\!] = 0$$

$$\mathcal{N}[\![1]\!] = 1$$

$$\mathcal{N}[\![N0]\!] = 2 \times \mathcal{N}[\![N]\!]$$

$$\mathcal{N}[\![N1]\!] = 2 \times \mathcal{N}[\![N]\!] + 1$$

Table 13.1   Semantics of Binary Numerals

input–output identifier. The input of the program is used as the initial value of the identifier, and the value of the identifier after executing the program becomes its output.

The following is an example of a program in this language:

> **program** (x);
> **begin**
> $y := x$;
> $p := ($**procedure** $x := x+1)$;
>   **if** $x=y$ **then** $x := x+(-1)$ **else** $x := 0$;
>   **call** p
> **end**.

For any numerical input, the output of the program is the same number; however, during execution of the program, the value of x is decreased and then increased. A truth value input produces an error message.

After the abstract syntax come the definitions of the semantic domains. For some of the domains, there is specified a distinctive symbol for the elements. For example,

$$b \in \mathbf{B} = \mathbf{T} + \mathbf{Z} \qquad \text{basic values}$$

specifies that symbol 'b', possibly with a subscript or a prime, always stands for some (perhaps unspecified) basic value, which may be either a truth value or an integer.

Stores were used in earlier chapters to describe updating assignments. For this language, identifiers may be associated directly with stored values (i.e., locations are not necessary), so that stores may be modelled by functions from identifiers to stored values:

$$s \in \mathbf{S} = \mathbf{Ide} \rightarrow (\mathbf{R} + \{unused\}) \qquad \text{stores}$$

For any identifier I, $s[\![I]\!]$ is the value at I in store s. An uninitialized identifier is associated with the special value *unused*, so that in the initial store for a program execution, every identifier (except the one specified for input–output) is associated with *unused*.

Procedures may be modelled by functions from stores to stores (or *error*):

$$p \in \mathbf{P} = \mathbf{S} \rightarrow \mathbf{G} \qquad \text{procedures}$$

If p is a procedure and s is a store, then $p(s)$ is the result of invoking the procedure with s as the initial store. Note that the domain definitions are (mutually) recursive:

$$\mathbf{R}=\cdots\mathbf{P}\cdots$$
$$\mathbf{S}=\cdots\mathbf{R}\cdots$$
$$\mathbf{P}=\cdots\mathbf{S}\cdots$$

The theoretical consequences of this were discussed in Section 3.3.2.

Three semantic functions are needed, for expressions, commands and programs. An expression yields a value (or *error*) when it is evaluated relative to a store. This is modelled by having expressions denote functions from stores to expression results; i.e., $\mathscr{E}: \mathbf{Exp} \to (\mathbf{S} \to \mathbf{E})$, so that if E is an expression, $\mathscr{E}[\![E]\!]$ is a function from $\mathbf{S}$ to $\mathbf{E}$, and $(\mathscr{E}[\![E]\!])(s)$ is either *error* or the value of E relative to store s.

To reduce the number of parentheses, it is convenient to assume that function application associates to the left and to omit parentheses around non-syntactic single-symbol arguments to semantic functions. Then $\mathscr{E}[\![E]\!]s$ is the value of E relative to store s. Also, it is assumed that the domain constructor "$\to$" associates to the right, so that the domains of arguments and results for $\mathscr{E}$ may be specified as follows:

$$\mathscr{E}:\mathbf{Exp} \to \mathbf{S} \to \mathbf{E}$$

and similarly for the other semantic functions.

Executing a command relative to a store yields a command result: either a new store or *error*. Consequently,

$$\mathscr{C}: \mathbf{Com} \to \mathbf{S} \to \mathbf{G}$$

where $\mathbf{G}=\mathbf{S}+\{error\}$, and $\mathscr{C}[\![C]\!]s$ is the result of executing C relative to store s. Finally, executing a program with some basic value as input yields an *answer*: either a basic value output or an error message, so that

$$\mathscr{M}: \mathbf{Pro} \to \mathbf{B} \to \mathbf{A}$$

where $\mathbf{A}=\mathbf{B}+\{error\}$, and $\mathscr{M}[\![M]\!]b$ is the answer output by executing M with input b.

The equations for the semantic functions use familiar operations on truth values and integers (*not, and,* $-$, $+$, $=$) without explicit definitions. Furthermore, several notational abbreviations are used.

(a)   For domain compatibility testing it is often necessary to test the "tag" component of elements of a domain sum, such as $\mathbf{B}=\mathbf{T}+\mathbf{Z}$. Define postfix predicates ' $\cdot$?$\mathbf{T}$' and ' $\cdot$?$\mathbf{Z}$' on $\mathbf{B}$ as follows:

$$b\,?\,\mathbf{T}=\begin{cases} true, \text{ if } b \text{ has been injected into } \mathbf{B} \text{ from } \mathbf{T} \\ false, \text{ otherwise,} \end{cases}$$

and similarly for $b\,?\,\mathbf{Z}$ and for other domain sums.

(b)   A ternary (i.e., three-argument) selection operation ' $\cdot \rightarrow \cdot , \cdot$ ' is defined as follows:

$$e \rightarrow x_1, x_2 = \begin{cases} x_1, \text{ if } e=true \\ x_2, \text{ if } e=false \\ error, \text{ if } (e\,?\,\mathbf{T})-false. \end{cases}$$

so that e selects either x_1 or x_2 if it is a truth value, and $error$ otherwise.

(c)   Strictly speaking, injection and projection functions should be used to map values into and from domain sums:

                 injections

                 projections

However, it is usually clearer to omit these mappings from semantic descriptions when they can easily be inferred from context. For example, equation

$$\mathscr{E}[\![-\mathrm{E}]\!]s = e\,?\,\mathbf{Z} \rightarrow -e \,, error$$
$$\text{where } e = \mathscr{E}[\![\mathrm{E}]\!]s$$

specifies that the value of a negation operation relative to store s is the negative of the value of the operand relative to s, provided that this is an integer; otherwise, the evaluation is in error. A sequence of projections of e into $\mathbf{R}$ and then $\mathbf{B}$ and then $\mathbf{Z}$ have been omitted, as well as injections of $-e$ back into $\mathbf{B}$, and then $\mathbf{R}$, and then $\mathbf{E}$.

(d)   An assignment command affects a store (i.e., a function from identifiers to stored values) at only one of its arguments. To describe this, we define a ternary operation ' $\cdot [\cdot \mapsto \cdot]$' for "perturbing" a function as follows: $s[\mathrm{I} \mapsto r]$ is the function that is like s except that argument I is mapped into r; that is, for all I',

$$s[I \mapsto r][\![I']\!] = \begin{cases} r, \text{ if } I = I' \\ s[\![I']\!], \text{ otherwise.} \end{cases}$$

Consequently, equation

$$\mathscr{C}[\![I := E]\!]s = e ? \mathbf{R} \to s[I \mapsto e] \, , \, \textit{error}$$
$$\text{where } e = \mathscr{E}[\![E]\!]s$$

specifies that the result of executing $I := E$ relative to store s is the perturbed store $s[I \mapsto e]$, where e is the value of E relative to s, provided that this is a storable value; otherwise, the execution is in error.

Note that auxiliary definitions of the form

$$\cdots \text{where } e = \cdots$$

can be used wherever convenient, but "non-mathematical" linguistic devices (updating assignments and sequencers) are *not* used in defining the semantic functions.

For the **while** construction a *recursive* auxiliary definition

$$\cdots \text{where } \mathbf{rec}, \text{ for all } s',$$
$$p(s') = \cdots p \cdots$$

is used. The recurrence of p specifies the effect of the whole loop at that point, but with a different initial store. The semantics of the **while** command can be expressed without circularity by using a limit construction of the kind discussed in Sections 3.3.2, 5.3.4, and 9.2.2:

$$\mathscr{C}[\![\textbf{while } E \textbf{ do } C]\!]s = \left[\lim_{i \to \infty} p_i \right](s) \qquad \text{where, for all } s',$$

$$p_{i+1}(s') = \mathscr{E}[\![E]\!]s' \to (g ? \mathbf{S} \to p_i(g) \, , \, \textit{error}) \, , \, s'$$
$$\text{where } g = \mathscr{C}[\![C]\!]s',$$

where p_0 is the meaning of commands whose executions never terminate. Note that if C_0 is any never-terminating command (for example, '**while** $0 = 0$ **do null**') and, for all i, C_{i+1} is command

if E **then begin** C; C_i **end else null**

then, for every i, p_i is the meaning of command C_i.

It should now be possible to read through the equations in Table 13.2 and verify that they express formally the semantics of the programming language. Note that the "propagation" approach described at the beginning of Chapter 10 is used to produce program result *error* if any evaluation or execution is in error. For example, equation

$$\mathscr{C}[\![C_1;C_2]\!]s = g?\mathbf{S} \to \mathscr{C}[\![C_2]\!]g \ , \ error \qquad \text{where } g = \mathscr{C}[\![C_1]\!]s$$

specifies that the result of executing $C_1;C_2$ relative to store s is the result of executing C_2 relative to the result of executing C_1 relative to s, provided that this is not in error; otherwise, the execution of $C_1;C_2$ is also in error. A neater treatment of errors will be possible in Section 13.4 using continuations.

Abstract syntax

$$I \in \mathbf{Ide} \quad \text{identifiers}$$
$$E \in \mathbf{Exp} \quad \text{expressions}$$
$$C \in \mathbf{Com} \quad \text{commands}$$
$$M \in \mathbf{Pro} \quad \text{programs}$$

E ::= 0 | 1 | −E | **not** E | E+E | E=E | I | **procedure** C | (E)

C ::= **null** | I:= E | **call** E | C ; C | **if** E **then** C **else** C
  | **while** E **do** C | **begin** C **end**

M ::= **program** (I); C.

Semantic Domains

$\mathbf{T} = \{true, false\}$	truth values
$\mathbf{Z} = \{\cdots, -2, -1, 0, 1, 2, \cdots\}$	integers
$b \in \mathbf{B} = \mathbf{T} + \mathbf{Z}$	basic values
$r \in \mathbf{R} = \mathbf{B} + \mathbf{P}$	storable values
$s \in \mathbf{S} = \mathbf{Ide} \to (\mathbf{R} + \{unused\})$	stores
$p \in \mathbf{P} = \mathbf{S} \to \mathbf{G}$	procedures
$e \in \mathbf{E} = \mathbf{R} + \{error\}$	expression results
$g \in \mathbf{G} = \mathbf{S} + \{error\}$	command results
$\mathbf{A} = \mathbf{B} + \{error\}$	answers (program results)

Table 13.2 Semantics of a Simple Programming Language

Semantic functions

$$\mathscr{E}: \mathbf{Exp} \to \mathbf{S} \to \mathbf{E}$$
$$\mathscr{C}: \mathbf{Com} \to \mathbf{S} \to \mathbf{G}$$
$$\mathscr{M}: \mathbf{Pro} \to \mathbf{B} \to \mathbf{A}$$

$\mathscr{E}[\![0]\!]s = 0$

$\mathscr{E}[\![1]\!]s = 1$

$\mathscr{E}[\![-E]\!]s = e?\mathbf{Z} \to -e$, *error*
    where $e = \mathscr{E}[\![E]\!]s$

$\mathscr{E}[\![\mathbf{not}\ E]\!]s = e?\mathbf{T} \to not(e)$, *error*
    where $e = \mathscr{E}[\![E]\!]s$

$\mathscr{E}[\![E_1 + E_2]\!]s = e_1?\mathbf{Z}$ *and* $e_2?\mathbf{Z} \to e_1 + e_2$, *error*
    where $e_i = \mathscr{E}[\![E_i]\!]s$ for $i = 1,2$

$\mathscr{E}[\![E_1 = E_2]\!]s = e_1?\mathbf{B}$ *and* $e_2?\mathbf{B} \to e_1 = e_2$, *error*
    where $e_i = \mathscr{E}[\![E_i]\!]s$ for $i = 1,2$

$\mathscr{E}[\![I]\!]s = s[\![I]\!]?\mathbf{R} \to s[\![I]\!]$, *error*

$\mathscr{E}[\![\mathbf{procedure}\ C]\!]s = \mathscr{C}[\![C]\!]$

$\mathscr{E}[\![(E)]\!]s = \mathscr{E}[\![E]\!]s$

$\mathscr{C}[\![\mathbf{null}]\!]s = s$

$\mathscr{C}[\![I := E]\!]s = e?\mathbf{R} \to s[I \mapsto e]$, *error*
    where $e = \mathscr{E}[\![E]\!]s$

$\mathscr{C}[\![\mathbf{call}\ E]\!]s = e?\mathbf{P} \to e(s)$, *error*
    where $e = \mathscr{E}[\![E]\!]s$

Table 13.2   (Continued)

$\mathscr{C}[\![C_1 \; ; \; C_2]\!]s = g\,?\,\mathbf{S} \to \mathscr{C}[\![C_2]\!]g \; , \; error$
$\qquad$ where $g = \mathscr{C}[\![C_1]\!]s$

$\mathscr{C}[\![\mathbf{if} \; E \; \mathbf{then} \; C_1 \; \mathbf{else} \; C_2]\!]s$
$\quad = \mathscr{E}[\![E]\!]s \to \mathscr{C}[\![C_1]\!]s \; , \; \mathscr{C}[\![C_2]\!]s$

$\mathscr{C}[\![\mathbf{while} \; E \; \mathbf{do} \; C]\!]s = p(s)$
$\qquad$ where $\mathbf{rec}$, for all s',
$\qquad\qquad p(s') = \mathscr{E}[\![E]\!]s' \to (g\,?\,\mathbf{S} \to p(g) \; , \; error) \; , \; s'$
$\qquad\qquad$ where $g = \mathscr{C}[\![C]\!]s'$

$\mathscr{C}[\![\mathbf{begin} \; C \; \mathbf{end}]\!]s = \mathscr{C}[\![C]\!]s$

$\mathscr{M}[\![\mathbf{program} \; (I); \; C.]\!]b$
$\quad = g\,?\,\mathbf{S} \; and \; g[\![I]\!]\,?\,\mathbf{B} \to g[\![I]\!] \; , \; error$
$\qquad\qquad$ where $g = \mathscr{C}[\![C]\!](s[I \mapsto b])$
$\qquad\qquad$ where, for all I', $s[\![I']\!] = unused$

Table 13.2   (Continued)

The treatment of procedures is especially important. The procedure abstract is evaluated by simply applying $\mathscr{C}$ to the body, without supplying a store. This equation might have been written

$$\mathscr{E}[\![\mathbf{procedure} \; C]\!]s = p \qquad \text{where, for all } s', \; p(s') = \mathscr{C}[\![C]\!]s'.$$

This makes it clear that the store s' for an *invocation* of the procedure need not be the store s of its *definition*. In general, it is possible to "right-cancel" arguments on both sides of a function definition (so long as there are no other occurrences of those arguments). Note that the equation for procedure invocation defines the meaning of that construct solely in terms of the value of its immediate constituent, and without referring to the abstract that defined the procedure.

13.3 ENVIRONMENTS

In this section the programming language of Section 13.2 will be extended to include *definitions*. Suppose that the abstract syntax is augmented to include two forms of definition and a command block, as follows:

$$D \in \textbf{Def} \quad \text{definitions}$$

$$D ::= \textbf{new } I=E \mid \textbf{val } I=E$$

$$C ::= \cdots \mid \textbf{with } D \textbf{ do } C$$

The **new** definition is an initialized declaration; the effect of the **val** definition is to bind the identifier to the *r*-value of the expression. The language is to use PASCAL-like (i.e., static) binding and scope conventions. For example, the output of the following program is 0, rather than 1:

> **program** (x);
>   **with val** $a=0$ **do**
>   **with val** $p=$**procedure** $x:=a$ **do**
>   **with val** $a=1$ **do**
>   **call** p.

The formal semantics of this language is given in Table 13.3. An abstract syntax and definitions of the domains of basic values are omitted.

In the definitions of the semantic domains, there are two major differences from Table 13.2.

(a) A domain **U** of *environments* has been introduced. An environment is a function that maps identifiers into the values they denote.

(b) Stores now map elements of a domain **L** of *locations* into the values they contain.

Note that the domain of *denotable* values (i.e., denotable by identifiers) differs from the domain of *storable* values (i.e., storable in a single location). Similar differences between value domains exist in almost every programming language.

The semantic functions for expressions, definitions, and commands are defined so that these constructs are interpreted relative to an environment as well as a store. For example,

$\mathscr{C}[\![C]\!]u$

is the store transformation denoted by command C in an environment u. Consequently,

$\mathscr{C}[\![C]\!]u\ s$

is the result of applying this store transformation to a store s, i.e., the resulting store (or *error*). Interpreting a definition yields a new environment, as well as a command result.

Semantic domains

$l \in \mathbf{L}$	locations
$r \in \mathbf{R} = \mathbf{B} + \mathbf{P}$	storable values
$s \in \mathbf{S} = \mathbf{L} \to (\mathbf{R} + \{unused\})$	stores
$p \in \mathbf{P} - \mathbf{S} \to \mathbf{C}$	procedures
$d \in \mathbf{D} = \mathbf{L} + \mathbf{R} + \{undefined\}$	denotable values
$u \in \mathbf{U} = \mathbf{Ide} \to \mathbf{D}$	environments
$e \in \mathbf{E} = \mathbf{R} + \{error\}$	expression results
$g \in \mathbf{G} = \mathbf{S} + \{error\}$	command results
$\mathbf{A} = \mathbf{B} + \{error\}$	answers

Semantic functions

$$\mathscr{E}: \mathbf{Exp} \to \mathbf{U} \to \mathbf{S} \to \mathbf{E}$$
$$\mathscr{D}: \mathbf{Def} \to \mathbf{U} \to \mathbf{S} \to (\mathbf{U} \times \mathbf{G})$$
$$\mathscr{C}: \mathbf{Com} \to \mathbf{U} \to \mathbf{S} \to \mathbf{G}$$
$$\mathscr{M}: \mathbf{Pro} \to \mathbf{B} \to \mathbf{A}$$

$\mathscr{E}[\![0]\!]u\ s = 0$

$\mathscr{E}[\![1]\!]u\ s = 1$

$\mathscr{E}[\![\textbf{not } E]\!]u\ s = e\,?\,\mathbf{T} \to not(e)$, *error*
    where $e = \mathscr{E}[\![E]\!]u\ s$

$\mathscr{E}[\![E_1 + E_2]\!]u\ s = e_1\,?\,\mathbf{Z}$ *and* $e_2\,?\,\mathbf{Z} \to e_1 + e_2$, *error*
    where $e_i = \mathscr{E}[\![E_i]\!]u\ s$ for $i = 1,2$

Table 13.3   Semantics With Environments

$$\mathscr{E}[\![E_1 = E_2]\!]u\ s = e_1?\mathbf{B}\ and\ e_2?\mathbf{B} \to e_1 = e_2\ ,\ error$$
$$where\ e_i = \mathscr{E}[\![E_i]\!]u\ s\ for\ i = 1,2$$

$$\mathscr{E}[\![I]\!]u\ s = d?\mathbf{L} \to s(d)\ ,$$
$$d?\mathbf{R} \to d\ ,\ error$$
$$where\ d = u[\![I]\!]$$

$$\mathscr{E}[\![\mathbf{procedure}\ C]\!]u\ s = \mathscr{C}[\![C]\!]u$$

$$\mathscr{E}[\![(E)]\!]u\ s = \mathscr{E}[\![E]\!]u\ s$$

$$\mathscr{D}[\![\mathbf{new}\ I = E]\!]u\ s$$
$$= e?\mathbf{R}\ and\ there\ is\ some\ l \in \mathbf{L}\ such\ that\ s(l) = unused$$
$$\to (u[I \mapsto l],\ s[l \mapsto e])\ ,\ (u, error)$$
$$where\ e = \mathscr{E}[\![E]\!]u\ s$$

$$\mathscr{D}[\![\mathbf{val}\ I = E]\!]u\ s = e?\mathbf{R} \to (u[I \mapsto e],s)\ ,\ (u, error)$$
$$where\ e = \mathscr{E}[\![E]\!]u\ s$$

$$\mathscr{C}[\![\mathbf{null}]\!]u\ s = s$$

$$\mathscr{C}[\![I := E]\!]u\ s = d?\mathbf{L}\ and\ e?\mathbf{R} \to s[d \mapsto e]\ ,\ error$$
$$where\ d = u[\![I]\!]$$
$$and\ e = \mathscr{E}[\![E]\!]u\ s$$

$$\mathscr{C}[\![\mathbf{call}\ E]\!]u\ s = e?\mathbf{P} \to e(s)\ ,\ error$$
$$where\ e = \mathscr{E}[\![E]\!]u\ s$$

$$\mathscr{C}[\![C_1\ ;\ C_2]\!]u\ s = g?\mathbf{S} \to \mathscr{C}[\![C_2]\!]u\ g\ ,\ error$$
$$where\ g = \mathscr{C}[\![C_1]\!]u\ s$$

$$\mathscr{C}[\![\mathbf{if}\ E\ \mathbf{then}\ C_1\ \mathbf{else}\ C_2]\!]u\ s$$
$$= \mathscr{E}[\![E]\!]u\ s \to \mathscr{C}[\![C_1]\!]u\ s\ ,\ \mathscr{C}[\![C_2]\!]u\ s$$

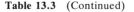

Table 13.3   (Continued)

The following points should be noted about the semantic equations.

(a)   By specifying that *any* location unused in the current store may be allocated, it is possible to avoid consideration of the details of storage management. For example, the equation for **new** I=E specifies that if the execution is not in error, the environment and store that result differ only in that I is bound to some location *l* that was previously unused, and *l* now contains the value of E.

$\mathscr{C}[\![\textbf{while } E \textbf{ do } C]\!]u\ s = p(s)$
   where $\textbf{rec}$, for all s',
     $p(s') = \mathscr{E}[\![E]\!]u\ s' \rightarrow (g?S \rightarrow p(g)\ ,\ error)\ ,\ s'$
      `where` $g = \mathscr{C}[\![C]\!]u\ s'$

$\mathscr{C}[\![\textbf{with } D \textbf{ do } C]\!]u\ s = g?S \rightarrow \mathscr{C}[\![C]\!]u'g\ ,\ error$
   where $(u',g) = \mathscr{D}[\![D]\!]u\ s$

$\mathscr{C}[\![\textbf{begin } C \textbf{ end}]\!]u\ s = \mathscr{C}[\![C]\!]u\ s$

$\mathscr{M}[\![\textbf{program } (I);\ C.]\!]b$
   $= g?S \text{ and } g(l)?B \rightarrow g(l)\ ,\ error$
     where $g = \mathscr{C}[\![C]\!](u[\![I \mapsto l]\!])(s[l \mapsto b])$
      where, for all I', $u[\![I']\!] = undefined$
      and, for all l', $s(l') = unused$
      and l is any location

Table 13.3   (Continued)

(b) For the block, a new environment is created for its body, but for other constructs, the immediate constituents inherit the given environment. In particular, this is true for the procedure abstract, so that free identifiers of a procedure are bound in the context of its definition, rather than its invocations.

(c) Evaluation of an identifier I using $\mathscr{E}$ includes a test of whether it denotes a storable value or a location. If I denotes a location, its current contents are returned; that is, $\mathscr{E}$ determines the r-value of its argument.

13.4 CONTINUATIONS

Continuations were used in Chapter 10 to describe the semantics of jumps. It may be recalled from Section 10.1 that the "normal" continuation for a computation is whatever should follow it, as a function of the expected "result" of that computation. We now introduce continuations into our *formal* descriptions.

    In the preceding sections, semantic functions returned "local" intermediate results, such as expression values or stores. Let us now define the semantic functions so that they always return the "global" result of the whole program. Each semantic function is defined relative to a *continuation* argument, in addition to an environment and a store. The continuation specifies what must be done with the intermediate result in order to produce the program answer (provided there is no error or jump).

For example, a command continuation specifies a computation that might follow execution of a command, as a function of the "normal" result of that execution. So a command continuation is a function whose argument is a store and which returns an answer (i.e. a program result):

$$c \in C = S \to A \qquad \text{command continuations}$$

where S is the domain of stores and A is the domain of answers. Then the semantic function for commands would be

$$\mathscr{C}: \textbf{Com} \to \textbf{U} \to \textbf{C} \to \textbf{S} \to \textbf{A}$$

where U is the domain of environments. (We shall see later why it is convenient to have the continuation argument precede the store argument.) So $\mathscr{C}[\![C]\!]u \ c \ s$ is the answer computed by the program of which C is a component. If the execution of C results in a new store s', then the continuation argument c will be applied to s' to produce the program answer.

For example, the semantic equation for the null command is

$$\mathscr{C}[\![\textbf{null}]\!]u \ c \ s = c(s)$$

This specifies that the answer produced by executing a null command relative to a continuation c is that obtained by applying c to the store argument s. Thus, program execution should continue without any change to the store. Note that the objects that are equated by this equation are answers (program results), and not "intermediate" results, like s.

An example of a semantic equation in which a continuation is defined as well as used is

$$\mathscr{C}[\![C_1;C_2]\!]u \ c \ s = \mathscr{C}[\![C_1]\!]u \ c' \ s$$
$$\text{where, for all } s', \ c'(s') = \mathscr{C}[\![C_2]\!]u \ c \ s'$$

This specifies that the sequential composition of commands C_1 and C_2 is to be executed as follows: first, C_1 is executed relative to a continuation c' that, if it is applied to some store s', will produce the answer obtained by executing C_2 relative to continuation c, i.e., the continuation of the whole construct. This is just a formal way of specifying the semantics expressed informally in Section 10.1.

Note that it is not necessary to test whether s' is *error* and then propagate the error, as was done in the preceding sections. When an error is discovered, the program answer *error* is selected, and the answer that would be obtained by following the "normal" continuation is ignored. An example of this approach to error handling in the semantics may be seen in the equation for the assignment command:

$$\mathscr{C}[\![I:=E]\!]u\ c\ s=\cdots d?\mathbf{L} \to c(s[d \mapsto r])\ ,\ error$$
$$\text{where } d=u[\![I]\!]$$

If the target identifier denotes a location, the answer is obtained by applying continuation c to an updated store; otherwise, the answer is *error*.

The same principles apply to other syntactic classes. For our language, the domain of expression continuations is

$$k\in\mathbf{K}=\mathbf{R} \to \mathbf{A}$$

Similarly, the domain of definition continuations is

$$q\in\mathbf{Q}=\mathbf{U} \to \mathbf{S} \to \mathbf{A}$$

(We will see later why this domain is more convenient than $(\mathbf{U}\times\mathbf{S}) \to \mathbf{A}$. It may be recalled from Chapter 3 that they are isomorphic.)

For example, equation

$$\mathscr{D}[\![\mathbf{val}\ I=E]\!]u\ q\ s=\mathscr{E}[\![E]\!]u\ k\ s$$
$$\text{where, for all } r,\ k(r)=q(u[I \mapsto r])(s)$$

specifies that a **val** definition is interpreted by evaluating the expression and then supplying the new environment and the store to the given definition continuation, q.

The language of Section 13.3 is re-defined using continuations in Table 13.4. It is possible to prove that the two definitions are effectively equivalent.

Some of the equations can be simplified by "right-cancelling" store arguments. For example, the equation for sequential composition of commands can be written

$$\mathscr{C}[\![C_1\ ;\ C_2]\!]u\ c=\mathscr{C}[\![C_1]\!]u\ c'$$
$$\text{where } c'=\mathscr{C}[\![C_2]\!]u\ c$$

Semantic domains

$$(\mathbf{B}, \mathbf{R}, \mathbf{S}, \text{ and } \mathbf{U} \text{ are defined as before})$$

$$\mathbf{A} = \mathbf{B} + \{error\} \qquad \text{answers}$$
$$c \in \mathbf{C} = \mathbf{S} \rightarrow \mathbf{A} \qquad \text{command continuations}$$
$$k \in \mathbf{K} = \mathbf{R} \rightarrow \mathbf{A} \qquad \text{expression continuations}$$
$$q \in \mathbf{Q} = \mathbf{U} \rightarrow \mathbf{S} \rightarrow \mathbf{A} \qquad \text{definition continuations}$$
$$p \in \mathbf{P} = \mathbf{C} \rightarrow \mathbf{S} \rightarrow \mathbf{A} \qquad \text{procedures}$$

Semantic functions

$$\mathscr{E}: \mathbf{Exp} \rightarrow \mathbf{U} \rightarrow \mathbf{K} \rightarrow \mathbf{S} \rightarrow \mathbf{A}$$
$$\mathscr{D}: \mathbf{Def} \rightarrow \mathbf{U} \rightarrow \mathbf{Q} \rightarrow \mathbf{S} \rightarrow \mathbf{A}$$
$$\mathscr{C}: \mathbf{Com} \rightarrow \mathbf{U} \rightarrow \mathbf{C} \rightarrow \mathbf{S} \rightarrow \mathbf{A}$$
$$\mathscr{M}: \mathbf{Pro} \rightarrow \mathbf{B} \rightarrow \mathbf{A}$$

$\mathscr{E}[\![0]\!]u \ k \ s = k(0)$

$\mathscr{E}[\![1]\!]u \ k \ s = k(1)$

$\mathscr{E}[\![\textbf{not } E]\!]u \ k \ s = \mathscr{E}[\![E]\!]u \ k' \ s$
  where, for all r, $k'(r) = r?\mathbf{T} \rightarrow k(not(r))$, *error*

$\mathscr{E}[\![-E]\!]u \ k \ s = \mathscr{E}[\![E]\!]u \ k' \ s$
  where, for all r, $k'(r) = r?\mathbf{Z} \rightarrow k(-r)$, *error*

$\mathscr{E}[\![E_1 + E_2]\!]u \ k \ s$
  $= \mathscr{E}[\![E_1]\!]u \ k_1 \ s$
  where, for all r_1, $k_1(r_1) = r_1?\mathbf{Z} \rightarrow \mathscr{E}[\![E_2]\!]u \ k_2 \ s$, *error*
  where, for all r_2, $k_2(r_2) = r_2?\mathbf{Z} \rightarrow k(r_1 + r_2)$, *error*

Table 13.4   Semantics With Continuations

in which the store arguments have been made implicit. Similarly, the equation for the block can be simplified to

$\mathscr{C}[\![\textbf{with } D \textbf{ do } C]\!]u \ c = \mathscr{D}[\![D]\!]u \ q$
  where, for all u', $q(u') = \mathscr{C}[\![C]\!]u' \ c$

$\mathscr{E}[\![E_1=E_2]\!]u \; k \; s$
$= \mathscr{E}[\![E_1]\!]u \; k_1 \; s$
    where, for all r_1, $k_1(r_1)=r_1 ? \mathbf{B} \rightarrow \mathscr{E}[\![E_2]\!]u \; k_2 \; s$, *error*
    where, for all r_2, $k_2(r_2)=r_2 ? \mathbf{B} \rightarrow k(r_1=r_2)$, *error*

$\mathscr{E}[\![I]\!]u \; k \; s = d ? \mathbf{L} \rightarrow k(s(d))$,
               $d ? \mathbf{R} \rightarrow k(d)$, *error*
                 where $d=u[\![I]\!]$

$\mathscr{E}[\![\mathbf{procedure}\; C]\!]u \; k \; s = k(\mathscr{C}[\![C]\!]u)$

$\mathscr{E}[\![(E)]\!]u \; k \; s = \mathscr{E}[\![E]\!]u \; k \; s$

$\mathscr{D}[\![\mathbf{new}\; I=E]\!]u \; q \; s = \mathscr{E}[\![E]\!]u \; k \; s$
    where, for all r,
        $k(r)$–there is some $l \in \mathbf{L}$ such that $s(l)=unused$
              $\rightarrow q(u[I \mapsto l])(s[l \mapsto r])$, *error*

$\mathscr{D}[\![\mathbf{val}\; I=E]\!]u \; q \; s = \mathscr{E}[\![E]\!]u \; k \; s$
    where, for all r, $k(r)=q(u[I \mapsto r])(s)$

$\mathscr{C}[\![\mathbf{null}]\!]u \; c \; s = c(s)$

$\mathscr{C}[\![I := E]\!]u \; c \; s = \mathscr{E}[\![E]\!]u \; k \; s$
    where, for all r, $k(r)=d ? \mathbf{L} \rightarrow c(s[d \mapsto r])$, *error*
            where $d=u[\![I]\!]$

$\mathscr{C}[\![\mathbf{call}\; E]\!]u \; c \; s = \mathscr{E}[\![E]\!]u \; k \; s$
    where, for all r, $k(r)=r ? \mathbf{P} \rightarrow r(c)(s)$, *error*

$\mathscr{C}[\![C_1 \; ; \; C_2]\!]u \; c \; s = \mathscr{C}[\![C_1]\!]u \; c' \; s$
    where, for all s', $c'(s')=\mathscr{C}[\![C_2]\!]u \; c \; s'$

$\mathscr{C}[\![\mathbf{if}\; E \; \mathbf{then}\; C_1 \; \mathbf{else}\; C_2]\!]u \; c \; s$
$= \mathscr{E}[\![E]\!]u \; k \; s$
    where, for all r, $k(r)=r \rightarrow \mathscr{C}[\![C_1]\!]u \; c \; s$, $\mathscr{C}[\![C_2]\!]u \; c \; s$

Table 13.4   (Continued)

This explains why it is convenient to have store arguments last and to "separate" the arguments of a definition continuation. For a language that allowed side effects, the domain of expression continuations would be $\mathbf{R} \rightarrow \mathbf{S} \rightarrow \mathbf{A}$.

$\mathscr{C}[\![$while E do C$]\!]u\ c\ s=c'(s)$
        where **rec**, for all s', $c'(s')=\mathscr{E}[\![$E$]\!]u\ k\ s'$
           where, for all r, $k(r)=r\rightarrow\ \mathscr{C}[\![C]\!]u\ c'\ s'$, $c(s')$

$\mathscr{C}[\![$with D do C$]\!]u\ c\ s=\mathscr{D}[\![D]\!]u\ q\ s$
                 where $q(u')(s')=\mathscr{C}[\![C]\!]u'\ c\ s'$

$\mathscr{C}[\![$begin C end$]\!]u\ c\ s=\mathscr{C}[\![C]\!]u\ c\ s$

$\mathscr{M}[\![$program (I); C.$]\!]b=\mathscr{C}[\![$C$]\!](u[\text{I}\mapsto l])\ c\ (s[l\mapsto b])$
        where, for all I', $u[\![\text{I}']\!]=undefined$
        and, for all l', $s(l')=unused$
        and, for all s', $c(s')=s'(l)?\mathbf{B}\rightarrow s'(l)$, $error$
        where l is any location

Table 13.4 (Continued)

With continuations in the semantic model, it is possible to add sequencers to the language. Suppose that the syntax is augmented by a labelled command and a sequencer, as follows:

        S∈**Seq**   sequencers

S ::=**goto** I

C ::= ⋯ | I: C | S

The scope of the label in a labelled command I: C will be restricted to this command itself.

For example, the following is a program in the extended language:

```
    program (x);
      begin
        x :=0;
loop: if not (x=1) then
        begin
          x :=x+1;
          goto loop
        end
          else null
      end.
```

It will output 1 after looping once.

The semantics of these facilities may be described formally by augmenting domain **D** to include command continuations:

$$d \in \mathbf{D} = \mathbf{L} + \mathbf{R} + \mathbf{C} + \{undefined\} \qquad \text{denotable values}$$

Then,

$$\mathscr{C}[\![I\colon C]\!] u \ c = c'$$
$$\text{where } \mathbf{rec} \ c' = \mathscr{C}[\![C]\!] (u[I \mapsto c']) \ c$$

which specifies execution of C relative to an environment in which the label identifier is bound to the continuation that begins with another execution of C. This continuation is defined recursively. Then,

$$\mathscr{C}[\![S]\!] u \ c = \mathscr{S}[\![S]\!] u$$

where $\mathscr{S}\colon \mathbf{Seq} \to \mathbf{U} \to \mathbf{S} \to \mathbf{A}$, and the equation for the sequencer is

$$\mathscr{S}[\![\mathbf{goto} \ I]\!] u \ s = d?\mathbf{C} \to d(s) \ , \ error$$
$$\text{where } d = u[\![I]\!]$$

so that the normal effect of a **goto** is to follow the continuation denoted by the destination identifier. Note that the semantic function for sequencers does not need a continuation argument.

13.5 CONTEXT-SENSITIVE SYNTAX

In Section 2.6.3, it was pointed out that BNF and similar notations for expressing concrete syntax do not make explicit the syntactic constraints imposed by static scope and type checking. The notation that we have been using to express semantics formally may also be used to specify context-sensitive constraints.

An example of this is given in Table 13.5 for the simple language that we have been using for illustration in this chapter. Because there are no type expressions in this language, the only constraints which can easily be tested for syntactically are that

(a) the target of an assignment must be either the input–output identifier of a program or bound by a **new** declaration,

$t \in \mathbf{Tp}$ types

$t ::= lv \mid rv \mid cv \mid undefined$

$x \in \mathbf{X} = \mathbf{Ide} \to \mathbf{Tp}$ contexts

$$
\begin{aligned}
\mathfrak{e}: \quad & \mathbf{Exp} \to \mathbf{X} \to \mathbf{T} \\
\mathfrak{d}: \quad & \mathbf{Def} \to \mathbf{X} \to (\mathbf{X} + \{error\}) \\
\mathfrak{s}: \quad & \mathbf{Seq} \to \mathbf{X} \to \mathbf{T} \\
\mathfrak{c}: \quad & \mathbf{Com} \to \mathbf{X} \to \mathbf{T} \\
\mathfrak{m}: \quad & \mathbf{Pro} \to \mathbf{T}
\end{aligned}
$$

$\mathfrak{e}[\![0]\!]x = true$

$\mathfrak{e}[\![1]\!]x = true$

$\mathfrak{e}[\![\mathbf{not}\ E]\!]x = \mathfrak{e}[\![E]\!]x$

$\mathfrak{e}[\![-E]\!]x = \mathfrak{e}[\![E]\!]x$

$\mathfrak{e}[\![E_1 + E_2]\!]x = (\mathfrak{e}[\![E_1]\!]x)\ and\ (\mathfrak{e}[\![E_2]\!]x)$

$\mathfrak{e}[\![E_1 = E_2]\!]x = (\mathfrak{e}[\![E_1]\!]x)\ and\ (\mathfrak{e}[\![E_2]\!]x)$

$\mathfrak{e}[\![I]\!]x = (x[\![I]\!] = lv)\ or\ (x[\![I]\!] = rv)$

$\mathfrak{e}[\![\mathbf{procedure}\ C]\!]x = \mathfrak{c}[\![C]\!]x$

$\mathfrak{e}[\![(E)]\!]x = \mathfrak{e}[\![E]\!]x$

Table 13.5   Context-sensitive Syntax

(b)   the destination identifier of a **goto** must be a command label, and

(c)   an applied occurrence of an identifier must be in the scope of a binding
occurrence of that identifier.

The constraints are specified formally by defining functions that check
phrase structures relative to a ***context*** (or "static environment", or "symbol
table") which maps identifiers into their types:

$x \in \mathbf{X} = \mathbf{Ide} \to \mathbf{Tp}$ contexts

$\mathfrak{d}[\![\textbf{new} \ I=E]\!]x = \mathfrak{e}[\![E]\!]x \to x[I \mapsto lv]$, *error*

$\mathfrak{d}[\![\textbf{val} \ I=E]\!]x = \mathfrak{e}[\![E]\!]x \to x[I \mapsto rv]$, *error*

$\mathfrak{s}[\![\textbf{goto} \ I]\!]x = (x[\![I]\!]=cv)$

$\mathfrak{c}[\![\textbf{null}]\!]x = true$

$\mathfrak{c}[\![I \ :=E]\!]x = (x[\![I]\!]=lv) \ and \ (\mathfrak{e}[\![E]\!]x)$

$\mathfrak{c}[\![\textbf{call} \ E]\!]x = \mathfrak{e}[\![E]\!]x$

$\mathfrak{c}[\![C_1 \ ; \ C_2]\!]x = (\mathfrak{c}[\![C_1]\!]x) \ and \ (\mathfrak{c}[\![C_2]\!]x)$

$\mathfrak{c}[\![\textbf{if} \ E \ \textbf{then} \ C_1 \ \textbf{else} \ C_2]\!]x$
$= (\mathfrak{e}[\![E]\!]x) \ and \ (\mathfrak{c}[\![C_1]\!]x) \ and \ (\mathfrak{c}[\![C_2]\!]x)$

$\mathfrak{c}[\![\textbf{while} \ E \ \textbf{do} \ C]\!]x = (\mathfrak{e}[\![E]\!]x) \ and \ (\mathfrak{c}[\![C]\!]x)$

$\mathfrak{c}[\![\textbf{with} \ D \ \textbf{do} \ C]\!]x = (\mathfrak{d}[\![D]\!]x \neq error) \ and \ (\mathfrak{c}[\![C]\!](\mathfrak{d}[\![D]\!]x))$

$\mathfrak{c}[\![\textbf{begin} \ C \ \textbf{end}]\!]x = \mathfrak{c}[\![C]\!]x$

$\mathfrak{c}[\![I: \ C]\!]x = \mathfrak{c}[\![C]\!](x[I \mapsto cv])$

$\mathfrak{c}[\![S]\!]x = \mathfrak{s}[\![S]\!]x$

$\mathfrak{m}[\![\textbf{program} \ (I); \ C.]\!] = \mathfrak{c}[\![C]\!](x[I \mapsto lv])$
     where, for all I', $x[\![I']\!] = undefined$

Table 13.5 (Continued)

For this language, the only types arc (a) *lv*, which is associatcd with thc domain **L** of locations, (b) *rv*, which is associated with the domain **R** of storable values, (c) *cv*, which is associated with the domain **C** of command continuations, and (d) *undefined*, which is the type of an unbound identifier. The types for a realistic programming language would be much more complex.

The semantic functions for expressions, sequencers, and commands simply check that, relative to some context, their argument satisfies the appropriate constraints. The function for definitions returns either a new context, or propagates an error indication. The phrase structure M of a complete program is then syntactically well-formed just if $m[\![M]\!] = true$.

13.6 SEMANTIC DOMAINS FOR PASCAL

This section describes the semantic domains for PASCAL. This will serve to illustrate how the approach to formal semantic description discussed in the preceding sections may be applied to a realistic programming language.

13.6.1 Basic Values

The basic (or "scalar") values in PASCAL are truth values, characters, integers, enumeration atoms, and real numbers:

$\mathbf{T} = \{false, true\}$	truth values
$\mathbf{H} = \{'A', 'B', \cdots, 'Z', '0', \cdots, '9', \cdots\}$	characters
$\mathbf{Z} = \{-maxint, \cdots, -2, -1, 0, 1, 2, \cdots, maxint\}$	integers
$\mathbf{At}$	enumeration atoms
$\mathbf{Re}$	real numbers

The domain of enumeration atoms can be any domain isomorphic to **N**. We shall not attempt to define **Re**. The domain of *indexing* values is the sum of all the basic value domains except **Re**:

$$\mathbf{I} = \mathbf{T} + \mathbf{H} + \mathbf{Z} + \mathbf{At} \qquad \text{indexing values}$$

13.6.2 Stores

In this section we shall define the domains **R** of storable values, **S** of stores, **Rv** of *r*-values, and **Lv** of *l*-values.

The values storable in a single location in PASCAL include all of the basic values, plus sets, files, and pointers. A *set* value is conveniently modelled by a function from indexing values to truth values, so that the domain of set values may be defined as follows:

$$\mathbf{St} = \mathbf{I} \rightarrow \mathbf{T} \qquad \text{set values}$$

That is, $i \in \mathbf{I}$ is a member of $s \in \mathbf{St}$ just if $s(i) = true$. As discussed in Section 4.5.2, a *file* value may be modelled by two sequences of *r*-values. (The "buffer" component of a file is selectively updateable and will be discussed later.) In the following, an additional component allows for differentiation between the "read" and "write" states of a file:

$$\text{Fl} = \text{Rv}^* \times \text{Rv}^* \times \{read, write\} \qquad \text{file values}$$

A *pointer* is either an *l*-value or the special value *nil*:

$$\text{Pt} = \text{Lv} + \{nil\} \qquad \text{pointer values}$$

The domain of storable values is then

$$\text{R} = \text{I} + \text{Re} + \text{St} + \text{Fl} + \text{Pt} + \{undefined\} \qquad \text{storable values}$$

where *undefined* is the contents of an uninitialized location. A *store* is a function from locations to storable values (or to *unused* for unallocated locations). Consequently,

$$\text{S} = \text{L} \rightarrow (\text{R} + \{unused\}) \qquad \text{stores}$$

where **L** is the domain of locations.

The domain of *r*-values may be defined recursively as the sum of the domains of storable values, records of *r*-values, and arrays of *r*-values:

$$\text{Rv} = \text{R} + (\text{Ide} \rightarrow \text{Rv}) + (\text{I} \rightarrow \text{Rv}) \qquad r\text{-values}$$

Record and array-structured *r*-values may be modelled by functions from identifiers or indexing values to component *r*-values. The domain of *l-values* is similarly constructed, but with locations as the primitive components:

$$\text{Lv} = \text{L} + (\text{Ide} \rightarrow \text{Lv}) + (\text{I} \rightarrow \text{Lv}) + (\text{Lv} \times \text{L}) \qquad l\text{-values}$$

The **Lv** × **L** term models file *l*-values: the **Lv** component is the file buffer, and the **L** component contains an element of **Fl** (after initialization).

13.6.3 Environments

An *environment* in PASCAL maps identifiers into *l*-values or procedures. (Identifiers may also be bound to types and *r*-values by **type** and **const** definitions, but these bindings are most conveniently represented in the contexts of a context-sentitive syntax.)

Procedures may be modelled by mathematical functions whose results are program answers, and that accept as arguments (one at a time)

(a)   a list of the values expressed by the actual parameters of the invocation,

(b)   a continuation to be followed after executing the body, and

(c)   a store.

Consequently, the procedure domains are

$$P = E^* \rightarrow C \rightarrow S \rightarrow A \qquad \text{command procedures}$$
$$F = E^* \rightarrow K \rightarrow S \rightarrow A \qquad \text{expression procedures}$$

where the following domains will be discussed later:

E	expressible values
C	command continuations
K	expression continuations
A	answers.

The domain of denotable values is then

$$D = Lv + P + F + (F \times L) \qquad \text{denotable values}$$

A **function** name denotes an element of $F \times L$ in the environment for the body of its definition; the location is for returning a value from the procedure.

The domain of *environments* is then

$$U = (Ide \rightarrow D) \times (N \rightarrow C) \qquad \text{environments}$$

The $N \rightarrow C$ component is for command labels. (It would be more consistent for this to be **Nml** $\rightarrow$ **C**, but most PASCAL implementations do not distinguish between, for example, 'goto 5' and 'goto 05'. However, 'goto $(2+3)$' and

```
const l=5;
   ⋮
goto l;
   ⋮
```

are *not* allowed.)

The domain of values *expressible* in PASCAL is then defined by

$$\mathbf{E=Lv+Rv+P+F} \qquad \text{expressible values}$$

13.6.4 Continuations

Continuations for commands, expressions, and definitions are needed in PASCAL. All accept a store and produce a program answer; expression and definition continuations also accept an expressible value or a new environment, respectively:

$\mathbf{A}$	answers
$\mathbf{C=S \to A}$	command continuations
$\mathbf{K=E \to S \to A}$	expression continuations
$\mathbf{Q=U \to S \to A}$	definition continuations.

The domain **A** of answers is implementation-dependent.

The entire collection of domain definitions is given in Appendix D. They provide a compact summary of the semantic structure of PASCAL, just as the abstract syntax summarizes its syntactic structure. It is a lengthy but relatively straightforward exercise to define the semantic functions that would complete the formal specification of the semantics of PASCAL.

13.7 DISCUSSION

In this section, we summarize and discuss properties of the method of formal semantic specification that was described and illustrated in the preceding sections.

Firstly, the semantics of a language is a *function* mapping (abstract) syntax to a domain of meanings. This has at least two important consequences:

(a) *Every* syntactic structure is mapped into a *unique* meaning, so that issues like incompleteness, inconsistency, and semantic ambiguity simply do not arise. (However, one question that should be addressed is whether the semantic model is *fully abstract*, that is to say, minimal. For technical reasons that are beyond the scope of this book, domains may contain "unnecessary" elements. This is currently a research problem.)

(b) Semantic functions and meanings are *mathematical* objects, so that standard mathematical techniques may be used to prove results about their properties.

A second important property of the method is that semantic functions are defined so that the meaning of any composite syntactic structure is expressed in terms of the meanings of its immediate constituents. This allows semantic descriptions to be remarkably compact and modular (allowing for the complexity or irregularity of the language being described). Also, we have seen that this characteristic makes it possible to model language features such as procedures and labels "abstractly", that is to say, without introducing artificial distinctions in the meanings of constructs that are syntactically different but semantically indistinguishable in all contexts.

The two properties of semantic descriptions discussed above are relevant to all kinds of language, and indeed originated in the methods developed by mathematicians to express the semantics of logical calculi. A feature that is distinctive to the semantics of *programming* languages is the use of recursive definitions of domains and domain elements. These may be rigorously justified using the theory of approximations, limits, and continuity that was outlined in Section 3.3.2 and which takes into account the limitations of discrete computation.

An important consequence of this theoretical foundation is that *arbitrary* mathematical sets and functions are not necessarily permissible in semantic models for programming languages. A convenient way to ensure that unsuitable domains or functions are not used is to formalize a "safe" meta-language for expressing semantic descriptions, just as it is possible to formalize the syntax and semantics of a syntax description language like BNF.

It has been shown by D. Scott that a very small language called LAMBDA is, in principle, adequate for expressing the semantics of *any* programming language: *all* and *only* the computable functions or functionals (i.e. functions whose arguments or results are functions) are definable in LAMBDA. Consequently, any language describable in LAMBDA must be implementable in principle. Furthermore, LAMBDA is a "mathematical" language in the sense that it has no updating assignments or jumps, and identifier binding is treated in a conventional mathematical way. This property makes it convenient to manipulate semantic specifications in mathematical proofs. The notation that was used in preceding sections for semantic specifications may by regarded as a convenient extension (or "syntactic sugaring") of LAMBDA, and the specifications could be translated into "basic" LAMBDA without much difficulty.

In practice, the four domain constructions and the semantic concepts of stores, environments, and continuations that were discussed are adequate to model all of the features of PASCAL and, indeed, nearly all of the language features discussed in this book. The exceptions are non-determinacy (including concurrency) and **newtype** bindings, which seem to require additional constructions and are subjects of current research. In short, this small set of constructions and concepts provides a simple but general framework for rigorous analysis, comparison, and formal specification of the semantics of a large class of complex and diverse programming languages.

13.8 APPLICATIONS

The primary application for formal semantic descriptions is to allow a language designer to set out a complete and precise specification of a programming language. This can be used by programmers as the final authority on the language and by language implementers as a guide to providing correct implementations. Of course, good informal descriptions are still desirable, particularly if they are based upon the formal description. Informal descriptions are quite adequate for pedagogical purposes and for ordinary use by programmers, but if differences of opinion arise over the interpretation of an informal description, it is essential to have a formal and implementation-independent specification as the ultimate standard.

In the following sections, several other applications of formal semantics will be briefly surveyed.

13.8.1 Soundness of Program Logics

In recent years programming theorists have put considerable emphasis on developing methods for formally *specifying* programs and *verifying* that programs meet their specifications. It is hoped that use of such methods will result in more reliable programs and reduce the need for testing and debugging.

It is possible to apply a semantic function of the sort discussed in preceding sections of this chapter to an individual program and then reason about the resulting meaning of the program. A system known as LCF ("Logic for Computable Functions") has been implemented to verify and partially mechanize the development of such proofs. Another approach is to prove properties of programs in a particular language by using a logical system specifically designed for this purpose. The formal semantics of the language may be used to prove the soundness of the specialized logic.

The best-known method of formal specification for commands is by means of formulas of the form

$$\{A_1\} \ C \ \{A_2\}$$

where C is a command and A_1 and A_2 are **assertions** (i.e. truth-valued expressions) about values of identifiers. The intended interpretation of this formula is as follows: whenever the value of A_1 relative to a state is *true*, and executing C relative to that state terminates without error, then the value of A_2 relative to the resulting state is *true*.

For example, here is a specification of a command that assigns the factorial of n ($n!$) to f:

```
{n≥0} begin
         i:= 0; f:= 1;
         while i≠n do
            begin
               i:= i+1;
               f:= f*i
            end
      end {f=n!}
```

Note that in assertions it is possible to use well-defined notation that is not in the programming language.

It is possible to verify in a formal and systematic way that the command meets its specification by using a logical system of *axioms* and *inference rules*. For example, an axiom scheme for simple assignment commands is

$$\{A'\} \ I := E \ \{A\}$$

where A' is A with all free occurrences of I substituted by E. (If necessary, identifiers must be changed to prevent clashes, as discussed in Section 8.2.) For example, formula

$$\{f*i=i!\} \ f := f*i \ \{f=i!\}$$

is an instance of this axiom scheme.

An example of an inference rule is the following one for sequential composition of commands:

$$\frac{\{A_1\} \ C_1 \ \{A_2\} \ , \ \{A_2\} \ C_2 \ \{A_3\}}{\{A_1\} \ C_1;C_2 \ \{A_3\}}$$

If the formulas above the horizontal line have been proved, then one may deduce the formula below the line.

Here is an instance of the use of this rule:

$$\frac{\{(f*(i+1)=(i+1)!) \quad \textbf{and} \quad (i+1:0..n)\} \quad i:=i+1 \quad \{(f*i=i!) \quad \textbf{and} \quad (i:0..n)\},}{\{(f*i=i!) \quad \textbf{and} \quad (i:0..n)\} \quad f:=f*i \quad \{(f=i!) \quad \textbf{and} \quad (i:0..n)\}}$$

$$\frac{\{(f*(i+1)=(i+1)!) \quad \textbf{and} \quad (i+1:0..n)\}}{i:=i+1; f:=f*i}$$
$$\{(f=i!) \quad \textbf{and} \quad (i:0..n)\}$$

The formulas above the line are instances of the axiom scheme for assignment, so that the inference rule allows us to deduce the formula below the line.

A very important inference rule is the following one for **while** loops:

$$\frac{\{E \text{ and } A\} \, C \, \{A\}}{\{A\} \, \textbf{while} \, E \, \textbf{do} \, C \, \{A \textbf{ and not } E\}}$$

Assertion A is known as an ***invariant*** of the loop. For example, if E is '$i \neq n$', C is

```
begin
    i:=i+1;
    f:=f*i
end
```

and A is '$(f=i!)$ **and** $(i:0..n)$', the proof of the formula above the line follows from our preceding example and the fact that $(i+1)!=(i+1)*i!$. Thus, the inference rule allows us to deduce the formula below the line. Note that (A **and not** E) implies $f=n!$, so that the rule for sequential composition and the fact that $0!=1$ may then be used to verify the specification of the whole command for computing the factorial of n.

But how do we know whether the axioms are valid and the inference rules sound? To be certain that our formal reasoning is semantically justified, this should be proved once and for all using the semantics of the programming language. To validate an axiom $\{A_1\} \, C \, \{A_2\}$ it must be proved that, for all stores s, if $\mathscr{A}[\![A_1]\!]s=true$ and $\mathscr{C}[\![C]\!]s?$ S, then $\mathscr{A}[\![A_2]\!](\mathscr{C}[\![C]\!]s)=true$, where $\mathscr{A}$ is an interpretation function for assertions and $\mathscr{C}$ is the usual semantic function for commands. To verify the soundness of an inference rule, it must be shown that it preserves validity, that is to say, that validity of the formula below the line follows from validity of those above the line.

Unfortunately, the assignment axiom is valid only for rather simple programming languages without side effects or aliasing. Furthermore, in languages with local scopes, formulas of the form

$$\{A_1\} \ C \ \{A_2\}$$

are almost always inadequate because they do not allow assumptions about free identifiers of the command to be made explicit in the specifications. This is particularly problematical when procedures are used. More elaborate logical systems are currently being developed that attempt to overcome these limitations by using semantic concepts such as environments.

13.8.2 Implementation

Another potentially important area of application for formal semantics is language implementation. Just as formal *syntax* and the theory underlying it have proved to be very useful for systematically writing or mechanically generating parsers for programming languages, it should be possible to use semantic descriptions to help produce interpreters or compilers. There exists a system known as SIS ("Semantics Implementation System") that produces implementations automatically by simply implementing the semantic meta-language, that is to say, by treating semantic specifications as *programs* for a simulated "LAMBDA machine". This approach is simple and general, but is far too inefficient to be practical.

Another direction of research focusses on validating implementation methods rather than producing implementations. It is possible to model implementation methods mathematically. These are known as **operational** models. It can then be proved that an operational model correctly implements the semantics of the language, that is to say, produces the same results in all circumstances.

We can illustrate operational models with one for the simple language of Section 13.2. Consider changing the semantic domains for that language as follows:

$$p \in \mathbf{P} = \mathbf{Com} \qquad \text{procedures}$$

A procedure will now be represented by the command part of the abstract that defined it. This models one approach to procedure implementation.

Then, the "semantic" functions for the operational model may be defined exactly as in Table 13.2, except for the following two equations:

$$\mathscr{E}[\![\mathbf{procedure} \ C]\!]s = C$$

$$\mathscr{C}[\![\mathbf{call} \ E]\!]s = e?\mathbf{P} \rightarrow \mathscr{C}(e)s, \ error$$
$$\text{where } e = \mathscr{E}[\![E]\!]s$$

Although these appear quite similar to the equations of Table 13.2, they are fundamentally different. For example, suppose that C_1 and C_2 are syntactically distinct commands such that $\mathscr{C}[\![C_1]\!] = \mathscr{C}[\![C_2]\!]$. But then according to this operational model,

$$\mathscr{E}[\![\textbf{procedure } C_1]\!] \neq \mathscr{E}[\![\textbf{procedure } C_2]\!]$$

even though the procedures are semantically indistinguishable.

The crucial difference between the two descriptions is that in the operational model, the meaning of the procedure invocation is expressed in terms of the meaning of a command (called 'e' in the equation) that is *not* one of its immediate constituents. Nonetheless, it can be proved that the operational model correctly implements the semantics of Table 13.2. More intricate implementation methods (such as the use of a stack for storage management and a display for environment management) have been validated.

Perhaps the most promising approach to semantics-directed language implementation is to develop general methods for systematically *transforming* semantic specifications into operational models that are directly implementable. The example discussed above is actually a simple case of a general transformation technique that allows a domain of *functions* (such as $S \rightarrow G$) to be represented by a domain of non-functional *data structures* (such as **Com**). Moreover, this and other transformations may be formalized and proved to be generally valid. This approach has been used to produce usable implementations of non-trivial programming languages in a fairly systematic way, but much work must be done before it can be used in practice.

13.8.3 Design

We began this book by observing that the problem of designing programming languages suited to both humans and computers is one of the most challenging of those faced by the computing scientist. Formal semantics can assist a language designer by allowing rigorous description of the semantics of his proposed language or language features. This makes evident any ambiguity, irregularity, or unnecessary complexity in the design, permits formal study of its properties, and facilitates comparison with other possible design approaches.

Of course, the role that formal semantics can play in language design must not be exaggerated. It is much like the role played by a programming language in program development. A language does not suggest what problems are worthwhile to solve, nor provide anything more than the framework for developing solutions. But a good language can protect a programmer from his own mistakes and help him to structure a solution in such a way as to help him cope with its complexity. Similarly, formal semantics is a tool which can help language designers achieve their objectives.

If this book has convinced the reader that a programming language designer needs the expertise of a scientist, the precision of a mathematician, and the taste of an artist as well as the pragmatism of an engineer, then it has achieved one of its objectives.

EXERCISES

13.1 Describe formally the semantics of binary numerals with fractions.

13.2 Use the semantics of Table 13.2 to verify the claims made in the text about the program example in Section 13.2.

13.3 Suppose that a multiple assignment command

$I_1, I_2 := E_1, E_2$

for $I_1 \neq I_2$ were added to the language of Section 13.2. Describe formally its (usual) semantics.

13.4 Suppose that an iterative command

repeat C **until** E

were added to the language of Section 13.2. Describe formally its (usual) semantics.

13.5 Commands C_1 and C_2 are equivalent just if $\mathscr{C}[\![C_1]\!] = \mathscr{C}[\![C_2]\!]$. Which of the following pairs of commands are equivalent according to the semantics of Section 13.2?

(a) I := I and **null**
(b) **null** ; C and C
(c) **call procedure** C and C
(d) **while** E **do** C and **if** E **then begin** C; **while** E **do** C **end else null**

13.6 Use the semantics of Table 13.3 to verify the claims made about the example program in Section 13.3.

13.7 Suppose that a definition form

var $I_1 = I_2$

were added to the language of Section 13.3. I_2 must denote a location and the effect of the definition is to bind I_1 to this location. Describe formally the semantics of this facility.

13.8 Suppose that parameters were added to the language of Section 13.3 as follows:

$$P \in \mathbf{Par} \quad \text{parameters}$$

$$P ::= \mathbf{val} \ I \mid \mathbf{new} \ I$$

$$E ::= \cdots \mid \mathbf{procedure} \ (P); \ C \mid \cdots$$

$$C ::= \cdots \mid \mathbf{call} \ E_1(E_2) \mid \cdots$$

The two parameter forms are to correspond semantically to the syntactically similar definition forms. Describe formally the semantics of these facilities, using the domain

$$p \in \mathbf{P} = \mathbf{R} \to \mathbf{S} \to \mathbf{G} \quad \text{procedures}$$

and an additional semantic function

$$\mathscr{P} : \mathbf{Par} \to \mathbf{U} \to \mathbf{R} \to \mathbf{S} \to (\mathbf{U} \times \mathbf{G})$$

What difficulty arises if the same approach is used for **var** parameters that are to correspond to **var** definitions as discussed in Exercise 13.7?

13.9 Modify the semantics of Table 13.3 to specify that free identifiers of procedures are to be bound *dynamically*.

13.10 Use the semantics of Table 13.4 and the equations for **goto** and labels to verify the claims made about the example program in Section 13.4.

13.11 Add sequencer **stop** to the language of Section 13.4 and define formally its (usual) semantics.

13.12 Replace sequencer **goto** I in the language of Section 13.4 by sequencer **leave** I, whose effect is to exit the command labelled by I. Describe formally the semantics of this facility, making whatever changes are necessary to the equations of other constructs.

13.13 Add expression form

        begin C **result** E

to the language of Section 13.4 and define formally its (usual) semantics, making whatever changes are necessary to the equations of other constructs.

13.14 Which of the domain compatibility tests in the semantic specification of Table 13.4 would be redundant for programs that satisfy the constraints of the syntax in Table 13.5?

13.15   Add type expressions to the language of Section 13.4 and specify a context-sensitive syntax that would make it possible to reduce the number of domain compatibility tests necessary during program execution.

PROJECT

Devise formal semantic models for

a.   selective *l*-expressions, such as L.I and L[E];

b.   the iterative control structure in ALGOL 68;

c.   name parameters in ALGOL 60;

d.   composite definition structures;

e.   definition and invocation of classes;

f.   coroutines;

g.   backtracking.

BIBLIOGRAPHIC NOTES

More on the subject of formal semantics and its applications may be found in papers by Strachey[13.28], Scott and Strachey [13.26], Scott [13.24, 13.25], Strachey and Wadsworth [13.29], and Tennent [13.30], and in books by Gordon [13.7], Stoy [13.27], and Milne and Strachey [13.16]. The problem of full abstraction of semantic models of programming languages was first discussed in a paper by Milner [13.17]. Formal semantics of non-determinism and concurrency is discussed in papers by Milne and Milner [13.15], Schwarz [13.23], Francez et al. [13.5], Hennessey and Plotkin [13.9] Back [13.2], and Park [13.19]; semantics of **newtype** bindings is discussed in a paper by Reynolds [13.21] and a thesis by McCracken [13.14].

LCF has been described by Gordon et al. [13.8]. The logic of formulas of the form $\{A_1\}$ C $\{A_2\}$ was first described by Hoare [13.10]; Apt [13.1] has surveyed this area. Validation of axioms and inference rules using mathematical semantics was first demonstrated by Ligler [13.13] and Donahue [13.4]. More powerful program logics are described in books by Reynolds [13.22] and de Bakker [13.3].

A description of SIS may be found in a paper by Mosses [13.18]. Verification of operational models has been treated by Milne and Strachey [13.16] and Gordon [13.6]. Transformations of language descriptions have been discussed by Reynolds [13.20]. Some current research on semantics-directed implementation may be found in a conference proceedings [13.11]. Tennent [13.30, 13.32] and Ligler [13.12] have discussed applications of denotational semantics in language design.

13.1   Apt, K. R. "Ten years of Hoare's logic, a survey", *Proc. 5th Scandinavian Logic Symposium* (eds., F. V. Jensen, B. H. Mayoh and K. K. Møller), pp. 1–44, Aalborg University Press (1979).

13.2   Back, R. J. "Semantics of unbounded non-determinism", Automata, Languages and Programming, *Lecture Notes in Computer Science*, **85**, Springer, Berlin (1980).

13.3   de Bakker, J. W. *Mathematical Theory of Program Correctness*, Prentice-Hall International, London (1980).

13.4   Donahue, J. E. "The mathematical semantics of axiomatically defined programming language constructs", *Proc. Int. Symposium on Proving and Improving Programs*, Arc-et-Senans, pp. 353–67, IRIA, Rocquencourt, France (1975).

13.5   Francez, N., C.A.R. Hoare, D. J. Lehmann, and W. P. deRoever. "Semantics of non-determinism, concurrency, and communication", *J. Comp. and Sys. Sci.*, **19**(3), 290–308 (1979).

13.6   Gordon, M. "Operational reasoning and denotational semantics", *Proc. Int. Symposium on Proving and Improving Programs*, Arc-et-Senans, pp. 83–98, IRIA, Rocquencourt, France (1975); also technical report CS-506, Computer Science Dept., Stanford University, Stanford, California (1975).

13.7   Gordon, M. *The Denotational Description of Programming Languages, An Introduction*, Springer, New York (1979).

13.8   Gordon, M., R. Milner, and C. Wadsworth. "Edinburgh LCF", *Lecture Notes in Computer Science*, **78**, Springer, Berlin (1979).

13.9   Hennessy, M.C.B., and G. D. Plotkin. "Full abstraction for a simple parallel programming language", Proc. Symposium on Mathematical Foundations of Computer Science, pp. 108–20, *Lecture Notes in Computer Science*, **74**, Springer, Berlin (1979).

13.10   Hoare, C.A.R. "An axiomatic basis for computer programming", *Comm. ACM*, **12**(10), 576–80, 583 (1969).

13.11   Jones, N. (ed.) Proc. of the Aarhus Workshop on Semantics-directed Compiler Generation, *Lecture Notes in Computer Science*, **94**, Springer, Berlin (1980).

13.12   Ligler, G. T. "A mathematical approach to language design, *Conf. Record of the 2nd ACM Symposium on Principles of Programming Languages*, pp. 41–53, ACM, New York (1975).

13.13   Ligler, G. T. "Surface properties of programming language constructs", *Proc. Int. Symposium on Proving and Improving Programs*, Arc-et-Senans, pp. 299–323, IRIA, Rocquencourt, France (1975).

13.14   McCracken, N. J. *An Investigation of a Programming Language with a Polymorphic Type Structure*, Ph.D. thesis, School of Computer and Information Science, Syracuse University (1979).

13.15   Milne, G., and R. Milner. "Concurrent processes and their syntax", *J. ACM*, **26**(2), 302–21 (1979).

13.16 Milne, R. E. and C. Strachey. *A Theory of Programming Language Semantics* (2 volumes), Chapman and Hall, London, and Wiley, New York (1976).

13.17 Milner, R. "Processes: a mathematical model of computing agents," *Logic Colloquium '73*, pp. 157–74, North-Holland, Amsterdam (1975).

13.18 Mosses, P. D. "Compiler generation using denotational semantics", Proc. Symposium on Mathematical Foundations of Computer Science, Gdansk, *Lecture Notes in Computer Science*, **45**, pp. 436–41, Springer, Berlin (1976).

13.19 Park, D. "On the semantics of fair parallelism", in *Abstract software specifications*, pp. 504–26, *Lecture Notes in Computer Science*, **86**, Springer, Berlin (1980).

13.20 Reynolds, J. C. "Definitional interpreters for higher order programming languages", *Proc. 25th ACM National Conf.*, pp. 717–40, ACM, New York (1972).

13.21 Reynolds, J. C. "Towards a theory of type structure", Proc. Colloque sur la Programmation, pp. 408–23, *Lecture Notes in Computer Science*, **19**, Springer, Berlin (1974).

13.22 Reynolds, J. C. *The Craft of Programming*, Prentice-Hall International, London (1981).

13.23 Schwarz, J. S. "Denotational semantics of parallelism", *Semantics of Concurrent Computation*, Proc. of the Int. Symposium, Evian, France, pp. 191–202, *Lecture Notes in Computer Science*, **70**, Springer, Berlin (1979).

13.24 Scott, D. S. "Mathematical concepts in programming language semantics", *Proc. 1972 Spring Joint Computer Conference*, pp. 225–34, AFIPS Press, Montvale, N.J. (1972).

13.25 Scott, D. S. "Data types as lattices", *SIAM J. on Computing*, **5**(3), 522–86 (1976).

13.26 Scott, D. S. and C. Strachey. "Towards a mathematical semantics for computer languages", *Proc. of the Symposium on Computers and Automata* (ed., J. Fox), pp. 19–46, Polytechnic Institute of Brooklyn Press, New York (1971); also technical monograph PRG-6, Programming Research Group, University of Oxford (1971).

13.27 Stoy, J. E. *Denotational Semantics: The Scott–Strachey Approach to Programming Language Theory*, MIT Press, Cambridge, Mass. (1977).

13.28 Strachey, C. "The varieties of programming language", *Proc. Int. Computing Symposium*, pp. 222–33, Cini Foundation, Venice (1972); also technical monograph PRG-10, Programming Research Group, University of Oxford (1973).

13.29   Strachey, C. and C. P. Wadsworth. *Continuations, a Mathematical Semantics for Handling Full Jumps*, technical monograph PRG-11, Programming Research Group, University of Oxford (1974).

13.30   Tennent, R. D. *Mathematical Semantics and Design of Programming Languages*, Ph.D thesis and technical report 59, Dept. of Computer Science, University of Toronto, Ontario (1973).

13.31   Tennent, R. D. "The denotational semantics of programming languages", *Comm. ACM*, **19**(8), 437–53 (1976).

13.32   Tennent, R. D. "Language design methods based on semantic principles", *Acta Informatica*, **8**, 97–112 (1977).

APPENDIX A
BIBLIOGRAPHY ON
PROGRAMMING LANGUAGES

ADA

1 "Preliminary ADA Reference Manual", *SIGPLAN Notices*, **14** (6), part A (1979).

2 Ichbiah, J. D. et al. "Rationale for the design of the ADA programming language", *SIGPLAN Notices*, **14** (6), part B (1979).

ALGOL 60

1 Naur, P. (ed.): "Revised report on the algorithmic language ALGOL 60"; *Comm. ACM*, **6** (1), 1–20 (1963); also *Comp. J.*, **5**, 349–67 (1963), and *Numerische Mathematik*, **4**, 420–52 (1963).

2 De Morgan, R. M., I. D. Hill and B. A. Wichmann. "A supplement to the ALGOL 60 Revised Report", *Comp. J.*, **19**, 276–88 (1976); erratum: *Comp. J.*, **21**, 282 (1978).

3 Eckman, T. and C. E. Froberg. *Introduction to Algol Programming*, Studentlitteratur, Lund, Sweden (1965); distributed by Petrocelli, New York.

4 Knuth, D. E. "The remaining trouble spots in ALGOL 60", *Comm. ACM*, **10** (10), 611–18 (1967).

5 Wichmann, B. A. *Algol 60 Compilation and Assessment*, Academic Press, London (1973).

ALGOL W

1 Wirth, N. and C. A. R. Hoare. "A contribution to the development of ALGOL", *Comm. ACM*, **9** (6), 413–32 (1966).

2 Sites, R. L. *Algol W Reference Manual*, technical report CS-230, Computer Science Dept., Stanford University, Stanford, California (1972).

3 Kieburtz, R. B. *Structured Programming and Problem Solving with ALGOL W*, Prentice-Hall, Englewood Cliffs, N.J. (1975).

ALGOL 68

1 Lindsey, C. H. and S. G. van der Meulen. *An Informal Introduction to ALGOL 68* (revised edition), North Holland, Amsterdam (1977).

2 McGettrick, A. D. *ALGOL 68: A First and Second Course,* Cambridge University Press, Cambridge, England (1978).

3 Hoare, C. A. R. "Critique of ALGOL 68", *ALGOL Bulletin*, No. 29, pp. 27–9 (1968).

4 Sintzoff, M. "A brief review of ALGOL 68", *ALGOL Bulletin*, No. 37, pp. 54–62 (1974).

APL

1 Wiedmann, C. *Handbook of APL Programming,* Mason and Lipscomb, London, and Petrocelli, New York (1974).

2 Falkoff, A. D. and K. E. Iverson. "The design of APL", *IBM J. Research and Development*, 17 (4), 324–34 (1973).

3 Abrams, P. S. "What's wrong with APL?", *Proc. APL 75 Congress*, pp. 1–8, ACM, New York (1975).

BCPL

1 Richards, M. "BCPL: a tool for compiler writing and system programming", *Proc. AFIPS Spring Joint Computer Conf.,* vol. 34, pp. 557–66 (1969).

COBOL

1 *American National Standard COBOL*, ANS X3.23-1974, American National Standards Institute, New York (1974).

2 Jackson, M. A. "COBOL", in *Software Engineering* (ed., R. H. Perrott), pp. 47–57, Academic Press, London (1977).

CONCURRENT PASCAL

1 Brinch Hansen, P. *The Architecture of Concurrent Programs,* Prentice-Hall, Englewood Cliffs, N.J. (1977).

FORTRAN

1 *American National Standard Programming Language FORTRAN*, ANS X3.9-1978, American National Standards Institute, New York (1978).

2 Wagener, J. L. *FORTRAN 77 Principles of Programming*, Wiley, New York (1980).

3 Brainerd, W. (ed.) "Fortran 77", *Comm. ACM*, **21** (10), 806–20 (1978).

LISP

1 McCarthy, J. "Recursive functions of symbolic expressions and their computation by machine, part 1", *Comm. ACM*, **3** (4), 184–95 (1960).

2 Siklossy, L. *Let's Talk LISP*, Prentice-Hall, Englewood Cliffs, N.J. (1976).

3 Allen, J. *Anatomy of LISP*, McGraw-Hill, New York (1978).

MODULA

1 Wirth, N. "Modula: a language for modular multiprogramming", *Software Practice and Experience*, **7** (1), 3–35 (1977).

2 Wirth, N. *MODULA-2*, Berichte des Instituts für Informatik No. 36, ETH, Zurich (1980).

PASCAL

1 Jensen, K., and N. Wirth. *PASCAL User Manual and Report*, Springer, New York and Berlin (2nd ed., 1974).

2 Welsh, J. and J. Elder. *Introduction to PASCAL,* Prentice-Hall International, London (1979).

3 Habermann, A. N. "Critical comments on the programming language PASCAL", *Acta Informatica*, **3**, 47–57 (1973).

4 Lecarme, O. and P. Desjardins. "More comments on the programming language PASCAL", *Acta Informatica*, **4**, 231–43 (1975).

5 Wirth, N. "An assessment of the programming language PASCAL", *IEEE Trans. on Software Engineering*, **1**, 192–8 (1975).

6 Welsh, J., W. J. Sneeringer and C. A. R. Hoare. "Ambiguities and insecurities in PASCAL", *Software Practice and Experience*, **7**, 685–96 (1977).

7 Addyman, A. M. "A draft proposal for PASCAL", *SIGPLAN Notices*, **15** (4), 1–66 (1980).

PASCAL PLUS

1 Welsh, J. "Pascal Plus, another language for modular multiprogramming", *Software Practice and Experience*, **9**, 947–57 (1979).

2 Welsh, J. and M. McKeag. *Structured System Programming*, Prentice-Hall International, London (1980).

PL/I

1 *American National Standard Programming Language PL/I,* ANS X3.53-1976, American National Standards Institute, New York (1976).

2 Nicholls, J. E. "Conflicting issues in programming language design", in *Software Engineering* (ed., R. H. Perrott), pp. 93–104, Academic Press, London (1977).

SIMULA

1 Dahl, O.-J., B. Myhraug and K. Nygaard. *SIMULA 67 Common Base Language*, S-22, Norwegian Computer Center, Oslo (1970).

2 Birtwistle, G. M., O.-J. Dahl, B. Myhraug and K. Nygaard. *SIMULA begin*; Auerbach, Philadelphia (1973), and Studentlitteratur, Lund, Sweden (1974).

3 Dahl, O.-J. and C. A. R. Hoare. "Hierarchical program structures", in *Structured Programming* (O.-J. Dahl, E. W. Dijkstra, and C. A. R. Hoare), pp. 175–220, Academic Press, London (1972).

SNOBOL 4

1 Griswold, R. E., J. F. Poage and I. P. Polonsky. *The SNOBOL 4 Programming Language* (second edition), Prentice-Hall, Englewood Cliffs, N.J. (1971).

APPENDIX B
ABSTRACT SYNTAX
FOR PASCAL

N   numerals
B   literals
O   operators
I   identifiers
L   *l*-expressions
E   expressions
K   static expressions
T   type expressions
Q   parameter specifiers
P   formal parameters
D   definitions
S   sequencers
C   commands
M   programs

$L ::= I \mid L.I \mid L[E] \mid E{\uparrow}$

$E ::= B \mid I \mid OE \mid EOE \mid I(\cdots,E,\cdots) \mid L.I \mid L[E] \mid E{\uparrow}$
$\quad\quad \mid [\cdots,E,\cdots,E\,.\,.\,E,\cdots] \mid (E)$

$K ::= B \mid I \mid OK$

$T ::= I \mid (\cdots,I,\cdots) \mid K\,.\,.\,K \mid {\uparrow}I \mid$ **set of** T
$\quad\quad \mid$ **array**$[T]$**of** $T \mid$ **file of** $T \mid$ **record**$\cdots;I{:}T;\cdots$**end**
$\quad\quad \mid$ **record**$\cdots;I{:}T;\cdots$**case** $I{:}I$ **of**$\cdots;K{:}(\cdots;I{:}T;\cdots);\cdots$**end**

$Q ::= I{:}I \mid$ **var** $I{:}I$
$\quad\quad \mid$ **procedure** $I(\cdots;Q;\cdots) \mid$ **function** $I(\cdots;Q;\cdots){:}I$

$P ::= I{:}I \mid$ **var** $I{:}I$
$\quad\quad \mid$ **procedure** $I(\cdots;Q;\cdots) \mid$ **function** $I(\cdots;Q;\cdots){:}I$

$D ::=$ **const** $I{=}K; \mid$ **type** $I{=}T; \mid$ **var** $I{:}T;$
$\quad\quad \mid$ **procedure** $I(\cdots;P;\cdots);C; \mid$ **function** $I(\cdots;P;\cdots){:}I;C;$

$S ::=$ **goto** N

C ::= | L:=E | I | I($\cdots$,E,$\cdots$) | C;C
   | **if** E **then** C | **if** E **then** C **else** C
   | **case** E **of**$\cdots$;K:C;$\cdots$**end**
   | **while** E **do** C | **repeat** C **until** E
   | **for** I:=E **to** E **do** C | **for** I:=E **downto** E **do** C
   | N:C | S
   | **with** L **do** C | $\cdots$D$\cdots$**begin** C **end** | **begin** C **end**

M ::= **program** I($\cdots$,I,$\cdots$);C.

Notes

(a) Several "abbreviations" (such as multidimensional arrays) have been omitted.

(b) **label** and **forward** declarations and **packed** types have been omitted.

APPENDIX C
SYNTAX DIAGRAMS
FOR PASCAL

PROGRAM

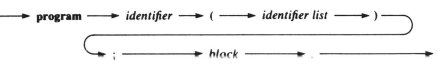

BLOCK

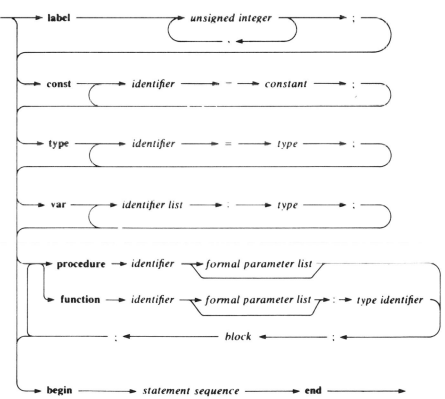

TYPE

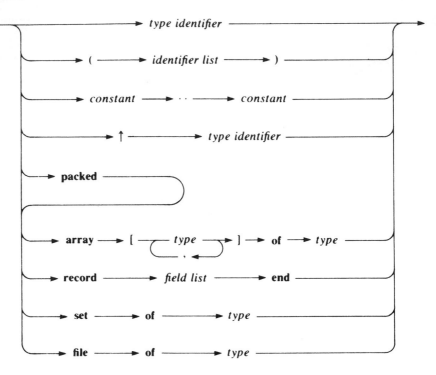

FIELD LIST

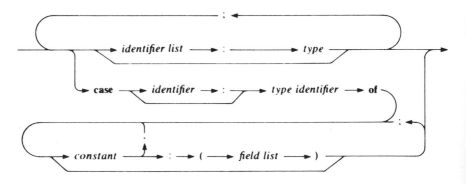

STATEMENT SEQUENCE

STATEMENT

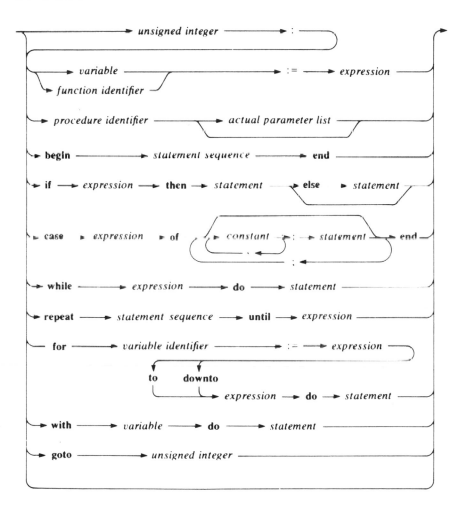

ACTUAL PARAMETER LIST

FORMAL PARAMETER LIST

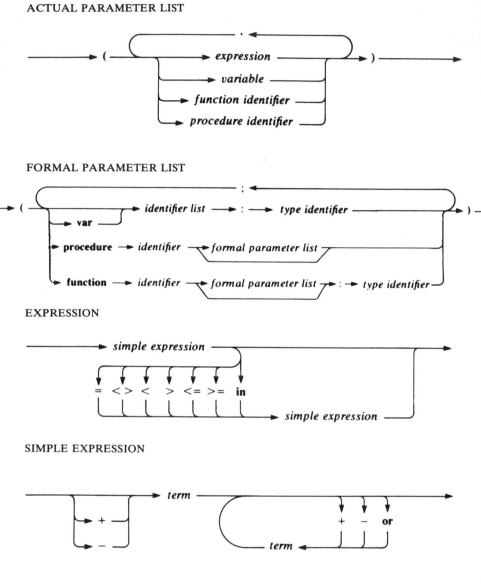

EXPRESSION

SIMPLE EXPRESSION

TERM

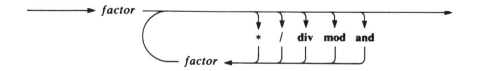

FACTOR

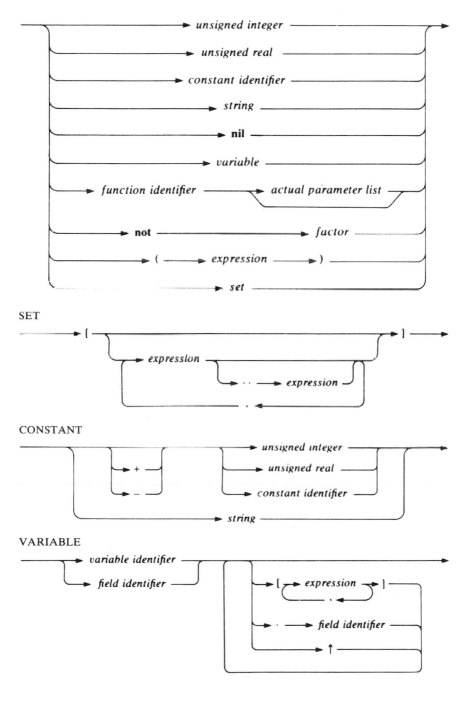

SET

CONSTANT

VARIABLE

IDENTIFIER LIST

IDENTIFIER

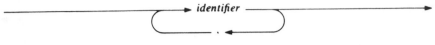

UNSIGNED INTEGER

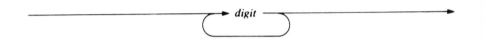

UNSIGNED REAL

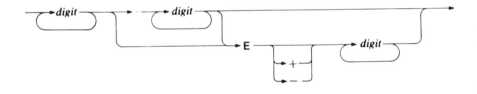

STRING

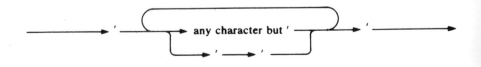

APPENDIX D
SEMANTIC DOMAINS
FOR PASCAL

BASIC VALUES

$\mathbf{T} = \{false, true\}$ truth values
$\mathbf{H} = \{'A', 'B', \cdots, 'Z', '0', \cdots, '9', \cdots\}$ characters
$\mathbf{Z} = \{-maxint, \cdots, -2, -1, 0, 1, 2, \cdots, maxint\}$ integers
$\mathbf{At}$ enumeration atoms
$\mathbf{I} = \mathbf{T} + \mathbf{H} + \mathbf{Z} + \mathbf{At}$ indexing values
$\mathbf{Re}$ real numbers

STORES

$\mathbf{St} = \mathbf{I} \rightarrow \mathbf{T}$ set values
$\mathbf{Fl} = \mathbf{Rv}^* \times \mathbf{Rv}^* \times \{read,\ write\}$ file values
$\mathbf{Pt} = \mathbf{Lv} + \{nil\}$ pointer values
$\mathbf{R} = \mathbf{I} + \mathbf{Re} + \mathbf{St} + \mathbf{Fl} + \mathbf{Pt} + \{undefined\}$ storable values
$\mathbf{L}$ locations
$\mathbf{S} = \mathbf{L} \rightarrow (\mathbf{R} + \{unused\})$ stores
$\mathbf{Rv} = \mathbf{R} + (\mathbf{Ide} \rightarrow \mathbf{Rv}) + (\mathbf{I} \rightarrow \mathbf{Rv})$ r-values
$\mathbf{Lv} = \mathbf{L} + (\mathbf{Ide} \rightarrow \mathbf{Lv}) + (\mathbf{I} \rightarrow \mathbf{Lv}) + (\mathbf{Lv} \times \mathbf{L})$ l-values

ENVIRONMENTS

$\mathbf{P} = \mathbf{E}^* \rightarrow \mathbf{C} \rightarrow \mathbf{S} \rightarrow \mathbf{A}$ command procedures
$\mathbf{F} = \mathbf{E}^* \rightarrow \mathbf{K} \rightarrow \mathbf{S} \rightarrow \mathbf{A}$ expression procedures
$\mathbf{D} = \mathbf{Lv} + \mathbf{P} + \mathbf{F} + (\mathbf{F} \times \mathbf{L})$ denotable values
$\mathbf{U} = (\mathbf{Ide} \rightarrow \mathbf{D}) \times (\mathbf{N} \rightarrow \mathbf{C})$ environments
$\mathbf{E} = \mathbf{Lv} + \mathbf{Rv} + \mathbf{P} + \mathbf{F}$ expressible values

CONTINUATIONS

$\mathbf{A}$ answers
$\mathbf{C} = \mathbf{S} \rightarrow \mathbf{A}$ command continuations
$\mathbf{K} = \mathbf{E} \rightarrow \mathbf{S} \rightarrow \mathbf{A}$ expression continuations
$\mathbf{Q} = \mathbf{U} \rightarrow \mathbf{S} \rightarrow \mathbf{A}$ definition continuations

INDEX